TEACHING MUSIC
IN THE
ELEMENTARY
CLASSROOM

TEACHING MUSIC IN THE ELEMENTARY CLASSROOM

CHARLES R. HOFFER

Indiana University

MARJORIE LATHAM HOFFER

Monroe County Community School Corporation,
Bloomington, Indiana

HARCOURT BRACE JOVANOVICH, INC.

New York   San Diego   Chicago   San Francisco   Atlanta
London   Sydney   Toronto

53557

ACKNOWLEDGMENTS

The poem "Who?" on page 194 was written by Edith Savage and is from Mary Val Marsh et al., *Spectrum of Music*, Grade 6, copyright © 1980 by Macmillan Publishing Co., Inc. The poem "Everyone Sang" on page 321 is from *Collected Poems* by Siegfried Sassoon, copyright 1920 by E. P. Dutton Co., copyright renewed 1948 by Siegfried Sassoon; reprinted by permission of Viking Penguin Inc.

PICTURE CREDITS

Cover and p.2: Talbot Studio, Bloomington, Ind.; **p.8:** Barbara Lautner/Wichita Symphony; **p.25:** Reimer et al., *Silver Burdett Music*, Book 3, © 1974 by the General Learning Corporation; **p.26:** M. Val Marsh et al., *Spectrum of Music*, Grade 2, Teacher's Annotated Edition. © 1980 by MacMillan Publishing Co.; **p.46:** Talbot Studio, Bloomington, Ind.; **p.123:** Magnamusic, Inc., St. Louis, Mo.; **p.152:** Talbot Studio, Bloomington, Ind.; **p.177:** Magnamusic, St. Louis, Mo.; **p.304:** Talbot Studio, Bloomington, Ind.; **p.319:** left, Joseph E. Seagram & Sons/Ezra Stoller © ESTO; right, Willy Ronis/Air France; **p.320:** United Nations; **p.323:** P. F. Brandwein et al., *Self-Expression and Conduct: The Humanities*, Red, © 1974 by Harcourt Brace Jovanovich, Inc.

ISBN: 0-15-588809-9

Library of Congress Catalog Card Number: 81-84013

Printed in the United States of America

To Allan and Martha, ours by birth
and
Donna and Don, ours by marriage

Preface

Teaching Music in the Elementary Classroom is a book about the ways in which classroom teachers and music specialists can effectively teach music to elementary school children. The suggested teaching procedures contained in it are based on the premise that music is a subject worthy of study by children, and that successful classroom experiences with music will increase their enjoyment of it.

Part One of the book discusses the value of music in the elementary school, the organization and operation of the elementary school in relation to music instruction, the roles of the classroom teacher and music specialist, and guidelines for planning music instruction.

Parts Two and Three describe practical methods for teaching music to children. These chapters are organized so that they consider the ages of the children while exploring the musical elements of rhythm, pitch, timbre, and loudness. Information is presented according to two general levels: primary and upper grades. Such a division recognizes the increases in musical learning that should be achieved as children progress through school, and yet it keeps the discussion from bogging down into lengthy lists of activities for each of six or seven grades. (Such specific lists are of limited value because they still have to be adapted to accommodate the many differences among classrooms and children.) The allocation of topics to either primary or upper grades corresponds in general to the appearance of those topics in current music series books and to conclusions drawn from research studies.

Part Four explores ways in which teachers can individualize certain aspects of music instruction, incorporate other fine arts into music teaching, tailor musical experiences to special students, and evaluate teaching and learning in music.

Although activities such as singing, creating, listening, and music reading are discussed and encouraged in this book, they are not in themselves the ultimate goal of music education in the elementary school. That goal is the gaining of musical understanding. For this reason, the book emphasizes the teaching of rhythm, melody, and other aspects of the music itself *through* activities such as playing instruments, singing, and moving to music. These activities can contribute to musical learning, but they should not substitute for it.

Throughout the book, the suggestions for teaching music are varied and realistic. Teaching procedures are carefully described, and many of them are demonstrated in dialogues from typical classes. All chapters conclude with review questions and with optional activities through which the reader can become directly involved in the topics being studied.

Because classroom teachers and music specialists possess different strengths and limitations when it comes to music instruction, this book takes those differences into account. First, the book does not assume prior study of music. Technical information is discussed in such a way that the material can be understood by nonmusicians, and an appendix on music notation is provided for those who need help in interpreting the written symbols of music. Second, because most elementary schools provide at least some help from specialized music personnel, the book advocates complementary roles to utilize most effectively the musical knowledge of the specialist and the classroom teacher's greater understanding of the children involved. Third, it encourages the utilization of elementary school music series books, because they provide instructional aids and are a resource in planning for the teaching of music.

The book is eclectic in its approach to the various methods of music teaching; it owes no allegiance to a particular system. Instead, it presents a balanced view of the various methods that are appropriate in elementary school music classes, including ideas adapted from the Orff-*Schulwerk*, the Kodály-Hungarian Singing School, Jaques-Dalcroze, and others when they seem pertinent. Nor does the book follow the curriculum sequence presented in any particular series of elementary music books. There is no way of knowing which series will be available to a beginning teacher. Further, such books are subject to frequent revision and to replacement because of changes in textbook adoption policies within a district or state.

In short, *Teaching Music in the Elementary Classroom* seeks to give prospective teachers a knowledge of principles, procedures, and materials that will be useful in a wide variety of music teaching situations.

We are grateful to the School of Music of Indiana University for the use of its library. We also want to thank the following persons for their reviews of the manuscript: Dorothy McDonald of the University of Iowa, Marilyn Vincent of Ball State University, and Linda Damer White of Indiana State University.

CHARLES R. HOFFER

MARJORIE LATHAM HOFFER

Contents

TEACHING MUSIC IN THE ELEMENTARY CLASSROOM

ONE

FOUNDATIONS FOR TEACHING MUSIC IN THE ELEMENTARY SCHOOL

Part One presents fundamental topics that influence the teaching of music in the elementary school. As a basis for examining these topics, it is necessary to consider the reasons for including music in the elementary school curriculum. Unless a substantial and satisfactory case for music is understood by teachers, attempts at music instruction will be of limited value, if they are undertaken at all. Chapter 1 examines the importance of music in the elementary classroom.

An understanding of the somewhat different roles of music specialists and classroom teachers can contribute to the success of music instruction in the elementary school. Since most schools designate a cooperative-complementary arrangement between specialists and classroom teachers, both types of teachers should understand what each can do better. These matters occupy much of the discussion in Chapter 2.

Later sections of this book describe specific procedures that have been successful in teaching music to children. The suggested methods are based on broad principles derived from educational psychology. Chapter 3 outlines the fundamental guidelines on which the recommended teaching methods are based.

Reasons for Teaching Music in the Elementary School

Music is important in human life. All over the world people spend countless hours listening to music and performing it, and they spend vast amounts of money for instruments, records, and record-playing equipment. People dance, sing, play instruments, and create new tunes in every part of the globe. It is estimated that in America more than 30 million people play musical instruments regularly. More than 54 million people attend concerts of popular music, and 27 million attend concerts of classical music.[1] That is a greater number than attend sports events such as major league baseball and college football games.

Music has also been present in every age. The walls of ancient Egyptian buildings show people playing instruments and singing, and the Bible tells how David soothed King Saul with his music. In the Middle Ages a courtly gentleman was likely to serenade the lady of his choice, and competitive guilds were organized to reward excellence in music performance. The breadth and depth of mankind's interest in music are indeed impressive.

Why are music and the other fine arts so important? There are several reasons, but a most significant one is that music and other arts represent a fundamental difference between existing and living. Animals exist in the sense that they manage to survive. Humans live; they attempt to make life interesting, rewarding, and satisfying. Humans are

4

not content merely to survive in a cave and grub roots for food. They notice sights and sounds and have feelings about them, and they find life richer because of these feelings and experiences.

The cave paintings at Lascaux, created during the Cro-Magnon period more than 15,000 years ago, show remarkable grace and artistry. The motivation for the work may have been functional—a way to invoke favor from a god of the hunt, or an illustrated lesson for young hunters. But for those functions, a stick figure of an animal would probably have been sufficient. The painter provided an aesthetic dimension, revealing a sensitivity to color, shape, and motion.

People have always been looking at beauty in the world about them. They are fascinated by the shifting surf, the color of a sunset, and the shape of a flower. They create beautiful and artistic objects. They value paintings, symphonies, and poetry, and they seek artistic quality in their everyday surroundings—in their clothing, homes, furniture, automobiles. A cardboard carton could serve as a lamp table, and it would have the virtue of being far cheaper than a piece of furniture. But humans do not want to live with objects that are merely functional. The human spirit needs to appreciate and create things of beauty. This compulsion to reach beyond immediate needs is not a luxury; it is a basic element of being human.

Why do humans seek the "good life," which includes music and other arts? Philosophers have pondered that question for a long time. It seems impossible to answer the question to everyone's satisfaction. One theory holds that in music and other arts, people reexperience in a symbolic way the feelings associated with events in life. This theory proposes that in the recurrent rise and fall of intensity in the music, the performer or listener relives in a roundabout way the emotions associated with personal experiences. Another theory claims that music is "transfigured Nature," transcending the world and revealing "the realm of the ultimate Will (God)," to cite two phrases from the nineteenth-century philosopher Arthur Schopenhauer.[2] Whatever the reasons, people do find life richer and better because of the arts.

WHY ARE MUSIC AND THE OTHER ARTS TAUGHT IN SCHOOL?

The role of the school is to teach the subjects and skills that enable a person to function successfully in society. When mathematics, music, science, and other school subjects move beyond a rudimentary level, they exceed the teaching capabilities of most families. There are too many things to learn and they are often complex. It is no coincidence that every society that seeks to progress beyond the tribal stage has established a system of schools. This has happened because no better way has been devised to equip individuals to function in a society.

Schools are also needed to transmit the culture of the society to each generation. That is what the Tanglewood Declaration (p. 7) refers to when it speaks of a "continuity . . . in . . . history." There exists a wealth of music, art, drama, poetry, and other literature that young people would not know without instruction in school. Interpreting mankind's great cultural achievements is an important mandate for all teachers.

At first glance, the arts may seem to be a frivolous, unnecessary component in the making of a productive citizen. School curriculums appropriately include subjects that are needed if one is to function in the contemporary world--reading, writing, arithmetic, and so on. But the concerns of most educators go beyond these subjects. They realize that giving children rudimentary skills is not enough today. Instead of asking, "What's the minimum level at which children can get by?", many educators are wondering, "What can we do to ensure the fullest possible life for each child?"

The notion that schools should be more than a training ground for the rudimentary needs of life has strong support. The American Association of School Administrators (AASA) has on three occasions gone on record in support of music and the other arts as necessary in the school curriculum. The first time was more than 50 years ago. Another statement was adopted in 1959. A portion of it reads:

> We believe in a well-balanced school curriculum in which music, drama, painting, poetry, sculpture, architecture, and the like are included side by side with other important subjects such as mathematics, history, and science. It is important that pupils, as a part of general education, learn to appreciate, to understand, to create, and to criticize with discrimination those products of the mind, the voice, the hand, and the body which give dignity to the person and exalt the spirit of man.[3]

A third statement of support by the AASA for the arts was adopted in 1973. It speaks explicitly against categorical budget cuts of "so-called 'peripheral' subject areas."[4]

Official educational agencies sometimes express a strong interest in the arts. In 1976 the Pennsylvania State Board of Education unanimously adopted the following policy statement:

> The State Board of Education affirms its position that experience in the arts is essential to the development of the human potential of every student in the Commonwealth. The arts, including but not lim-

ited to music, art, drama, dance, film and creative writing, serve and express the needs, aspirations and acts of humanity. Therefore, the arts, in both separate and interdisciplinary modes, should occupy a central place in the educational programs of all public schools.[5]

The views of the Pennsylvania State Board of Education are in full agreement with those of the Music Educators National Conference (MENC), which is the professional association of school music teachers in the United States. In 1967 the MENC sponsored a symposium at Tanglewood in Massachusetts. Leaders from all walks of life met to discuss the role of music in American society. A portion of the Tanglewood Declaration issued at the conclusion of the Symposium reads:

> We believe that education must have as major goals the art of living, the building of personal identity, and the nurturing of creativity. Since the study of music can contribute much to these ends, *we now call for music to be placed in the core of the school curriculum.*
>
> The arts afford a continuity with aesthetic tradition in man's history. Music and other fine arts, largely nonverbal in nature, reach close to the social, psychological, and physiological roots of man in his search for identity and self-realization.[6]

Much has been written in recent years about nurturing the uniqueness of each child. Terms such as "self-actualization" and "creative environment" have been employed to verbalize this idea. Educators are saying not only that learning should move beyond the rudimentary and routine, but that each child should be encouraged to explore, express, and experiment so that he or she can develop potential abilities to the fullest extent. The artistic, aesthetic area is certainly one in which children should be given a chance to test their aptitudes and explore their interests. Music, art, dance, drama, and literature are recognized avenues for creative expression, and the schools are uniquely equipped to provide guidance and encouragement in such endeavors. When music and other arts are omitted from the curriculum, children are being deprived of a valuable part of their preparation for living today and in the twenty-first century. Perhaps the American patriot and second President of the United States, John Adams, summarized best the value of the arts in a letter he wrote to his wife, Abigail, during the Revolutionary War:

> I must study politics . . ., that my sons may have liberty to study mathematics and philosophy, geography, natural history and naval architecture, navigation, commerce, and agriculture, in order to give their children a right to study painting, poetry, music, architecture, statuary, tapestry, and porcelain.[7]

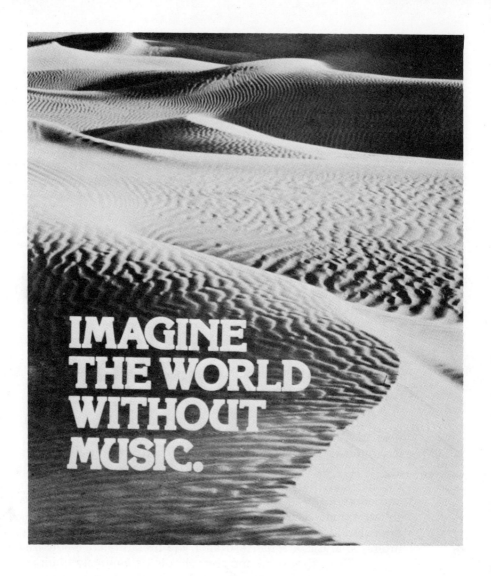

IMAGINE THE WORLD WITHOUT MUSIC.

MUSIC AS A SUBJECT

Although music may <u>provide greater opportunities for self-expression than most school subjects</u>, it is a field of study—an academic discipline—like other subjects in the curriculum. It involves a body of information and skills with which every child should be familiar, at least to some degree. There are concepts related to the structure of music, as well as specialized techniques for performing and creating it. There is also much to be learned about the repertoire of music (called music literature) and about the syntactical patterns of the various types of music. It is a vast and varied field.

Like other subjects, music is learned through effort and concentration. Some people regard music primarily as an activity in which one participates for recreation. This is valid in many situations, but there is a difference between just singing through a song for entertainment and singing a song to gain a greater understanding of its musical properties. One is a pastime, while the other is a means of learning music. This is not to say that music should be only hard work instead of fun. Rather, it means that a person's enjoyment is heightened as understanding increases and skills are mastered.

The fact that music is enjoyable has both helped and hindered its acceptance in the schools. Its inherent appeal has tended to discourage educators from considering it as a subject worthy of serious effort. This is unfortunate, because lasting satisfaction and enjoyment in music are the result of solid understanding and accomplishment, which do not often occur without effort on the part of both teachers and students.

Another characteristic of music as a subject is the fact that many of its facets are unlikely to be learned by children outside the school. Popular music is heard virtually everywhere by children, so their familiarity with it is assured without formal instruction. The larger world of music, however, is less accessible to most children, so they are unlikely to learn about it unless they receive specific instruction.

NONMUSICAL VALUES OF MUSIC

Music has often been advocated for its contributions to reasoning ability, language arts, character, leisure activity, health, and so on. In the first part of this chapter, music and the other fine arts were cited as contributing to the quality of human life. The benefits of music are not confined to the art of music itself.

Transfer effects

If engaging in one activity causes behavioral changes in another area, the first activity is said to transfer to the second area. Does music instruction transfer to other areas of the school curriculum? If so, to which areas, and to what extent? One can read varied opinions about the transfer effects of music instruction. However, because research findings represent the best means available for securing solid information, this brief review is based on research results.

Several major attempts have been made to assess the results of arts instruction on general learning ability. In some cases, notably the Interdisciplinary Model Program in the Arts for Children and Teachers (IM-PACT) and the Dallas "Learning to Learn through Music" program, positive results were achieved, but other data indicate that the enriched programs made little difference.[8,9] Another study provided encouraging evidence of transfer.[10] Similarly mixed conclusions can be drawn about the claims for the transfer to general learning of the Kodály-Hungarian Singing School programs; the results offer encouragement, but the conclusions must be tempered because of the inadequacies of the studies.[11,12]

The area most likely to benefit from transfer of music instruction appears to be language arts. Two studies conclude that certain aspects of music instruction transfer to some aspects of reading achievement.[13,14]

It has been known for some time that many stutterers sing without their usual hesitations. The likelihood that singing can improve some speech disorders suggests a positive transfer effect, but more research is needed in this area.

Only a few studies have been conducted to assess the connection between music study and skills in mathematics or social studies. Very little relationship has been found.[15]

The limited amount of research on the effects of music instruction on self-concept has yielded inconclusive results. Generally, little difference is observed as the result of music instruction.[16] Similar conclusions are obtained from analyzing the results of the few studies of music instruction and personality change.[17,18]

There is evidence of expanded chest and lung capacity when regular music instruction includes singing.[19] Information is not available regarding other physical changes that may occur as a result of music instruction. In any case, the physical benefits of music study are small when compared to those of physical education and health instruction.

This discussion of the transfer effects of music instruction can best be summarized by citing the conclusions reached by Karen I. Wolff after her review of research on the topic.

> The weight of evidence gleaned from the research leads one to believe that there may be measurable effects of music education on the development of cognitive skills and understanding. This seems to be true for both general transfer, i.e., "learning how to learn," and specific transfer. Specific transfer is particularly apparent in its effect on performance in the language arts . . . .
>
> While it is true that most of the research related to the non-musical outcomes of music education has produced positive results, the conclusions drawn generally remain unconvincing. This is due largely to obvious inadequacies in the experimental designs and also to the incomplete and equivocal descriptions of the experiments themselves.[20]

Attitude toward school

It has been demonstrated that a classroom program enriched by instruction in the arts provides a more interesting school environment for children. Absenteeism is often reduced.[21] Advocates of behavior modification techniques have demonstrated on several occasions the success of offering music as a reward for work completed in other areas of the school curriculum.[22]

The reported influence of music and the arts in improving the outlook of children toward school should not be surprising in view of the long history of music in schools as a means of adding variety to classroom routines. In 1837, when Lowell Mason was finally given approval to institute music instruction in the Boston public schools, the subject was justified, by the Board of Education committee that evaluated the proposal, on the basis of its contributions to reading and speech. The committee also concluded that music provided "a recreation, yet not a dissipation of the mind—a respite, yet not a relaxation,—its office would thus be to restore the jaded energies, and send back the scholars with invigorated powers to other more laborious duties."[23] Music does add variety to the school day, although it certainly is not the only means of introducing a change of activity into the classroom.

Other values

Two other nonmusical benefits of music instruction should be mentioned. Although music does not always have the power to "soothe a savage breast," music therapy has demonstrated that the mind can respond to the curative powers of music. The desire to use music for the release of feelings is stronger in some people than in others, but it is nevertheless a significant function of music, even for those who do not have serious emotional problems.

Music also offers many options for filling nonworking hours with constructive and interesting activity. While life expectancy is increasing, the average work week is decreasing. This means that leisure time is assuming a larger role in contemporary life. Music is an important avocational activity in most societies, including America. Participation may involve playing in a community orchestra, singing in a church choir, listening to recordings, or attending concerts. Again, music is not the only subject in the school curriculum that can enrich nonworking hours, but its avocational values are great.

It is important to keep the nonmusical benefits of music instruction in perspective. There are valid and supportable reasons for including music in the elementary school curriculum, apart from any nonmusical benefits. The additional benefits can be considered as "bonuses" arising from the music instruction that the schools should be offering anyway. The place of music in the elementary school does not depend on these benefits, but its position may be stronger because of them.

IMPLICATIONS FOR THE ELEMENTARY SCHOOL MUSIC PROGRAM

The idea that music is a subject worthy of study rejects the view that elementary school music is primarily a training ground for musical organizations in the secondary schools. A good music program in the elementary school will of course improve the quality of the secondary school instrumental and choral groups. But that improvement is a desirable result, not a major justification for teaching music in the early grades. An elementary school music program designed to be of maximum benefit to the secondary school groups would not include the variety and types of activities that are usually recommended for children. Instead, it would consist of heavy doses of drill on specific performance skills such as music reading. Probably efforts would also be made to eliminate the less talented children from the instruction.

Music in elementary schools is more than a diversion, a frill, or a respite from the rigors of other instruction. It is a respected and time-honored field of study that should not be eliminated if time or money grows short.

For all of the reasons presented in this chapter, music should be a vital part of the curriculum of every elementary school classroom.

NOTES

1. *U.S. News and World Report*, Vol. 82, No. 20 (May 23, 1977), p. 63.
2. Arthur Schopenhauer, *The World as Will and Idea*, trans. R. B. Haldane and J. Kemp, 4th ed., Vol. 1 (London: Kegan, Paul, Trench, Trubner and Co., Ltd., 1896), p. 333.
3. *Your AASA in 1958-1959*, American Association of School Administrators, Official Report for the Year 1958, (Washington: AASA, 1959), pp. 248-49.
4. "Curriculum Balance" (Reston, Va.: Music Educators National Conference, 1973).
5. Basic Education Circular 60-76, Pennsylvania Department of Education, adopted September 10, 1976.
6. Robert Choate, ed., *Documentary Report of the Tanglewood Symposium*, (Reston, Va.: Music Educators National Conference, 1968), p. 139.
7. Charles Francis Adams, ed., *Letters of John Adams Addressed to His Wife*, (1841), Vol. II, letter 78 (1780).

8. J. David Boyle and Robert L. Lathrop, "The IMPACT Experience: An Evaluation," *Music Educators Journal*, Vol. 59, No. 5 (January 1973), p. 42.
9. *Learning to Learn Through Music Sampler* (Dallas: Dallas Independent School District, n.d.).
10. Diana Nicholson, "Music as an Aid to Learning" (Ph.D. dissertation, New York University, 1971).
11. J. L. Haynes, "The Effects of Musical Training on General Educational Development" (Master's thesis, Culham College, England, 1972), p. 28.
12. Irving Hurwitz et al., "Nonmusical Effects of the Kodály Music Curriculum in Primary Grade Children," *Journal of Learning Disabilities*, Vol. 8, No. 3 (March 1975), pp. 167-74.
13. Edwin A. Movsesian, "The Influence of Teaching Music Reading Skills on the Development of Basic Reading Skills in the Primary Grades" (Ph.D dissertation, University of Southern California, 1967).
14. Nellie Marie Maze, "A Study of the Correlations Between Musicality and Reading Achievement at First Grade Level in Athens, Georgia" (Ed.D. dissertation, University of Georgia, 1967).
15. Karen I. Wolff, "The Nonmusical Outcomes of Music Education: A Review of the Literature," Council for Research in Music Education Bulletin No. 55 (Summer 1978), p. 14.
16. Donald E. Michel and Dorothea Martin, "Music and Self-Esteem Research with Disadvantaged, Problem Boys in an Elementary School," *Journal of Music Therapy*, Vol. 8 (Winter 1970), pp. 124-27.
17. Wincie Lowe Blanton, "An Experimental Application of Language Theory, Learning Theory, and Personality Theory to Evaluate the Influence of Music in Language Learning" (Ph.D. dissertation, University of Texas, 1962).
18. Burrel S. Hood, "The Effect of Daily Instruction in Public School Music and Related Experiences upon Nonmusical Personal and School Attitudes of Average Achieving Third-Grade Students" (Ed.D. dissertation, Mississippi State University, 1973).
19. Marta Nemesszeghy, "The Importance of a Daily Music Curriculum in Total Education," paper presented at the University of Bridgeport Summer Course of Kodaly Music Training Institute, Inc., 1971.
20. Wolff, op. cit., pp. 19, 21.
21. Robert Rodosky, "Arts IMPACT: Final Evaluation Report" (Columbus, Ohio: Columbus Public Schools Department of Evaluation, Research, and Planning, June 1974), p. 2.
22. Clifford K. Madsen et al., "Effect of Music Via Television as Reinforcement for Correct Mathematics," *Journal of Research in Music Education*, Vol. 24 (Summer 1976), pp. 51-59.
23. Edward Bailey Birge, *The History of Public School Music in the United States* (Reston, Va.: Music Educators National Conference, 1966), p. 43.

REVIEW QUESTIONS

1. What objective evidence indicates that human beings value music and the other fine arts?

2. Why shouldn't the teaching of music be left to the family and to social institutions other than the school?

3. Name a few of the governmental and educational organizations that strongly support the inclusion of music in the elementary school curriculum.

4. How has the fact that music is an enjoyable activity hindered its inclusion in the elementary school curriculum?

5. Examine the photograph on page 8 that contains the words "Imagine the world without music." What is the message of that picture and that sentence?

6. Suppose that music has no nonmusical benefits. Should it still be taught in the schools? Why?

7. Does music training appear to have any transfer to other areas of the curriculum? What subjects and skills appear to receive the most benefits from music instruction?

8. How does music study seem to influence the attitudes of children toward school?

9. What nonmusical values other than transfer appear to accrue from music instruction?

ACTIVITIES

1. Develop a ten-minute presentation on the topic "Why music should be a part of the elementary school curriculum." Assume that it is to be presented at a school board meeting. In preparing your rationale:
   a. Determine what points you will stress.
   b. Decide how you will make each point, using pictures, a lecture, a demonstration, or supporting statements.
   c. Anticipate doubts and questions from the board members about providing adequate financial support for music in the elementary schools.

2. Referring to the research data cited on pages 10-11, read one of the studies on the transfer effects of music instruction. Prepare a brief summary report of the study, and share it with the class.

Music Instruction
and the
Classroom Teacher

Who is responsible for music instruction in the elementary schools? Under what arrangements is music taught? These questions are significant in determining the kind of instruction future classroom teachers and music specialists are given in their undergraduate preparation. If, for example, elementary classroom teachers almost never lead their classes in singing, then instruction in song-leading can be omitted from their music methods course. Because the roles of the classroom teacher and the music specialist are different, both future classroom teachers and music specialists need to be aware of the way in which music instruction is generally conducted "on the job."

PERSONNEL RESPONSIBLE FOR MUSIC INSTRUCTION

Music specialists

Music specialists are teachers who hold certification in the subject area of music. Usually their undergraduate training has included special instruction in teaching music in the elementary and middle/junior high schools, as well as student teaching at these levels. In some universities, music education majors spend about half of their undergraduate program in the major area of music, taking courses in music theory, music history and literature, applied study on an instrument or in voice, music methods, conducting, and ensembles. Their subject-matter knowledge and performance skills are superior to those of most elementary education majors, who normally take only one or two courses in music.

Despite the expertise of the specialists, they seldom have sole responsibility for music in the elementary classroom. In actual school situations, they normally are able to spend only about 30 minutes twice a week with each classroom- hardly an overwhelming amount of time. They would like to meet each class more often, but seldom can the budget of a school district allow for the employing of enough specialists. Therefore, although their competence may be great, the time they have for teaching any one class is limited.

There are other limitations as well. Music specialists must operate on a strict schedule if they are to get around to all of the classes and schools for which they are responsible. This means that they cannot be flexible about the amount of time they spend or when they spend it. A classroom teacher may decide that two o'clock on Wednesday would be a good time for the children to sing some songs about pioneer life in the United States. But if the music specialist is scheduled with the class at nine o'clock on Tuesdays and Thursdays, the songfest will have to occur then, unless the classroom teacher can lead the singing at the desired time. Occasionally a music specialist can arrange a schedule change to accommodate a special event for a class, but that cannot be done often.

Furthermore, it is difficult for the specialist to integrate the music instruction with the social studies or language arts projects of a classroom that is not visited daily. It is not that the specialist is uncooperative, but it is hard for two busy teachers to remain in full communication about the current activities of any class. The problem is compounded by the number of classes for which the specialist is responsible. It is almost impossible for any specialist to devise a different plan for each of the several classes at all of the grade levels that are visited each week.

It is difficult for specialists, who usually see several hundred students each week, to know each child; it takes a few weeks just to learn their names. Again, it is not that the specialists care less about children than classroom teachers do. It is just the practical problem of dividing time and attention equitably among so many children.

Music consultants

A consultant is one who possesses expertise in an area and offers help on request. Music consultants are specialists who are responsible for helping teachers, usually those in the elementary classroom. The ratio of music consultants to children is generally much greater than that of specialists, who do the actual teaching. Although the teaching of children is not their main assignment, consultants are also strong in subject matter preparation.

In actual practice, some specialists who are designated as "consultants" are teachers, and others designated as "teachers" serve mainly as consultants. The terms are not applied consistently.

A continuing problem for consultants is that their advice is seldom requested, except by a few teachers who are already strong in music. The teachers most in need of help often do not realize that their efforts could be improved, so they are unlikely to ask for assistance. For this reason, consultants usually just offer their suggestions and hope that they will be followed. Most consultants have no administrative authority, so they cannot require that their ideas be implemented. Their role is simply to share their subject matter expertise in an advisory capacity.

Often consultants are responsible for so many schools that they can have little personal contact with the teachers. Sometimes they can visit a classroom only a few times during the year. Written curriculum guides and memos containing suggestions and exhortations must take the place of personal contacts. Sometimes consultants organize in-service workshops for classroom teachers in the district. These sessions serve not only as a help to the teachers, but also as a device for coordinating music instruction within the district.

Music supervisors

A supervisor is more likely to work with music teachers as an administrator, and to serve as a liaison between music teachers and the central administration of the school district. The term is sometimes used interchangeably with "consultant."

Classroom teachers

Classroom teachers enjoy some advantages over music specialists in the teaching of music. They know their students better, and they can be more flexible about incorporating music into a particular learning situation. There is no problem about singing the songs of the pioneers at two o'clock on Wednesday if that seems best. Classroom teachers can integrate music with any area of the curriculum whenever they are so inclined.

Although the music preparation of most classroom teachers is much less extensive than that of a music specialist, the expedient of simply adding more hours of music to a college's elementary education program is not a viable solution. Someone once asked representatives from each academic area what they considered to be the *minimum* preparation that classroom teachers should receive in their particular academic discipline. When the recommended minimum requirements were totaled in terms of course hours, they amounted to more than 200 semester credits—the equivalent of seven years of college. A seven-year program is not a realistic possibility, of course, but the results of the survey point out the serious compromises that must be made in terms of the subject matter preparation of classroom teachers.

The limited preparation of classroom teachers in music led the professional association of school music teachers, the Music Educators National Conference, to recommend that music in the elementary schools be taught by music specialists. The 1972 *Teacher Education in Music: Final Report* of the MENC reads: "The Commission recommends that music in the elementary schools be taught by music specialists."[1] However, the report goes on to say, ". . . even when there is a specialist assigned to a school, there will be times when the classroom teacher must take some responsibility for classroom musical experiences."

Over the years, the music education profession has wavered in its assessment of the music teaching abilities of classroom teachers. In the 1940s and 1950s, a large segment of the profession promoted the idea of music teaching by classroom teachers. With the increasing interest in subject matter in the 1960s, the trend moved away from that view. This shift in position has come about partly because of today's greater demands on the classroom teacher in other areas of the curriculum, and these responsibilities in turn decrease the attention that the teacher can give to music. Another reason for the change in thinking is that many music educators thirty years ago had unrealistic expectations of what a classroom teacher could accomplish in teaching music. Eventually they realized that a course or two and some workshops are not enough to enable most classroom teachers to feel confident in their teaching of music. In short, the roles for specialists and classroom teachers had not been defined realistically, an oversight that resulted in frustration and unfulfilled expectations.

It is not only a feeling of inadequate preparation that leads some classroom teachers to prefer minimal involvement with music teaching. They learn that it is hard to find sufficient time to plan for the many subject areas for which they are responsible. The subjects put off until last, both in teacher planning and in actual class time consumed, are often the "special" subjects like music. An imminent performance for parents or public is often a spur to intensive short-range work. But a balanced program of music instruction requires a sustained, varied, and long-range effort, and this requires a consistent investment of time.

It sometimes happens that classroom teachers are willing to devote class time to music, but the children still do not receive an organized program of music instruction. The occasional singing of a song or two, with a reference to music in a social studies lesson now and then, turns out to be the extent of the music curriculum. It should not be assumed that the lack of organized music instruction is the fault of the classroom teacher. True, the curriculum statements of the school district may mandate a specific and rather sizable amount of time for music, and they may even include guidelines for course content and minimum music competencies for children at each grade level. But unless the principal or curriculum director makes clear that the district regards music as important in the education of children, and commends the music curriculum guidelines to the teachers, a sketchy music program may still prevail.

These facts, coupled with the realities of limited preparation and class time, work against the teacher who wants to do a more thorough job of teaching music. In order to teach music adequately, the classroom teacher must have above-average ability and a strong commitment to a well-rounded education for the children.

Value of classroom teachers in music instruction

Even if there were enough music specialists to teach all of the music in all of the elementary classrooms in the United States, the interest and participation of classroom teachers in the music instruction would still be necessary, as noted in *Teacher Education in Music: Final Report.* The reasons can be summed up in two words: attitude and completion.

The attitude of classroom teachers toward music may be as significant as their ability to teach it. Children are quick to detect how their teacher feels about a subject. When a music specialist visits the classroom, a lack of interest or support from the classroom teacher can undercut what the specialist tries to accomplish. For example, when the time for music arrives, a few teachers think, "Am I ever ready for a break!" as they hurry off to the teachers' lounge. Other teachers say with dismay, "Oh, it's not time for music *again*, is it?" Some classroom teachers who are responsible for music instruction will cancel the music lesson if academic work is not completed. Others will merely go through the motions of teaching music by letting the children make all of the choices, or they may elect to sing a song or two or perhaps listen to something on the record player. A few teachers fail to prepare the children to be attentive in music; they are likely to turn their unruly classes over to the music specialist with the comment, "They're really wild today. Lots of luck!" Such actions are detrimental to the children's attitude toward music, and indirectly affect how much they will learn about it.

The teacher, whether a specialist or a classroom teacher, needs to serve as a positive model for the children's interest in music. Albert

Bandura, a noted psychologist, has conducted research studies that indicate children do indeed imitate the examples set by adults, especially teachers.[2] Therefore, the teacher needs to be positive about music and the children's efforts in music class. To convey this attitude, the teacher should first see that the children enjoy music; the instruction need not be tedious and unpleasant for learning to take place. The teacher also needs to be optimistic about the children's potential success in learning music. Research by Robert Rosenfeld and others has demonstrated how teachers' predictions and beliefs about their students' abilities can influence the results.[3] Children tend to fulfill the expectations that parents and teachers have of them. So teachers should assume that, yes, the children will learn in music. The musical genius is rare and will succeed with or without school music instruction. Music success should not be gauged by that standard. The great majority of children can learn about music and perform it so that it will enrich their lives. With that goal in mind, it certainly is worthwhile to have a positive viewpoint.

The word "completion" was used earlier to describe the follow-up or continuity of effort that can be provided by the classroom teacher. Without this help, the music instruction offered the children will usually be incomplete. Even if music specialists had more time than the usual 50 or 60 minutes per week with each class, there would not be time to complete successfully all of the activities that should be included in music instruction. It is beneficial, for example, for the children to review a song on a day when the specialist is not in the building, to hear the rest of a recording that was begun during the music lesson, and to practice reading some pitch or rhythm patterns. Children benefit especially from limited amounts of daily work in skill areas such as reading or singing. The classroom teacher can be a valuable asset by following up activities and projects begun by the specialist.

Combination arrangements

Arrangements for teaching music can involve both the music specialist and the classroom teacher. Such combinations range from situations in which the specialist does little while the classroom teacher is responsible for most of the teaching, to situations in which the specialist does virtually all of the music instruction with little help from the classroom teacher.

It is difficult to obtain data about the various arrangements for teaching music in the nation's elementary schools. There are many variations from state to state, and a degree of confusion exists about the terminology that designates various teacher roles. One survey by the National Education Association provided these data:

The practice reported by . . . about 40 percent [of the schools]
was to have the classroom teacher teach music with help from a music
specialist. . . . The elementary-school classroom teacher had to teach
music on his/her own in almost as large a percentage of schools in grades
1, 2, and 3, but in grades 4, 5, and 6, the teacher carried the full responsibility for music in less than a third of the schools. Music specialists
alone did the teaching in about one-fifth of the schools in grades 4-6,
and in 12 to 15 percent of the schools in grades 1-3.[4]

A combination arrangement alleviates the disadvantages encountered when there is complete reliance on either specialist or classroom
teacher. The specialist contributes subject knowledge and skills, while
the classroom teacher provides schedule flexibility and familiarity with
the individual children.

The combination arrangement has merit beyond its obvious educational virtues. Economic factors also encourage it. As one professor
observed about the university where he worked, "Around here, money
doesn't talk; it screams!" Most educational institutions are hard-pressed
financially, so they cannot hire as many specialists as they would like.

There is also the matter of released time for classroom teachers,
as required in many states by regulation or by the master contract between the teachers' union and the school board. Teachers need some
time each day to collect their thoughts and relax, away from the children. Since youngsters cannot be left unattended, other teachers must
be instructing or supervising them while the regular teacher has released
time. Special teachers fill this role automatically while teaching the children a legitimate subject. In some cases, the need to cover for teachers
while they are on released time has been the impetus for hiring music
specialists, thereby providing a good example of doing the right thing
for the wrong reason.

Differences in the roles of classroom teachers and music specialists

Not only do classroom teachers and music specialists differ in
training and competencies, but their assignments also differ. Music
specialists are expected to devote their full attention to the education
of children in one subject, while classroom teachers are expected to
oversee many subject areas. Music specialists work at several levels within their academic discipline as it progresses from kindergarten through
the higher grades, while classroom teachers must concentrate on the
grade level at which they are teaching.

Basically, music specialists have the role of designer, and classroom teachers fill the role of technician or artisan. The two roles are

analogous to those of a doctor (the expert in medicine) and a nurse (the technician), or an architect and a bricklayer. The expert-technician roles are complementary, not competitive. If carried out successfully, they lead to a better program of instruction in music than can be achieved by either specialists or classroom teachers working alone. The complementary nature of their roles can be summarized in this way:

Music Specialist	Classroom Teacher
Assumes a leadership role	Assumes a supportive role
Formulates objectives	Helps to achieve objectives
Makes plans	Implements plans
Introduces areas of study	Follows up areas of study

As an example of their respective functions, it is the specialist who decides if, when, and how hand signs should be taught, recorder skills should be mastered, and theme and variation technique should be introduced. The classroom teacher supports these endeavors by helping the children as they practice hand signs, review their recorder-playing skills, and listen to a recording of music that demonstrates theme and variation technique.

The need for cooperation

For the best results to be achieved, a cooperative relationship needs to be established between music specialists and classroom teachers. That is easier said than done, but it still should be accomplished. Part of the problem is the difficulty in finding time to communicate and discuss the music instruction. Music specialists may need to work with twenty or more teachers in two or more buildings. Because of their traveling assignments, they are not full-time members of any one building faculty, so it is hard for them to attend faculty meetings or to see other teachers in the lunchroom or faculty lounge. These absences cause some building principals and other teachers to wonder about the loyalty and interest of the specialists, who in fact may be missing lunch each day in the rush to get to the next school. Sometimes music specialists must communicate by written memos, which tend to seem impersonal. Not all of the difficulties in communication can be fully overcome, but mutual understanding can help.

Classroom teachers have a right to expect that they will receive clear and reasonable suggestions for appropriate follow-up activities. The suggestions should be realistic in terms of what the children are likely to accomplish within the limited time available for follow-up. Music specialists have the right to expect that classroom teachers will remain with their classes during at least a portion of the music instruction. In this way the classroom teacher can gain some idea of what the children are learning in music, and can follow up more effectively.

ASSISTANCE AVAILABLE IN MUSIC SERIES TEXTBOOKS

This discussion is not a critique or evaluation of the several series of music textbooks available for the elementary grades. Rather it is an exploration of the many ways in which these books are designed to be helpful, especially to classroom teachers.

Four publishers currently market extremely attractive series of graded music books: Silver Burdett Company, Macmillan Publishing Company, Inc., Holt, Rinehart & Winston, Inc., and American Book Company.* The books are replete with color illustrations, and their content is carefully prepared with the help of expert consultants to ensure authenticity. Each music series includes a teacher's edition for each grade level, and sets of recordings of all the music presented in the books. The material should not be followed slavishly, but should be adapted to the needs of a particular class or school. The books contain more songs and activities than most classes can cover in a year, so teachers are given a choice of what to include in their music classes.

Although books are not necessary for the teaching of music, they are helpful, for the following reasons.

1. They offer a selection of topics, songs, and activities that expert authors have compiled, so a teacher is spared the major effort of rooting around in search of songs and ideas for music instruction.

2. The books provide a minimum or "bedrock" program of music learning, which is especially helpful when no music specialist or district curriculum is available for the teacher's guidance. Often the book's content is organized around topics or units, and these provide a natural sequence for the music instruction.

3. The teacher's edition of each book suggests points to stress and questions to raise. Reference material is included, and musical terms are defined. Through the use of colored inks or explanatory material in the margins, the teacher's edition provides background information concisely and quickly.

4. Simple piano accompaniments for most of the songs in the book are included. The accompaniments are beyond the ability of a rank amateur, but students or teachers with a modest background in piano can play most of them.

*See Appendix B for more complete information on these series.

5. The books include ideas for incorporating classroom instruments and orchestral instruments into the song accompaniments.

6. Pronunciation guides for all foreign language songs are included. Translations are also provided if they are not present as alternative verses of the song.

7. The recorded performances are of high quality. The instrumentalists employed for them are among the top performers available, because the rules of the American Federation of Musicians make it no more expensive to hire the best than to hire less able musicians. In the past decade there has been a trend toward recording children's singing on many of the songs. These performances provide an excellent model of good singing for the children to hear. Fine adult singers are also recorded for the albums. The musical arrangements of the songs are tasteful, interesting, and quite authentic, with folk instruments utilized when appropriate.

8. The books offer supplementary suggestions for extending the learning activities into other arts and other academic disciplines. For teachers familiar with the special music methods devised by Carl Orff and Zoltan Kodály, there are recommendations for incorporating those teaching techniques into the children's music experience.

9. The songs are indexed in several ways, according to title, type, country of origin, musical concepts, appropriateness for special occasions, and involvement of instruments.

To provide a clearer idea of the appearance of a teacher's edition and the help it can provide, two pages are reproduced here—one from the third-grade book published by Silver Burdett, and the other from the second-grade book published by Macmillan.

On the page from the Silver Burdett book (opposite), the questions for the teacher to discuss with the class are printed boldly in black. The cues for the teacher are lighter because they are in blue type, although the color is not reproduced here. The round circle next to the song title indicates that a recording is available. The keyboard fragment of two black and three white keys, given beside "Teacher's Edition," indicates that a piano accompaniment is available, and tells where it can be found in the teacher's edition. A reduced copy of the student book is included in the teacher's edition.

In the Macmillan book (see p. 26), the top of the page tells the teacher the key and starting note of the song, the page number for the piano accompaniment, and information about the recording that is provided. Statements of objectives, materials, and teaching procedures appear at the side of the page. Additional suggestions are given at the bottom of the page; in this case, an idea for relating the words to language arts instruction is offered. Extension of the lesson and statements about the responses desired from the children appear on the

When you play records at home, you can *hear* whether men, women, or children are singing without seeing them. Listen to the tone color of the voices on this recording. What makes the contrast between sections A and B?

Children sing section A; a man sings section B.

"Little David, Play on Your Harp," Recording 4

This time, sing section A. How many times will you sing it?

Section A returns, so the children sing it twice.

"Little David, Play on Your Harp," Recording 4

Teacher's Edition, page 172

You know that both shapes and letters can show the form of a song.

Which drawing in your book shows the form of "Little David, Play on Your Harp"?

Circle, square, circle (ABA)

Pupil's Book, page 77

Here is another song in ABA form. Follow the long and the short phrases in each section as you listen.

SPECIMEN PAGE—*SILVER BURDETT MUSIC*

Source: Elizabeth Crook et al., *Silver Burdett Music,* Book 3 (Morristown, N. J.: General Learning Corporation, 1974).

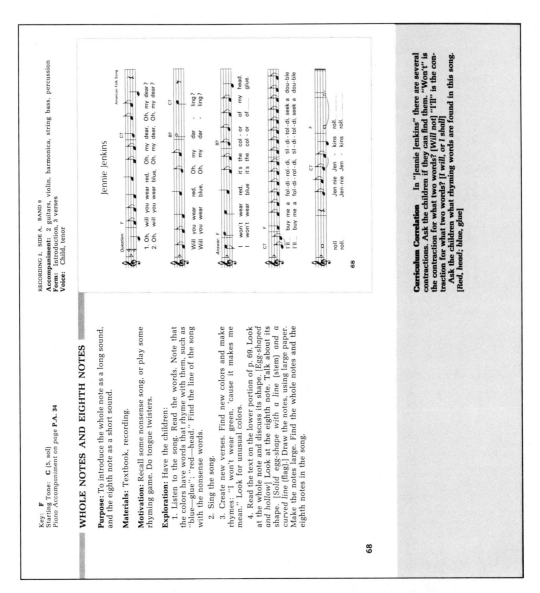

SPECIMEN PAGE—MACMILLAN *THE SPECTRUM OF MUSIC*

Source: May Val Marsh et al., *The Spectrum of Music,* Book 2 (New York: Macmillan, 1980).

next page, along with additional learning activities. As in the Silver Burdett series, a reduced copy of the page from the student book is included for the teacher's convenience.

Classroom teachers are important to the program of music instruction in the elementary school. Their role in music teaching is challenging, but sources of assistance are available, including specialist help and well-planned music series books. Classroom teachers should not be expected to organize the complete music instructional program, but by taking advantage of the help and material available, they can teach music effectively and contribute much to their students' enjoyment of music.

NOTES

1. Robert H. Klotman, ed., *Teacher Education in Music: Final Report*, (Reston, Va.: Music Educators National Conference, 1972), p. 20.
2. Albert Bandura and F. J. McDonald, "Influence of Social Reinforcement and the Behavior of Models in Shaping Children's Moral Judgments," *Journal of Abnormal and Social Psychology*, Vol. 67 (1963), pp. 274-81.
3. Robert Rosenthal and L. Jacobson, "Teacher's Expectations as Self-Fulfilling Prophecies," in R. C. Sprinthall and N. A. Sprinthall, eds., *Educational Psychology: Selected Readings* (New York: Van Nostrand-Reinhold, 1969), pp. 295-300.
4. *Music and Art in the Public Schools*, Research Monograph 1963-M3 (Washington, D. C.. National Education Association, 1963), p. 12.

REVIEW QUESTIONS

1. a. What are the advantages and disadvantages of having music specialists be responsible for all of the music instruction in the elementary schools?
   b. What are the advantages and disadvantages of having classroom teachers be responsible for all of the music instruction in the elementary schools?

2. What are the differences in roles between a music specialist and a music consultant?

3. In what ways are the interest and participation of classroom teachers important to the success of the music instruction?

4. a. If the benefits of a coordinated effort between the music specialist and the classroom teacher are to be realized, what roles need need to be adopted?
   b. What conditions need to be met for a cooperative relationship to exist between the music specialist and the classroom teacher?

5. Cite five ways in which the use of music series books can be helpful to the teacher.

6. Describe how a page from a teacher's edition in either the Macmillan or the Silver Burdett book series can aid the teacher.

ACTIVITIES

1. Find out the arrangements for music instruction in the elementary schools of a particular school district. (The districts near your college can be examined, as can your home school district.) Gather information on the following:
   a. Who teaches music?
   b. How much time for music does each classroom receive each week?
   c. Is a curriculum guide or other information on teaching music available?
   d. What music book series is used, if any?
   e. If a music consultant is employed, by what means does the consultant communicate ideas and suggestions to the teachers?
   f. If music specialists are employed, how many children do they see each week? How many classrooms in how many schools?
   g. Ask two classroom teachers and one music specialist what they believe to be the main problems with the music program in their schools.

2. On page 22, in the paragraph beginning "As an example . . . ," there are practical examples of actions that might be taken by music specialists and classroom teachers as they implement their respective roles of expert and technician. Team up with another class member to develop three additional examples in the area of music.

3. To the extent that elementary music series books and materials are available to you, examine and compare them, especially the teacher's editions, record albums, and other materials such as charts or tapes. In the teacher's editions, look for:
   a. classifications in the index
   b. outline of units or minimum program
   c. teaching suggestions, both general and specific
   d. piano accompaniments

Guidelines for Planning and Teaching Music in the Elementary School

The phenomenon of learning is an intriguing aspect of human behavior, and it has inspired considerable study. Research continues to reveal new insights into assumptions of the past. Below is a true-false quiz containing some common beliefs about learning music. The correct responses will be disclosed at various points in the chapter.

T (F) 1. The most effective way to develop an initial understanding of a rhythmic pattern is for the teacher to describe its rhythmic values verbally.

T (F) 2. Repeating a point is the best way to make sure the students remember it.

T (F) 3. Practice in solving difficult mathematical problems will bring about improved thinking ability in other academic areas.

T F 4. Concepts are usually remembered better than particular facts.

T F   5. If the students cannot get a portion of a song right, they should go over it again and again until they can do it correctly.

T F   6. In learning a song, a class should first get the notes right, then work on understanding its musical qualities.

T F   7. There is one best way to teach a song in a music class, and the prospective teacher should use that method.

T F   8. Because concepts are developed from knowing many facts, teachers should stress detailed information more than broad, conceptual understandings.

T F   9. Students will learn better if they understand the reason for what they are doing.

T F   10. A student who wants to learn to play the guitar or other instrument should practice for an hour and 45 minutes one day a week rather than for 15 minutes every day.

Although there is a little truth in most of the ten statements, eight of them are false. Which ones are true and which are false is not important at this moment. The important point is that each answer calls for an assumption about how music is best learned. Whether they realize it or not, teachers make decisions based on their fundamental beliefs about learning. These assumptions exert a strong influence on what happens in the music class.

The guidelines presented in this chapter are intended to serve as a checklist for the teacher in planning and teaching music. While there is more to teaching a successful music class than simply following the principles presented here, these points will help establish a basis for good music teaching.

Two qualifications should be observed when following the guidelines. First, none of them is absolute, and none should override the others. Reason and judgment are needed in applying them. Second, some of the guidelines do not apply to all types of learning. Developing concepts and acquiring skills require different approaches. The idea that there is only one right way to teach music is incorrect, so the answer to question 7 is "false." The appropriate method depends on the situation, the students, and what they are trying to learn.

Learning is a many-sided word. To some people it means memorization ("John has learned the multiplication tables"). To others it indicates acquiring a skill ("John has learned how to type"). Sometimes people use the word to mean that insight has been gained ("John has learned the relationship between nutrition and health"). Sometimes "learn" means that a problem has been solved ("John has learned how to put together the works of a clock").

LEARNING IN MUSIC

When applied to music, the word "learn" is just as diffuse. There is factual, cognitive information to be learned, often involving memorization. Skills are evident in careful listening habits and in music-reading proficiency, as well as in the actual physical techniques required for singing or playing an instrument. Learning also occurs as insights and concepts are derived from experience with many examples of music. Finally, learning allows problems to be solved, as when decisions are made about the interpretation of a song.

But there is something more in music—an aspect that is elusive and difficult to describe. It is the learning of the patterns of music, its syntax. There are some successful musicians, especially in the folk and popular idiom, who are not formally educated in music but who possess a highly developed sense of how musical sounds are organized in a particular style. Awareness of musical syntax is one of the first things that a youngster needs to learn, because it is the basis from which the child evaluates ensuing musical experiences. Gaining a sense of sound patterns is made more difficult by the fact that they cannot be explained in words. Verbal descriptions of music are boring and ineffective.

There is another facet of music that is difficult to verbalize. The flow of sound with its changing levels of intensity and its varied tone qualities stirs the emotions of the performer and listener. People do not usually laugh or cry when they hear music that moves them, because they have learned to control the expression of their feelings. Philosophers and scholars agree that the emotional response to music is beyond the ability of words to describe. It may be that music breaks through the limits of words by allowing each individual to express whatever is within. In any case, learning in music includes becoming more sensitive to the expressive qualities in music.

Start where the students are

The principle of adjusting the content and methods of a class to the knowledge and interests of the students is certainly a truism in education, but its application is often difficult because of the differences that exist within any group of children. Some youngsters are more verbal, more analytical, or more experienced in a given area than others. These differences are noticeable in music, a subject in which some children receive private instruction outside of school. It is hard to design a lesson that is interesting to the more advanced children without confusing the less experienced in the class, or to work with the less able children without boring the more able ones. Nevertheless, the teacher must assess the various levels of ability within the class, and plan the instruction so that it includes suitable learning activities and significant content.

Determining an appropriate level of instruction is difficult for another reason: it requires an amalgamation of the children's needs with the teacher's own interests and abilities in the subject. In the case of classroom teachers, music is not usually a field of special training. While expertise in matching student ability with a balanced course content in music is not a realistic expectation for elementary education majors, this book does offer suggestions for improving that skill. Classroom teachers tend to underestimate the musical potential of their students, while music specialists tend to have high expectations, probably as a reflection of their own special interest and training.

GUIDELINES FOR TEACHING MUSIC

The guidelines that apply to the actual teaching of music classes are presented first, so that the later suggestions for developing plans can be viewed in the context of these guidelines.

Provide experiences

Have you ever tried to describe to someone what the color green looks like? It's nearly impossible. To know what green looks like, one has to see it, to experience it. Words cannot give an adequate description of any color. The same situation exists in music, especially for such fundamental aspects as beat, pitch, tone color, loudness, harmony, and so on. Children can memorize a definition of "melody," but they understand little of what the words mean until they hear the concept in actual musical sounds. They need to experience melodies in pieces of music, and then—the order is important here—they can be given a term for the phenomenon of consecutive cohesive pitches. Experience should come first, then a verbalization such as, "A melody is a series of pitches that seem to belong together." The answer to question 1 in the true-false quiz is "false."

The need for experience as a basis for learning is especially important for children of elementary school age. The psychologist Jean Piaget spent his professional career conducting research on the mental development of children. Although one may question certain of his specific ideas, in general they verify what parents and teachers have observed for generations.[1] When children enter elementary school they are still in what Piaget terms the "intuitive or preoperational" stage. Between the ages of seven and eleven, children are in the stage he terms "concrete operations." In neither of these stages is the conceptualizing of abstractions very successful. "Just give me the facts" is the typical attitude of an elementary school child. Literalness based on concrete experience is especially meaningful to children at this level. These concrete experiences become the basis for later intellectual concepts.

Two precautions should be noted with regard to the need for experiencing. First, the experience must be suitable for whatever it is the children are to learn. Playing chords on an autoharp will do little to further a knowledge of melodies. Second, not all experiences are equally valuable in terms of what the children learn from them. A teacher should consider the amount of time and effort required, and balance this against the probable benefit to the children.

In many ways, learning in music is analogous to mastering a language. A child learning to speak will imitate the sounds applied to concrete objects—"dog," "dada," and so on. No formal definition of "dog" is provided, nor is there a concern about grammatical correctness. Parents are delighted when a two-year-old says, "Dog bark," even though a smoother construction would be "The dog is barking." Furthermore, three or four years of speaking and understanding a language precede any attempt to write words. The principle of experience-before-symbolization is clear in the language-learning process, and it applies to music as well.

Use a multisensory approach

Some years ago, examiners in the Belgian Department of Education noticed that students from a certain small rural school were consistently scoring unusually high on the national examinations in mathematics. Investigation proved that the teacher at that school had a superior method of teaching mathematics to children. The method featured small sticks that are called "Cuisenaire rods." Each of the ten sizes is a different color, and they are proportioned so that ten of the "one" rods equal one "ten" rod in length, and so on.

Why are the Cuisenaire rods so successful? One reason is that the children can see *and* feel 2 + 2 = 4; no longer are the numbers abstractions, manipulated without comprehension. The rods provide a concrete experience, as recommended in the preceding paragraphs. In addition, seeing and feeling provide a stronger impression than either experience alone. Another principle of learning, then, is that the more ways in which something is experienced, the more likely it is to be learned.

One application of this guideline can be seen in the use of visual aids such as films, film strips, and overhead projectors. Teachers can help children to associate sound and notation through the use of books, chalk and flannel boards, and similar means. The guideline suggests that seeing an opera or ballet is better than merely hearing the music for it.

Provide valid musical experiences

Music is often defined as "organized sound." It is an aural art. Therefore, if learning is to be true to the nature of music, it must relate directly to organized sound.

There are several ways in which activities in music classes may fail to meet this guideline. One is when the music study becomes so cerebral that it loses its association with actual sound. Sometimes teachers attempt to explain the rhythmic values of notes by treating them as mathematical problems containing fractions. For example, $½ + ½ = 1$, so half of a beat plus half of a beat equals one beat. Intellectual understanding of note durations is helpful, but it must be related to actual sound, because arithmetic skills in themselves do not guarantee an understanding of rhythm. A similar lack of connection with sound occurs when a class engages in purely cerebral exercises, perhaps working extensively to spell words in music notation (C A B B A G E, B A G G A G E, etc.).

Another way in which the sensing of music as organized sound can be missed is when the singing or playing becomes simply a mechanical undertaking. Musical sensititivy is lost when there is a preoccupation with performance techniques, such as how one fingers a scale or breathes when singing. Just producing the notes of a song is not enough. Even seals in a circus can play tunes on horns (a feat for which they are rewarded with a fish, in lieu of artistic satisfaction). The difference between the rendition of a piece by a human being and by an animal should be the element of awareness that makes the human sensitive to the organization of the sounds as they form music. Admittedly, musicianship cannot be conveyed when mechanical flaws are distracting. It is sometimes necessary, therefore, to isolate technical passages for practice purposes. But the passage should be reinstated into its musical context as soon as possible. In this way, musical considerations will not appear to be "tacked on" after the piece is prepared. The answer to question 6 is "false." Technical accuracy and musical understanding should generally be developed together.

A more subtle temptation is the appeal of planning a full-blown musical production in which musical factors take last place behind the excitement of designing costumes, building stage sets, learning dialogue, planning choreography, and preparing publicity. Most accoutrements of show business are quite unrelated to musical considerations.

Involve the students

In one research study, students were given two sets of arithmetic problems. On the first set they were provided with principles to help them solve the problems. On the second set they had to deduce the principle for themselves. A week later they were tested on their ability to solve the two types of problems. The results: Students did better on the problems for which they had to deduce the principles than they did on the problems for which they had been given the principles.[2]

What do the results of this and similar studies indicate? They show that what people do for themselves is learned better and is more likely to be remembered. What they get "free" just doesn't mean as much. For this reason, children should feel that they have an investment in their own learning. This guideline has long been known to observant teachers, and it has in recent years received renewed attention under the heading "discovery method," sometimes inaccurately called the "Socratic method." One reason for the success of the programmed learning format is the fact that it requires involvement through frequent responses from the student.

Student involvement includes letting the children in on the reasons for mastering what they are trying to learn. People learn more effectively when they understand why they are being asked to do something—a fact that makes question 9 in the quiz "true." Children are often admonished to sit up straight when they sing. Do they know why? The teacher needs to introduce postural experiments so that the children can demonstrate for themselves that an erect rib cage allows more room for breath, which in turn aids in producing a good singing tone.

What is the difference between the guidelines of "experiencing" and "involvement"? With experiencing, the teacher is largely responsible for the decisions and leadership. Involvement implies that some of the obligation is transferred to the children, so that they become responsible for directing a portion of their learning. The notion of more student responsibility and initiative is often associated today with the "open classroom" philosophy. Examples of student involvement include deciding which instruments and style of accompaniment are appropriate for a song, offering ideas for singing a song expressively, and discussing the similarities and differences between two songs or pieces of music. Most of the teaching examples presented later in this book call for the involvement of the students.

Promote conceptual learning

A concept is "an abstract or generic idea generalized from particular instances."[3] There is, for example, a concept that is represented

symbolically in the English language by the word "dog"; it is a generalization about a certain type of animal. The characteristics of "dog" as a
concept include an animal with four legs and a tail, the ability to bark,
an acute sense of smell and hearing, inability to climb trees or see in
the dark, and so on. Children make a generalization individually from
seeing several animals that people identify for them as "dog," and from
those experiences they form general conclusions about "dogs." At first
they may mistake a cat for a dog, but they soon learn to refine their
concept of "dog" by eliminating from that category all animals that
meow instead of bark.

Why are concepts important in learning, as well as in thinking and
communicating? First, concepts can be applied to more than one situation. Second, concepts and general understandings are far more likely
to be remembered. Therefore, the answer to question 4 in the quiz is
"true." In fact, studies indicate that the ability to interpret and apply
basic ideas does not diminish significantly after a course is over, a stability that is not characteristic of detailed, factual information.[4] Because basic ideas are retained well, in addition to some specific information, the answer to question 8 is "false." Teachers should encourage
children to develop general understandings rather than memorize a
large amount of detailed information.

Memory. Effective learning means retaining what has been learned.
Some people downgrade the importance of remembering by charging
that students who demonstrate adequate retention are merely "regurgi-
tating facts." Without memory, however, people would exist only on a
level of instinct, impulse, and perpetual trial-and-error. The issue is not
whether students should remember, but rather what they should
remember.

Certain techniques and practices can help children to remember
the content of a lesson. Here are a few memory-aiding suggestions:

1. Make the material as interesting as possible, and apply it to the
children's present experiences. People on a sinking ship will concentrate on lifeboat instructions more intensely than will the jovial pas-
sengers just sailing out of the harbor. Although the material covered
in a classroom seldom appears to be of life-saving importance, the
teacher should still treat it with a sense of immediacy. Even the information offered in Chapter 1 can be shared with children in such a way
as to impress them with the timelessness and universality of music in
civilization. There is a common thread of human experience that relates
music of different times and places to the present, and children can
become sensitive to this quality.

2. Structure the original learning so that it is thorough and vivid.
Often what is forgotten was never really learned in the first place. It is

not necessary to make the children go over the same material again and again, if there is adequate clarity and comprehension when the material is first taught. Films and other visual aids—even placing key words on the chalkboard—are helpful techniques for catching the attention of the class from the beginning.

3. Present new material so that it relates to what the children have previously learned. Nonsense material, so educational researchers have discovered, is much less likely to be retained, probably because it does not relate to anything else.[5] For example, knowing that the composer Joseph Haydn was born in 1732 is of little value to most children. But if it is pointed out that 1732 was the same year in which George Washington was born, they are more likely to remember that Haydn and Washington lived in the same historical period.

4. Review previously learned material. Most of what is forgotten is lost soon after it is learned, usually within one hour. The rate of forgetting looks something like a ski jump: a rapid descent followed by a gradual flattening out. The amount of material remembered will vary according to the conditions pointed out previously in this discussion, but the essential pattern of forgetting remains the same. The need for review is not a sign of bad teaching or lazy students. True, some things are remembered after only one presentation, but most items are retained only because they are encountered several times.

Review should not be confused with sheer repetition. Repeating for its own sake is seldom effective because it tends to "turn off" the children. This fact makes question 2 in the quiz "false." The parent who complains, "If I've told you once, I've told you a thousand times . . ." may be right, but the method is ineffective.

5. Test the class on the material learned. Sometimes tests are scorned because it is felt that the children learn only to pass the examination. As long as the test material is useful and reasonable, such learning does not seem to be a bad result. The effectiveness of testing as a learning device depends primarily on whether the concepts have been adequately taught. As long as the attitudes of the teacher and children remain open and relaxed, the organizing of newly learned ideas for purposes of a test does aid in remembering.[6]

Conditions for transfer. For many years educators believed in automatic transfer from one formal discipline to another. That is, they believed that engaging in difficult mental tasks such as mathematics or foreign language strengthened a person's general mental powers in much the same way that physical exercise develops muscular strength. The misplaced faith in automatic transfer and formal discipline stemmed from a basic misconception about the brain. The brain is not a muscle that can be built up through exercise. If one engages in intensive practice in geometry problems, an improvement in the ability to solve geometry problems will be noted, but no general gain in academic ability or logical thinking is likely.[7] Therefore, the answer to question 3 in the quiz is "false."

What does this fact indicate about transfer? It means that there is no such thing as *automatic* transfer. Transfer depends on the degree of similarity between the two areas and the extent to which the instruction is designed to achieve maximum transfer. The greater the similarity, overlap, or number of common elements between two topics, the greater the possibility of transfer. This fact partially explains the possible transfer value of music to the language arts, which was mentioned in Chapter 1. Also, the more the teacher stresses the application and transfer of what is being taught, the greater is the likelihood of its application in other situations. Suggestions for achieving greater transfer in music classes are offered throughout this book, especially in some of the sample lessons.

Develop musical skills

Up to this point, the chapter has been primarily devoted to the learning of information and intellectual understandings, or what is termed the "cognitive domain." Attention now turns to the learning of skills, or what is termed the "psychomotor domain."[8] Skills involve not only the mind but also the senses and muscles. Playing the piano, singing on pitch, and hearing music accurately are examples of skills. Because different processes are involved in acquiring skills, somewhat different guidelines are needed.

Distributed effort. Educational psychologists have found that it is far more efficient to learn a skill in numerous short sessions than in a few long sessions. This fact is referred to as "distributed effort" or "distributed practice" or "spaced practice." The research data are impressive. In one experiment the subjects learned stanzas of poetry. When two stanzas were learned in one sitting, the assignment required .38 of a minute per stanza. However, when 100 stanzas were learned in one session, the assignment took 3.85 minutes per stanza, *ten times as long for each stanza.*[9] It is clearly more efficient to distribute the learning of skills and memorization tasks. Furthermore, it has been shown that more learning takes place in the first ten minutes of the session than takes place in the next ten, and so on. Because of the effectiveness of distributed effort, the answer to question 10 is "false."

In teaching, it is better to leave something unfinished and come back to it another day than to overwork on it. The idea of staying on a problem until it is corrected, no matter how long it takes, often produces negative results. Therefore, the answer to question 5 is "false."

On the other hand, distributed effort should not be misinterpreted as an excuse for avoiding hard work. Persistence should not be confused with dull and mechanical repetition.

The maximum amount of time that should be spent on any one activity varies with the amount of concentration required, the age of the children, and their interest in the activity. Elementary school children can concentrate for perhaps ten minutes on a musical skill, then a change of activity or piece of music is beneficial. Shorter times are needed for younger children.

Singleness of concentration. A person can concentrate on only one point at a time. If you know how to rub your stomach and pat your head at the same time, you will recall that you first had to establish the pattern for one arm so that it could move independently before starting the other. The mastery of more complex activities requires similar concentration. For example, a person driving a car for the first time needs to think of each step: turn on the ignition, set the transmission, step on the accelerator, turn the steering wheel, push the brake, and so on. Eventually these actions become automatic, and the driving can continue while the driver is thinking of other matters.

Although the developing of music skills is not bound by a rigid sequence of step-by-step actions, much of the skill-learning in music is simply the building of good habits. People need to have a large quantity of breath to sing well, so proper breathing should be made a habit. Good posture and clear enunciation should also become habitual. The habit of careful listening is necessary for producing a good tone quality, singing in tune, and staying exactly together with others. Because no one can simultaneously concentrate on all of the music skills needed for performance, each skill needs to be isolated occasionally to reinforce the habit being developed. When good habits are well established, they will be maintained even in stress situations such as performing before an audience. There is no need to worry that the rendition will be mindless and mechanical; the good habits that have been built will help the performers to feel more confident, and will free their attention to focus on the musical qualities of their performance.

Encourage positive attitudes

The way children feel about music and music classes is a more important consideration than it is with many of the "academic" subjects. People must read and write almost every day, regardless of whether they enjoy reading and writing. They must balance checkbooks and compute income taxes regardless of how they feel about arithmetic. Not so with music. If people don't like music, they can refrain from buying recordings and attending concerts; if forced to listen to music in a supermarket, they can psychologically "tune it out." Much of the ultimate success of a music class depends on how the class affects the children's attitudes about music. And their attitudes will be affected. The question is not *will* the children have feelings about what they are doing, but rather *what* feelings will they develop?

Attitudes and knowledge are complementary. People cannot have intelligent reactions to something with which they are unfamiliar. If asked, "Do you like aardvarks?" they will probably answer, "I don't know." The teacher's main task is to share knowledge with the children so that at the least they can form intelligent reactions, and at best they can experience what the educator-philosopher Harry Broudy calls "enlightened cherishing."[10]

Human nature is contradictory in its approach to the unknown. It is human to mistrust the unfamiliar, but it is also human to appreciate new insights about something not previously known. Most children, whether they admit it or not, do not want to be left out of anything in life, including music and other arts. Children have a curiosity—a natural desire to know about the world in which they live.[11]

Attitudes and feelings are learned indirectly; they are "caught" rather than "taught" in a direct way. Beliefs and feelings cannot be forced on people. Attitudes are shaped by many factors, including the teacher's personality and interest in the subject, as was noted in Chapter 2.

PLANNING THE MUSIC CLASS

Because the help given classroom teachers for music teaching varies in amount and type from one district to another, there can be no single best way for a teacher to plan the music instruction. The help from two sources—music specialists and music series books—was discussed in Chapter 2.

A third resource for assistance in planning is a curriculum guide. Many school systems and virtually all state education agencies publish curriculum guides for music. These are especially helpful to the classroom teacher because their suggestions are practical and stated in nontechnical terms. The main complaint heard from state music consultants and school curriculum writing teams is that the fruits of their labor are not fully utilized. Perhaps the presence of a state curriculum creates concern about loss of a teacher's individuality. This is a groundless concern, however, because a curriculum guide is not intended to be restrictive. On the contrary, it includes a wide range of workable suggestions that have been proved effective in a variety of situations. A beginning teacher will benefit by trying the ideas, adapting them as needed, and using them as a springboard for developing further ideas.

Principles of planning

Good music instruction is based on a fundamental principle: *Every music activity should be designed to increase the children's understanding of music or to improve their musical skills.* It is not enough just to "put in time" singing songs or listening to recordings; the intent to further the children's education in music needs to be present.

Although no "perfect" plan exists for teaching, certain factors should be considered when planning for music instruction.

1. Build on what has been learned in previous music classes. Begin by recalling what the children have done in music over the last week or two. If recent classes were taught by a music specialist, the observing of at least a part of each music class is a prerequisite for good planning by the classroom teacher. Think about what the children did well and did not do well, what they liked, what did not seem clear to them, and what they know that can serve as a basis for further learning.

2. Choose two or three specific concepts or skills to teach in the lesson. This suggestion assumes that the class is not being operated in an "open," individualized situation, suggestions for which are presented in Chapter 18. Music classes usually last from 20 to 40 minutes in elementary schools, with 30 minutes being the most frequently encountered length. Probably at least three different activities should be included in each class period. Children, especially in the primary grades, tend to become restless, and consequently do not learn as much, when they stay too long on one activity.

The points to be learned should be stated in specific terms. An objective such as "To learn about the music of Mexico" is too vague. An objective such as "To recognize, from hearing, the consecutive thirds found in Mexican music" is much clearer, and the children's success in learning can be evaluated more accurately.

3. State the objectives for the class in terms of what the children should be able to do as a result of the instruction. Outcomes stated in such terms are called "behavioral objectives." Unless the children can provide evidence of how much they have learned, it is hard for the teacher to determine what should be taught in subsequent music classes. Some objectives can apply to skills: for example, "The class will learn to sing 'La Paloma' with accurate pitch and rhythm." Other objectives can apply to cognitive learning: for example, "Ninety percent of the class will be able to describe two characteristics of Mexican music."

4. Select appropriate materials. A teacher who decides to stress the consecutive thirds (known as parallel movement) in Mexican music can look through the books available and select a song that seems best for teaching that aspect. The music series books are a convenient resource, with their indexes arranged by activity (dances, singing games), song subject, country of origin, musical features, and so on. The teacher's editions offer further suggestions for instrument-playing and other activities.

5. Decide how to teach the content. Suppose that parallel thirds in Mexican music is the concept that the class is to learn. There are several ways to teach this. If the class has sung a song with thirds, a review activity can emphasize the singing of that interval. Another approach is to examine the melodic features of Mexican songs and to add the notes a third below when they fit in a particular song. Recordings can be played, enabling the class to hear the sound of parallel thirds in a piece of Mexican music. If the children possess the necessary skills, they can play thirds on recorders or bells. Or they can discover the interval for themselves by examining the notation or by listening carefully to a song that features parallel lines of thirds. All of these procedures are appropriate under the right circumstances. Knowing beforehand which of the several possibilities will be employed leads to more confident and more effective teaching.

6. Evaluate the success of each portion of the lesson. If the objectives have been stated in terms of what the children are able to do as a result of their learning, this step should not be difficult. Evaluation does not mean that a formal test must be administered. Evaluation can be simply the observation of a representative sample of the individuals in the class. If the first few children called on can respond appropriately to a review of the point being stressed, it is reasonable to assume that most of the others in the class have learned that point. Remember that the purpose of this evaluation is to determine the results of instruction rather than to grade the class. Evaluation is needed whether or not the children are graded in music. A more complete discussion of evaluation in music is presented in Chapter 21.

The foregoing suggestions stem from the basic questions that should be asked about any type of teaching at any level: What? To whom? How? With what result? If these four questions have been answered clearly, good planning has been achieved. There is of course a fifth question related to all teaching: Why? The reasons for studying music, as outlined in Chapter 1, should undergird the planning and implementation of all music instruction.

7. When the preceding six suggestions have been followed, begin the next planning cycle. The results achieved in the preceding class should influence a teacher's decision to advance to the next step or activity, to reinforce a point previously covered, to try a different approach, or to spend more or less time on some aspect. Teaching and planning are a cycle. Each class period should relate to what preceded it and what will follow it; it does not exist alone.

Before teaching a music lesson, the teacher should think through his or her plan and consider these questions:

   a. Will the points in the lesson be of reasonable difficulty for the class?
   b. Will the children experience music, or just talk about it?
   c. Will they be involved in the learning activity?
   d. Will the teaching techniques involve several senses and different modes of presentation?
   e. Do the children have an adequate aural foundation for what they will be asked to learn?
   f. Will they gain general understandings in addition to useful facts?
   g. Will a special effort be made to help the children remember what they have learned?
   h. Will a special effort be made to help them apply what they have learned to other musical situations?
   i. If the learning involves skill acquisition, will the effort be spread out over a span of time? Will the attention of the class be focused on one point at a time?
   j. Will the learning be presented attractively, to encourage positive attitudes toward music?

Finally, will a balance among the guidelines be maintained? Good teaching means achieving the proper synthesis of the significant factors —the subject matter, the children's needs and interests, and an understanding of the way people learn. Good music teaching is a skill developed through persistent effort over many months and years.

NOTES

1. Richard C. and Norman A. Sprinthall, *Educational Psychology: A Developmental Approach*, 2nd ed. (Reading, Mass.: Addison-Wesley, 1977), pp. 121-24. See also Marilyn P. Zimmerman, *Musical Characteristics of Children* (Reston, Va.: Music Educators National Conference, 1971), pp. 15-20.

2. Henry Clay Lindgren, *Educational Psychology in the Classroom*, 3rd ed. (New York: John Wiley & Sons, 1967), p. 271.
3. *Webster's New Collegiate Dictionary* (Springfield, Mass.: G. & C. Merriam Company, 1974), p. 233.
4. Ralph W. Tyler, "Permanence of Learning," *Journal of Higher Education*, Vol. 4 (1933), pp. 203-04.
5. Hermann Ebbinghaus, *Memory*, trans. H. A. Ruger and C. E. Bussenius (New York: Teachers College, Columbia University, 1913), pp. 68-75. First published in German in 1885.
6. George J. Mouly, *Psychology for Effective Teaching*, 2nd ed. (New York: Holt, Rinehart & Winston, 1968), p. 371.
7. Sprinthall, op. cit., p. 325.
8. Benjamin Bloom et al., *Taxonomy of Educational Goals, Handbook I: The Cognitive Domain* (New York: David McKay, 1956) and Benjamin Bloom et al., *Taxonomy of Educational Goals, Handbook II: The Affective Domain* (New York: David McKay, 1964).
9. D. O. Lyon, "The Relation of Length of Material to Time Taken for Learning and the Optimum Distribution of Time," *Journal of Educational Psychology*, Vol. 5 (1914), pp. 85-91.
10. "The Tanglewood Symposium: Music in American Society," *Music Educators Journal*, Vol. 54, No. 3 (November 1967).
11. H. F. Harlow, J. L. McGaugh, and R. F. Thompson, *Psychology* (San Francisco: Albion, 1971), pp. 271-72.

REVIEW QUESTIONS

1. Which guidelines are violated by these teachers?
   a. Mary Finch plans for her class to learn note names and rhythmic values by filling out worksheets.
   b. Ralph Jones requires his students to memorize the definitions for musical terms before these concepts are experienced in the music.
   c. Shirley Mason teaches her class about rhythmic values by comparing the durations to portions of a pie: a quarter note equals one pie, an eighth note is half a pie, and so on.
   d. Helen Andrews tells the children which of their songs should be fast and which ones should be slow. She believes the children are too young to arrive at their own understandings or make musical judgments on their own.
   e. Marshall Hill keeps his class working intensively on one song throughout the 30-minute period.

2. How can a teacher help children remember what they have learned?
3. What factors determine the amount of learning that will transfer from one subject to another?
4. Why is the topic of student attitude especially important for music?
5. What are some sources of suggestions for teaching music in the elementary classroom?

ACTIVITIES

1. Observe a music class in an elementary school, then respond to the following questions to determine how closely the guidelines in this chapter were followed:
   a. Were the points in the lesson of reasonable difficulty for the class?
   b. Did the children experience music, or just talk about it?
   c. Were they involved in the learning activity?
   d. Did the teaching techniques involve several senses or different modes of presentation?
   e. Did the children seem to have adequate previous musical experience for what they were asked to learn?
   f. Did they gain general understandings in addition to useful facts?
   g. Was a special effort made to help the children remember what they had learned?
   h. Was a special effort made to help them apply what they learned to other musical situations?
   i. If the learning involved skill acquisition, was the effort spread out over a span of time? Was the attention of the class focused on one point at a time?
   j. Was the learning presented attractively?

2. Select one song or other activity in the class you observed, and describe how it might have been taught more effectively.

PART TWO

TEACHING MUSIC IN THE KINDERGARTEN AND PRIMARY GRADES

Part Two contains specific techniques for teaching music. The presentation is divided into two general levels—primary and upper grades—so that reasonably specific suggestions can be given for the objectives and teaching procedures pertinent to each of the two levels. To offer recommendations for every individual grade would be unrealistic and cumbersome. Classes and children vary too much for more detailed suggestions to be of practical value.

The teaching suggestions in Chapters 4 through 17 of this book are based on the premise that activities in the classroom should have an educational purpose. The organization of topics is designed to focus attention on specific aspects of learning. Skills are treated in chapters dealing with singing and the playing of simple instruments. Intellectual understandings are classified into four basic elements of music: rhythm (duration), tone quality (timbre), pitch, and dynamic level.

The sections dealing with the teaching of various aspects of music contain realistic illustrations of possible teaching methods. These examples are only short segments, not complete lessons. To consider them as mandatory procedures for teaching would be to mistake their purpose in this book.

Singing and Playing: Re-creating Music

Music teaching shares this basic principle with other areas of the elementary school curriculum: Experiences are the foundation on which intellectual understandings are built. As Chapter 3 pointed out, conceptualizing is likely to be flawed when it is unrelated to experience. The performance of music through singing and playing instruments, therefore, is a necessary beginning for an education in music. Furthermore, such performance should include both traditional music and music devised by the children themselves. The present chapter deals with teaching children to perform music that others have created—in other words, to re-create it. Chapter 5 is devoted to the creative musical efforts of the children, and subsequent chapters suggest ways to develop understandings from these experiences.

Intellectual concepts in music and experiences with music must be closely coordinated if the learning activity is to be of value. The performance of music provides the basis for lasting understandings, and such understandings, in turn, help children to perform music better. For this reason, it should not be assumed that children must spend the first several months learning to perform and create music before they can move on to understanding what they have been doing. The relationship should be a reciprocal one, with technical skill and musical insight each contributing to the other.

Most music experiences involve performing or listening to music previously created by someone else. That body of music is large almost beyond comprehension. It includes the folk, art, and religious music of all cultures in all historic periods. Because of this diversity in styles and media—both vocal and instrumental—insight is increased if the children can develop enough skill to be involved by re-creating the music with some degree of satisfaction.

In this book, as in the elementary classroom, the fundamental skills are considered to be singing, playing simple instruments, and, to some extent, reading music notation. The development of music skills in the early grades is not primarily for the purpose of enabling children to render music faultlessly. Instead, the skills of singing, playing, and reading music are a *means* to greater understanding. Certainly performance skills in music should be developed as fully as possible, given the time available for instruction and the abilities of the class. But the main concern is to see that children learn about the music and enjoy it, rather than that they demonstrate an advanced level of singing or playing.

SINGING

Singing is the basic means of performing music in the primary grades. Every child has a voice that he or she has been using for talking, and sometimes singing, by the time music instruction begins in kindergarten or first grade. No financial outlay is required to possess this means of making music, and technical problems are few because there are no fingerings or other overtly mechanical procedures to learn. Perhaps most important, the voice is an extremely personal means of expression. It displays a sensitivity to emotion and a responsiveness that are difficult to achieve on an instrument. Words are usually sung with a melody, and this contributes further to the expressiveness of singing.

Children's voices

It is traditional to describe the quality of children's voices with words like "light," "free," and "clear." These words are as good as any, although none truly describes the quality of the sound. Children at the ages of five through eight are not big enough physically to produce a full, rich tone; they do not have the vocal mechanism or breath capacity for it. To sing more loudly, they must "force" the quality of their voices and produce a distorted sound that is often not in tune. The result is a quality closer to shouting than to singing. If continued, such singing can injure the voice.

Unfortunately, there are not many good examples of children's singing to emulate. The best source appears to be provided by the elementary music series books (see Appendix B), which have accompanying recordings that contain songs sung quite well by children. It is this tone quality that children should attempt to copy, rather than the forced style that is heard so often in popular music.

When properly produced, the singing of children gives an impression of being "floated" out, not forced. It is as though the breath being used for singing would support a feather fluttering a few inches away from the mouth. To achieve this, children need to stand or sit erect, with no slouching, when they sing. Standing is an excellent way to attain the straight spine that allows for sufficient breath. The breath should be inhaled as if it is being directed to the area below the rib cage, so that the wall of the abdomen moves *out* as the breath is taken *in* and slowly moves in as air is expelled. The expansion needed for the breath comes not from puffing up the chest or raising the shoulders; instead it results when the diaphragm moves down toward the waistline.

The mouth should be quite open. Some teachers maintain that the teeth should be far enough apart to allow two fingers aligned vertically to be inserted between the upper and lower teeth. The actual height of the opening varies according to the word being sung. Except for the wall of the abdomen, there should be little tension, especially in the throat. The attention of the singer should be on maintaining a steady flow of air, not on manipulating the voice box. The idea should be to sing *through* the larynx, not *with* it.

The range of most children's voices extends approximately from middle C to the C an octave higher, although many children encounter difficulty in singing around G or A above middle C.* Some children force their voices in an effort to sing higher or lower than their comfortable ranges, but such singing should not be encouraged. As the children mature and learn to sing better, their ranges slowly increase. For many children and adults, a range of about one octave is the usual limit for comfort and pleasant sound.

Even young children can appreciate the difference between singing and talking. The vowels are sustained in singing, but not in speaking. In fact, the vowels in singing should be regarded as being connected to one another in a continuous "stream" until the conclusion of a phrase. This point may need to be worked on in a variety of songs over a period of weeks. One simple procedure is to sing the song or phrase on a neutral syllable instead of with the words. When the flow of singing tone has been achieved, the song should be sung with words and with the same stream of sound. If a steady flow of sound is not achieved, the result is a chopped style in which each syllable is separated briefly from the next. The result is a puffing or panting effect.

Selection of songs

The songs in the music series books are graded and carefully selected, but a teacher can be flexible in borrowing music recommended for another grade level. There is room for disagreement among reasonable people as to whether a certain song is better for one grade or for another.

*A glossary and an appendix on musical notation (Appendix A) are given at the end of the book.

Although there are no exact criteria to employ in making grade-level distinctions, four general factors appear to determine the placement of a song in the music series books. One is the length of the song. Young children are more likely to lose interest when the song is long, so most of the material suggested for this age level is short.

A second factor in determining an appropriate grade level is the amount of repetition in a song. If lines or phrases are repeated, that condition makes learning easier. An example of such a song is "Old MacDonald," in which the response "Ee-i-ee-i-o" appears after each phrase of the text. The children can learn the nonsense phrase quickly and then chime in on it as the entire song is sung by the teacher. Also, the remainder of the song presents only a limited number of musical ideas. "Old MacDonald had a farm" and "On that farm he had some chicks" are sung to the same melody. The "chick-chick" segment is sung almost entirely on one note.

OLD MACDONALD

American Song

1. Old Mac - Don - ald had a farm, Ee - i - ee - i - o, And on that farm he had some chicks, Ee - i - ee - i - o. With a chick - chick here, and a chick - chick there, Here a chick, there a chick, ev - 'ry - where a chick - chick, Old Mac - Don - ald had a farm, Ee - i - ee - i - o.

2. Old Mac - Don - ald had a farm, Ee - i - ee - i - o, And on that farm he had some ducks, Ee - i - ee - i - o. With a quack - quack here, and a quack - quack there, Here a quack, there a quack, ev - 'ry - where a quack - quack, Old Mac - Don - ald had a farm, Ee - i - ee - i - o.

3. Old Mac - Don - ald had a farm, Ee - i - ee - i - o, And on that farm he had some pigs, Ee - i - ee - i - o. With an oink - oink here, and an oink - oink there, Here an oink, there an oink, ev - 'ry - where an oink - oink, Old Mac - Don - ald had a farm, Ee - i - ee - i - o.

The song "John the Rabbit" features a two-word refrain that stays on the same pitch and appears six times. The children can join in on the "oh yes" statement with emphasis and feeling.

JOHN THE RABBIT

A third consideration regarding the selection of songs for children is the text. If possible, it should involve something that the children have experienced. It is for this reason that many of the songs in primary grade music books deal with topics of the home, school, and adult occupations that are readily visible in the community. The words in the text should also be understandable to the children. Long, complicated words should be avoided, unless they are vital to the humor of the text— a use epitomized by "supercalifragilisticexpialidocious."

A fourth factor in song selection is the degree of musical complexity. Singing in parts is seldom attempted before the third grade, so songs that depend for their effectiveness on two or more simultaneous melodic lines are best introduced in the later grades. A good preparation for part singing is the experience of performing rounds. Because most rounds are not difficult, and because the entire class sings the same music (but of course at different times), rounds are easier for children to sing than songs with two or more different musical lines. The singing of rounds, however, does require the children to know the melody thoroughly and to keep the tempo steady. Initially, it is often more successful for the teacher to sing one part of the round while the entire class sings the other part.

Singing by the teacher

Many classroom teachers are reluctant to sing for their students. This hesitancy is seldom due to an actual lack of singing ability, especially among those teachers who had some music training as a part of their undergraduate preparation. Of course this background does not ensure that they will sing as well as a music major who has had years of special instruction in voice. But there are four facts that should be remembered by every classroom teacher who needs encouragement in singing. First, a singer with an operatic quality is not needed in the elementary grades. In fact, an overly mature voice quality complete with full vibrato is not the most suitable model for children because it is too different from the way they sound when they sing. Second, the children don't compare a classroom teacher to some fine soloist. Such models are so infrequent that they are not part of the children's frame of reference. Youngsters are satisfied when the song is sung accurately with a pleasing voice quality. Third, practice by actually "doing" will produce improvement in the teacher's singing as well as in the children's singing. Gradually there will be greater ease in singing, better tone quality, and wider range. Finally, and most important, a teacher's willingness to sing with the children, in spite of initial misgivings, shows them that music is to be shared and enjoyed by people of all ages.

Sometimes teachers prefer to use the piano or a simple instrument such as a set of bells to teach a song. This is acceptable only if the teacher's singing is poor. The tone quality of an instrument differs from the quality of a voice and therefore is not the best example for children to copy. Also, percussive instruments such as the bells and the piano do not sustain pitches well. Their tones begin to fade immediately after being sounded, so they do not produce the continuous stream of sound that is desirable when singing. Finally, children find it more difficult to locate the correct pitch from most instrumental sounds than from most singing voices, a fact that is especially true of bell instruments that sound one or two octaves higher than the voice. An instrumental rendition is better than nothing, but the teacher's singing is the more desirable option.

Teaching songs from recordings

Students in music methods classes often ask, "What about teaching songs from recordings? Isn't that just as good as singing, especially since I'm not a very good singer?" The answer is usually "no." A rendition of a song "live" by the teacher is better for teaching children than is a recording, for the following reasons:

1. Because the teacher is presenting a live performance for the children, it has a greater impact on them than merely hearing a recording. Children have many opportunities to listen to recordings, but seldom do they hear a song sung "in person" just for them.

2. The teacher can start and stop at the ends of phrases and isolate places that need work. It is impossible to locate exact places on a long-playing record. A song learned from a recording must be mastered by hearing the complete song again and again.

3. Many elementary classrooms do not have sound-reproducing equipment of a quality that does justice to the fine recordings that accompany the music series books. The abilities of recording artists may fail to come through because of inadequate equipment.

4. The accompaniment on a recording may make it more difficult for the children to learn the melody of the song. However, in some stereo recordings it is possible to emphasize either the melody or the accompaniment by moving the balance knob to make one channel predominant.

If a recording is to be used, the learning of a song can be aided by first printing its words on the chalkboard, if the children are old enough to read and if the words are not in music books that the children can hold. One or two presentations of the words before the children listen to the recording will allow them to devote more of their attention to the music when it is finally played for them. It is best if they do not sing along with the recording the first time it is played. When they do sing with the recording, they should sing softly enough so that they can continue to hear it.

The recordings in the music series albums are helpful not only as aids to teaching songs and as models of singing for the children to imitate, but also as sources for instrumental sounds. The accompaniments for many of the recorded songs are played by excellent musicians and acquaint the children with a variety of instrumental tone colors. Such an accompaniment is rarely possible in the elementary classroom except on a recording.

Introducing a new song

It is a good idea to introduce a new song by promoting those aspects that are most likely to attract the interest of the class. Some thought in the text may be especially appealing. In the following lesson the teacher builds on the children's interest in babies.

"Today we're going to learn a song that a mother might sing to her baby to help it fall asleep. I'll bet that some of you have little brothers and sisters who have trouble falling asleep sometimes. Maybe your mother sings to them to help them feel sleepier."

HUSH, LITTLE BABY

American Folk Song

Hush, lit-tle ba - by, don't say a word, Pa-pa's gon-na buy you a mock-ing-ing-bird.
If   that mock-ing - bird won't sing,   Pa-pa's gon-na buy you a   dia-mond ring.

A song may be introduced by first teaching the children a repeated portion of it. For example, in the song on page 57, the words "All night, all day" are sung to exactly the same music each time the phrase appears. The words "Day is dying in the west" and "Sleep, my child, and take your rest" are sung to the same melody, which is merely a more elaborate version of the first four half notes.

In other cases the children might first learn the words and then say them as expressively as they can. Or they might start by listening to a recording of the song. On other occasions they might learn part or all of a song on the bells or some other simple instrument prior to singing it.

If the text is unusual or more difficult than normal, it may be printed on the chalkboard or made visible to the class by other means. The children can first read through the words with the teacher's help.

Procedures for starting a song

The teacher does not usually conduct children when they sing in a classroom situation. Since the purpose of the singing is to learn about music rather than to prepare for public performance, conducting is not necessary. In addition, conducting suggests a formality that is out of place when the group is small and the children can easily hear voice directions. There is also the practical problem that is encountered when children try to read words and music from a book while watching a teacher's conducting motions.

To help the class start singing a song together, it is best to follow a consistent verbal routine. The particular words involved are not crucial. What matters is that the same routine be followed consistently so that the children become accustomed to it. Before starting to sing a song, they need to know the pitch of the first note, the tempo, and when to start. The pitch can be given by humming or singing the first note on a neutral syllable, or by sounding the note on a bell or piano if necessary. The teacher then sings or speaks *in the tempo of the song* a phrase such as "Rea-dy, sing" or "Rea-dy, go." These directions are usually given on the two beats before the song starts. If the song begins with a pickup note of less than one beat, the music starts at the appropriate moment after the signal. Here is an example of one such beginning.

Sometimes it is helpful to sing the notes of the tonic chord one after another, or to play the chord on the bells or piano. Such a procedure helps the children to sense the key of the music. After the tonic chord is given, the teacher can follow the usual procedure for starting the song with sung or spoken directions.

Procedures for teaching a song

There are several effective ways to teach a song. The choice depends on the nature of the song and the interests and abilities of the children and teacher. In the primary grades, most songs are taught by rote. That is, the teacher sings the song or a phrase of the song while the children listen, and then they attempt to sing it. The procedure is repeated until the entire song is learned. The length of the phrase sung for the children depends on their abilities and on the difficulty of the music. If a song is quite short, it may be sung without interruption. Longer songs are usually broken into phrases.

For example, the song "All Night, All Day" is probably too long to be learned in one segment. The teacher may find it helpful, however, to sing the entire song for the children at first, to give them an idea of how it goes. The rote teaching begins when the teacher sings "All night, all day" (if the children are young and inexperienced) or "All night, all day, angels watching over me, my Lord" (if the children are older and more experienced). The phrase should be sung twice for the children before they attempt to sing it themselves. When that phrase is learned satisfactorily, the teacher moves on to the next phrase and repeats the procedure just described. With each new phrase, the previously learned phrases are included at least once in the children's response. When the song is completed in this manner, it should be set aside for the rest of the period. It can be refined on subsequent days.

As the class sings back the song or phrase the teacher has just presented, the work of eliminating mistakes begins. Almost all of this work is done "on the spot" without the benefit of prior planning. The teacher hears what the children sing, and takes that as a basis for de-

ALL NIGHT, ALL DAY

Smoothly, with feeling   Spiritual

All night, all day, an-gels watch-ing o-ver me, my Lord.___

All night, all day, an-gels watch-ing o-ver me,

1. Day is dy-ing in___ the west, An-gels watch-ing o-ver
2. Now I lay me down to sleep, An-gels watch-ing o-ver

me, my Lord._____ Sleep, my child, and
me, my Lord._____ Pray the Lord my

take___ your rest, An-gels watch-ing o-ver me.
soul___ to keep, An-gels watch-ing o-ver me.

ciding what points in the song need attention. The teacher needs to be analytical enough to detect the errors and to know what to do to correct them. The extent to which a classroom teacher is able to do this depends on his or her training and ability in music. Most classroom teachers can improve in correcting musical errors if they work at it.

Here is how one teacher attempts to identify and correct the places at which the children are not singing accurately.

> "Your tone quality was just right that time. But there's one thing we can improve. We didn't all get the third note right. It's the one after 'night.' Listen while I sing the first three notes very slowly . . . .
>
> "Now, while you sing the same notes, hold your hand in front of you like a shelf, like this, and move it up and down as you think the pitch of the note goes. If you think a sound goes up, move your hand up. If you think a sound goes way up, move your hand way up toward the top of your head. Show me with your hand where you think your voice should go. Rea-dy, sing . . . ."

The potential errors for even a rather short song like "All Night, All Day" are numerous. Pitch is liable to be the most troublesome factor for young children, although rhythmic accuracy and interpretive details may also need attention. Ways to help the children find the right pitch are discussed in Chapter 8. Suggestions for correcting rhythmic errors are presented in Chapter 6, and techniques for improving tone quality and producing differences in dynamic level are presented in Chapters 7 and 9, respectively.

Another aspect of the class effort that may need attention is the expression with which a song is sung. Determining the best tempo and style for a song requires an examination of the text and music. For example, "Hush, Little Baby" (p. 55) is a lullaby, so the tempo should not be rushed, nor should the tone quality be harsh and loud. The children should be encouraged to offer their opinions as to the most appropriate style and expression for a song. Here is an example of how this might be done.

> "In 'Hush, Little Baby' let's pretend that we're singing to a real baby. Joel, should we sing the song loudly like this?" [The teacher sings the song boisterously.] "Or should we sing this way?" [The teacher sings softly.]
>
> "Sherri, should the song go fast like this?" [The teacher sings a phrase at a rapid tempo.] "Or should it move gently like this?" [The teacher sings at a leisurely tempo.]

When the teacher asks for an opinion from the children, it is good to reach general agreement on the point of interpretation. If a child seems mistaken in a choice, a bit of probing—"Why do you think so?"—may uncover a different way of thinking about the song. The teacher should not pass judgment by saying the answer is right or wrong, but should merely ask other children for their ideas, in the hope of securing a more fitting response. If none is given, the teacher should demonstrate an alternative to let the class see its merits. Providing a choice, as the teacher did in the preceding example, helps the children arrive at an appropriate decision. Often children are not sure what the word "fast" means in terms of a song. They need to hear different speeds and styles in order to understand what the descriptive words mean.

The recordings that accompany the book series can serve as examples for appropriate style. In fact, that is one of the values of these recordings. The class should listen carefully to how the song is performed before the children sing along with the recording or try to imitate the style. As with so many other aspects of music, performing with the proper expression is—initially at least—a matter of listening and imitating. It is impossible to describe verbally all the subtleties of how a song should be sung. Most songs, even those that appear to be simple, are too complex to be explained by words that attempt to describe the many nuances of rhythm, tone color, and dynamic level.

Helping out-of-tune singers

Many children in kindergarten and first grade experience difficulty in singing a song on pitch. In fact, one study estimates that 36.6 percent of children in first grade experience some problem in singing accurately on pitch.[1] The problem gradually disappears for most children, so that by the end of sixth grade that percentage has dropped to about 10 percent. It is encouraging to observe that with music instruction the difficulties with out-of-tune singing are greatly reduced as children progress through school. Less encouraging is the fact that in the meantime a significant number of them may be acquiring a negative attitude about their musical interests and abilities. Like adults, children tend to dislike activities in which they do not do well, and to enjoy activities in which they can achieve.

Why do children so often have trouble singing on pitch when they enter first grade? There are a number of reasons.

1. Many parents do not sing to their children as infants. Research data indicate that the amount of music activity in the home has much to do with the child's music capabilities on entering school.[2] Children who have had a limited music background simply need time and experience to gain the ability to sing on pitch.

2. Some children have not yet gained the concept of high and low pitch. They do not understand what they are to do with their voices.

3. Some children seem unable to pay attention well enough to learn a song. It is performed for them, but they fail to concentrate when listening or trying to sing.

4. Some children have not learned the muscle movement necessary to make their voices change pitch accurately. They tend to drone within a narrow pitch range because they are unable to get the voice to sing higher (or occasionally lower).

5. Some children cannot hear the difference between pitches. True monotones—those who are unable to distinguish between pitches at all—are rare. It is true that some people hear pitch more accurately than others, but almost everyone can learn to carry a tune.

6. A few children have vocal problems, such as nodules on the vocal cords, that prevent them from singing well. The nodule condition can be corrected with therapy and/or surgery. If a teacher suspects nodules on a child's vocal cords—a condition manifested by a persistent-

ly husky voice quality—the child should be encouraged to sing only very softly, or to stop singing altogether, until a medical examination can be conducted.

7. A few children demonstrate good pitch discrimination except when they themselves sing. Apparently they lack the normal aural feedback of their own voices. Many of these children can eventually succeed in instrumental performance.

What can be done to help out-of-tune singers? First, they should never be given the idea that something is seriously and irrevocably wrong. After all, most such children will eventually overcome the problem. Children who have trouble carrying a tune should not be singled out in front of their peers. The teacher should not bend over them and sing into their ears, nor should the youngsters be asked to sing in front of the group or to remain silent because their singing doesn't "contribute to the class." If they volunteer to sing a phrase or song alone, they should be encouraged to do so. But the teacher should not mislead them by saying, "That's fine!" when in fact their singing is poor. It is much more productive and honest to offer such comments as, "I'm glad you volunteered to sing for us," or "Your words were clear and easy to understand." Even in first grade, children can sense when their singing is faulty. And if they don't sense it, their classmates often let them know about it! If a child is aware that there is a problem, the attitude of the teacher should be, "Let's work to make it better."

Probably the best way to help out-of-tune singers is to work with them privately or in a small group. This can take place during recess or lunch period, so long as the children do not regard the sessions as punishment.

Music specialists differ somewhat on how to begin helping nonsingers. Some teachers believe the first step in getting these children on pitch is to help them discover what it feels like and sounds like to be in unison with a given pitch. That is what the teacher in this example is trying to do. In this case the teacher sings the pitches, but they may also be played on the piano.

> "Peter, sing what you think is your best note—the one that feels most comfortable for you and sounds best to you. When you find it, hold it while I sing that same note. . . .
>
> "Okay. Now listen carefully to how it sounds when you and I are exactly together on that note. The two sounds seem to agree. Try it again." . . . "That's the idea." . . . "Now let me sing the note again and you match it." . . . "Better. Do it again. . . .
>
> "Now let's move up one note from the pitch that we've been singing. Think of moving your voice up just a short step."

If the child is able to move up a step and match pitch, then another note, perhaps the next step higher, can be attempted. Sometimes it helps if the child rather than the teacher plays the note on the piano. Also, the child may find that putting a hand over one ear helps focus attention on his or her own voice.

Other music specialists have observed that children in the first grade seem to have two types of voices, a "chest" or "speaking" voice and a "head" or "singing" voice.[3] The "singing" voice is about five notes higher than the "speaking" voice. After the children learn to recognize the difference between the two voices, they can be encouraged to use the singing voice for music. A teacher might say to a child who is droning in a chest voice, "That's your speaking voice; now try it with your singing voice." Either the pitch-matching procedure or the "singing voice" procedure appears to work when applied consistently.

After the sensation of unison pitch-matching or using the singing voice has been experienced, other techniques can be tried.

1. Ask the child to imitate a siren by gradually raising and lowering the pitch level of his or her voice. This promotes the concept of changing pitch level without requiring the child to match exact pitches.

2. Invite the child to indicate with his or her hands the approximate pitch level of what is being heard or sung. One pattern can be sung to the words "Bounce my ball." As the words are sung, the child makes a bouncing motion with his or her hands, palms down, but with the height above the floor regulated by the relative pitch levels. A wide interval, even an octave, works well in this routine because the rhythmic flow gives a feeling of energy and momentum, and the sudden leap in pitch encourages vocal flexibility.

Bounce   my   ball!

3. Give the out-of-tune singer extra practice on the echo patterns that are sung in music class to help all children sing pitches more accurately. (See p. 119.)

4. Tape record the out-of-tune singer during these practice sessions, if the child does not become self-conscious. Listening to oneself on a recording makes self-evaluation more objective.

5. Suggest that the out-of-tune singer make up a short tune to sing. Sometimes a child who sings on only one pitch will make up tunes that require singing on a variety of pitches.

6. Ask the child to imitate animals, especially the sound of a cuckoo. This is the descending interval found in so many children's songs around the world.

7. Invite the out-of-tune singer to pick out familiar tunes at the piano or on the bells. These instruments provide visual and physical reinforcement of the distance between pitches.

Some children may need special help for several months. They may achieve the unison sensation once or twice, only to lose it by the next day. Patience is needed to help the children who find it hard to sing on pitch. The efforts at helping them are well worth the teacher's attention, however, because their outlook toward music in later years will benefit from early correction of singing difficulties.

PLAYING CLASSROOM INSTRUMENTS

Instruments make a valuable contribution to music instruction in the elementary school, primarily because they are an excellent means of learning about tone qualities. Methods for helping children explore instrumental sounds are presented in Chapter 7; the use of instruments in children's creative activities is discussed in Chapter 5.

Instrument playing is included in elementary music classes so that the children can learn to supplement and enrich a song, not so that they can gain technical facility for its own sake. Instrumental activity is time-consuming, requiring assignment of instruments, instruction in their use, and taking turns so that several children can share the experience. Time seems to be in short supply in most elementary classrooms, and must be allocated carefully. Nevertheless, experience with instruments is of sufficient value to warrant the extra time and inconvenience that this type of activity entails.

In kindergarten and first grade, much of the instrument playing is done by the teacher. Gradually the children are introduced to playing short phrases and easy parts on an instrument. The guideline to follow in selecting or creating instrumental parts for primary school children to play is: *Keep it simple.* At first, only one or two instruments should be played at the same time. The greater the number of instrumental parts, the greater becomes the likelihood of mistakes.

An example of how instruments can be worked into music instruction can be seen through the song "Are You Sleeping?", which appears on page 96. The song is in the key of F. That pitch can be sounded on the first beat of each measure throughout the song. If the child playing the instrument senses the beat clearly, he or she can think (and even say softly), "Play, rest, play, rest," and so on. If that procedure does not work, the teacher can point to the child each time the note is to be sounded. Several different instruments can sound the note F for "Are You Sleeping?", including bells and piano.

The suggestion in the preceding paragraph—that the teacher direct the child each time a note is to be played—is typical of the amount and type of help that needs to be given when children first begin to play instruments. Much of the teacher's attention will need to be devoted simply to keeping the player on the beat so that an incorrectly played part does not confuse the singers. To limit the amount of distraction, it is important that the class have the song learned thoroughly before an instrumental part is added. Also, it is often necessary to take a minute or two of class time to "rehearse" the instrument player on the part, even though that part may seem extremely simple to the teacher.

The teacher should give each child an equal opportunity to play the instruments. This means that the less musically able youngsters, as well as the talented children, must have a chance to play. It is advisable to select the more able students to perform the part the first time or two it is played. This gives the class an idea of how the music should sound, and helps the other children learn the part so they can play it better when their turn comes.

The song "All Things Bright and Beautiful" sounds good with a descending scale—one note per measure—played on the bells.

Despite the presence of eight different notes, the part is relatively easy because each note is played "in order." One child might play all eight notes, or eight children might be invited to play one note each. Bells are more appropriate than a sustained vocal sound for this scale passage, because in several measures the initial note creates dissonance with the chords implicit in the last half of the measure. Again, the children may need to be given a clear signal for each note they are to play. The scale pattern may also be played so that the notes occur in ascending order as an introduction, coda (ending), or interlude between verses.

Some children have started to take piano lessons by the time they are in first or second grade. These children should be given the opportunity to play with the class. Such an activity reinforces what they have learned, demonstrates to the other children the practical advantages of piano study, and contributes to the music class. Even children not studying piano can be taught to play a simple one-finger part like the one-note repeated accompaniment suggested for "Are You Sleeping?" (p. 96).

ALL THINGS BRIGHT AND BEAUTIFUL

Words by Cecil F. Alexander   William Tyndale

1. All things bright and beau - ti - ful, All crea - tures great and small,
2. Cold wind in the win - ter, The pleas - ant sum - mer sun,

All things wise and won - der - ful, The Lord God made them all.
Ripe fruits in the gar - den; He made them ev - ery one.

Music copyright © 1966 by Gulf Music Co. Used by permission.

Most of the instruments that are played in the primary grades are of the xylophone type. Such instruments are sold under different trade names, but they are basically called "bells" and consist of bars that conform to the pattern of the piano keyboard. Some sets have bars that can be removed so that unwanted bars will not be struck accidentally. Another type of instrument found in primary grade classrooms are bells of the traditional shape, with a handle, and these are shaken individually. A piano is an asset, and can be played by the teacher or an experienced student.

Another useful instrument is the autoharp, on which the player sounds a chord merely by pressing a button and strumming across the strings. The two tasks can be given to two children simultaneously if they both want to play the instrument within a short time span. The autoharp has a pleasant tone and produces many notes with little effort (although the initial tuning is time-consuming). It is a good supplement for songs in the primary grades, even though the topic of harmony—for which it is an excellent learning tool—is not a significant aspect of music instruction at this level.

The song "Hanukah" indicates the three chords that harmonize best with the melody. An autoharp accompaniment would be an appropriate addition after the class has learned the song. Assigning two children to the autoharp—one to strum and one to press the chord bars—not only will give more children a chance to play but will simplify the complexity of playing three different chords, particularly if the teacher gives finger cues to the child pressing the chord bars. The signals might be as follows: one finger held up by the teacher indicates a C chord, four fingers represent the F chord, and five fingers indicate the G^7 chord. Although young children do not need to know the significance of the finger numbers, the teacher may find it helpful to remember that in C major, the C chord is known as I, the F chord is IV, and G^7 is V^7.

HANUKAH

Melody instruments such as the recorder (and the related Tonette and Flutophone) and plucked string instruments like the guitar are too difficult for most primary grade children. Such instruments are best retained for presentation in the upper elementary grades.

Percussion instruments are useful in music instruction in the primary grades, and techniques for incorporating them into the classroom situation are presented in Chapter 6.

MUSIC READING

Music reading refers to the ability to look at music notation and to render in sound what the notation indicates. This skill is not essential for the performance of music, but it is a valuable aid and a desirable outcome of music instruction in the elementary school. When children can read music, they can learn new songs more quickly and more independently, with less help from the teacher. The ability to read music expands the child's opportunities for participating in music and enjoying it.

Reading music notation is more complex than reading language. Music notation indicates both pitch and rhythm, and offers some idea as to how the music should be performed. Most of these directives are in a nonverbal code. Pitch is represented in a graph-like arrangement of lines and spaces, and rhythm is indicated by a series of symbols. Song words are divided by hyphens when they are more than one syllable long, and are placed below the staff of music. This placement requires the eyes to move up and down, as well as laterally from left to right.

Music reading, even in the best school music programs, is taught for much less time than the reading of language, perhaps because the advantage of music reading in the world outside of school is not nearly as evident as is the need to read words. Children see adults read newspapers, books, and signs much more often than they see them read music. Even with large amounts of skilled instruction and a high level of reinforcement by society, many children have trouble learning to read language well. Therefore, because of the greater difficulty of music reading and the smaller amount of time and importance given it, it is not surprising that few children in the primary grades possess the ability to read music.

Music reading can be taught through singing or playing simple instruments, or both. The voice requires less technical skill development on the part of the children than do most instruments; there are no keys to push down or bars to strike. When singing, however, the children do not have the benefit of the fixed pitches found on most instruments. Nor do they have the additional reinforcement of the physical sensation of spatial distance that occurs when they produce an interval on a keyboard-like instrument.

Procedures for teaching music reading

When does instruction in reading music begin? In a way, it begins when the child first hears music, just as learning to read begins when a child first encounters speaking. Aural experience is the basis for a successful reading effort in both music and language.

Direct instruction in music reading usually begins in a limited way in the first grade, when the children are shown selected notation symbols in large print, as well as illustrated material in books. As with reading language, intensive efforts must wait until there has been sufficient development of the eye muscles to allow for focusing on smaller print.

Some "primer" type music books are available for children in kindergarten and first grade, but books are not usually placed in the children's hands until second grade. In no sense are second graders expected to *sightread* the music; that is, to perform it unaided on first encounter, solely by observing the notation. Rather, the books contain the song words, which many of the children can read, as well as the notation. The presence of the notation acquaints the children with its appearance and gives them an impression of how the system represents pitches and rhythms.

Learning to read music is similar to learning to read language, in that both skills require the development of sound/symbol associations. A child learns that a dog is a particular type of animal and that a certain vowel-consonant combination of sounds stands for that animal. Later the child learns that the letters d-o-g, when combined, are a visual representation of that sound and concept.

There is an additional complication in music reading, however. Music reading involves understanding relationships as well as learning fixed meanings. The notes E and G on the staff are fixed designations and can be identified rather easily by someone with a rudimentary knowledge of note names. It is harder to sense an interval in terms of sound and to reproduce the two notes accurately. Music notation also presents relationships in its rhythm values. A child may be able to identify a quarter note at sight, but useful reading will not occur until the child can interpret that symbol by reproducing a sound of the proper duration in the context of a given meter and tempo. Specific techniques for teaching the reading of rhythm and pitch are found in Chapters 6 and 8.

As with most skill-learning, frequent practice is necessary if children are to develop their ability to read music. The eyes must learn to move efficiently, the mind must learn to interpret the symbols quickly, and the ear must learn to anticipate the sound that is intended by the visual code. There is no magic process in learning to read music, nor is there only one way in which it can be accomplished. Any one of several different approaches will do the job, *if* it is practiced persistently. Once a system for music reading has been started, it should not be mixed with other systems. Consistency of approach will reduce the amount of confusion for the children.

Skills are acquired gradually, not in one or two large breakthroughs. The teaching of music reading in the primary grades is the beginning of a process that will extend over several years, and the amount of music reading skill eventually achieved will vary from one student to another. Most people can detect some meaning from looking at notation, but almost no one can read difficult music flawlessly.

NOTES

1. A. Oren Gould, *Finding and Learning to Use the Singing Voice: A Manual for Teachers* (Washington, D.C.: Office of Education, OEC 6-10-016, 1968).
2. Ibid.
3. Mary Goetze, "The Development of Children's Singing Voices," *Indiana Musicator*, Vol. 36, No. 2 (January 1981), p. 12.

REVIEW QUESTIONS

1. Why is singing the basic means of performing music in the primary grades?

2. What is the approximate range of children's voices in the first and second grades? What are the characteristics of their voices?

3. What types of song texts are especially suitable for children in the primary grades?

4. Describe the movement of the abdominal wall when a person is singing correctly.

5. Why is an operatic voice not especially appropriate as a model for children?

6. For teaching purposes, why is a live vocal performance of a song preferable to a rendition on the bells? to hearing the song on a recording?

7. What are the basic procedures for teaching a song by rote?

8. Approximately what percentage of all children entering first grade can be expected to have trouble singing on pitch?

9. What are some reasons for pitch problems in children's singing?

10. Cite five techniques for helping children learn to sing on pitch.

11. What musical instruments are most likely to be available in primary grade classrooms?

12. In what ways is learning to read music similar to learning to read language?

13. At what grade level are music books usually made available to the children?

14. What are some reasons for the fact that reading music is more difficult than reading words?

15. Why is it desirable for children to start learning to read music in the primary grades?

ACTIVITIES

1. Examine one of the music series books designed for first, second, or third graders. Select one song to teach to the methods class. Decide what steps you will take to ensure that the class will learn the song easily and sing it well.

2. Practice the procedures for singing. Referring to the song you selected for activity 1, decide how you might teach the methods class to sing better by applying the principles of good vocal technique to specific aspects of that song.

3. Select one round from a music series book designed for a primary grade. Learn the round, then teach it to the methods class.

4. Work with another class member and learn his or her song. Sing it to the best of your ability and let your partner offer suggestions for improvement. Reverse roles and repeat the procedure.

5. Select another song, one for which you can introduce a simple instrumental part. (The index of a music series book will help you locate such arrangements.) Teach the song to the methods class, then select students to play the instrumental part.

6. Evaluate the performance of two songs sung by the methods class.

Improvising and Composing: Creating Music

Creativity is a troublesome word because it is used in many ways. Sometimes it is intended to define the tangible result of a monumental effort, like writing a novel or composing a symphony; sometimes it implies only that an idea or product is original to a given person; at times it seems to be a synonym for "different" or "offbeat."

People may not be sure what creativity is, but most persons seem to be strongly in favor of it. One can hardly pick up an educational journal or popular magazine without reading about the need for more creative living, creative thinking, creative relationships, creative teaching, creative decorating, and creative salads.

NATURE OF CREATIVITY

Part of the problem with defining creativity is that it may not be a single entity. J. P. Guilford and other psychologists who have worked in this area have concluded that what is referred to as creativity is actually a combination of at least three mental traits.[1] Guilford terms one of these traits *fluency;* it refers to the ease with which people can make associations of words or ideas. A second trait comprising creativity is called *flexibility;* it involves the ease with which people can change procedures to solve a problem. The third trait is named *originality* by Guilford; it involves the ability to think in new and different ways or to see the relationships in a situation that others have not seen. Some people who are considered creative may be strong in only one or two of these traits. It is also true that some people who are good at learning prescribed material are not strongly creative. In other words, those who score high on conventional intelligence tests may or may not score high on measures of creativity.

Difficult though it may be, it is necessary to devise a definition of creativity for use in this book. A short, practical definition is: "a thought, product, or action that is original to the person who produces it." According to this definition, the child who makes a sandcastle is being creative, even though a million other children have made sandcastles. The child who copies another person's sandcastle is not being creative.

In music, there are two types of creative experience: *composing* and *improvising.* The difference between these words is the amount of thought and planning that goes into the creative effort. Composing implies careful, thoughtful preparation of music. Such preparation means either writing the music down on paper or preserving the composition on tape. A person who improvises, on the other hand, makes up music extemporaneously without prior planning. The performance setting is likely to be casual, with no attempt to preserve the musical result. Improvising is usually based on pre-existing guidelines for the type of music being performed, so the performer/improvisor does not make up music out of thin air. Both composing and improvising are important in the world of music, and can be incorporated in a rudimentary form into the elementary classroom.

THE VALUE OF CREATIVITY IN THE CURRICULUM

There is little disagreement about the value of the creative efforts of people like Ludwig van Beethoven, Thomas Edison, and Leonardo da Vinci. The human race has been bettered by their accomplishments. But what about the value of the creative efforts of most people, especially those of youngsters? Is a child struggling with bells in some way to be compared with the great Beethoven? Are the painted paper plates that children bring home from school as valuable as paintings by Rembrandt or Cezanne?

From the standpoint of inherent artistic worth, the phrases on the bells and the painted paper plates are of virtually no value. However, creative activities are included in music instruction not for the artistic product that may result, but for the benefits that accrue to the child through the act of creating.

One value of creative effort in music is that it encourages individuals to express their own musical thoughts. When trying to create music, people are drawing on their own ideas and manipulating an art form in a personal way. This is an enriching experience in life. Music involves learning not only to reproduce or listen to what others have created, but also to organize sounds for one's own satisfaction. Children should have opportunities to try out their musical ideas.

A second reason for creative activity is the fact that what a child makes seems more valuable to him or her. The paper that third-grader Amy writes on "What I Did Last Summer" is more meaningful to her than what someone else wrote on the topic. By creating something that is uniquely hers, she has contributed to her self-image as a productive and competent person.

A third value of creative effort is the contribution that it makes toward learning music better. When a person is creating music, whether it be a one-measure ostinato with two pitches or an entire cantata, the mind is engaged in much trial and error in considering sounds and how they can best be organized to express what the person has in mind. In short, when people are trying to create music, they are thinking intently about sounds and their organization, which is the essence of music. They are doing such thinking to a greater degree than they usually do when studying what someone else has composed or performed.

For these reasons, then, opportunities to create music should be a part of each child's education.

ADDING CREATIVE ELEMENTS TO EXISTING MUSIC

The idea of asking children to create music may seem like an unrealistic hope. How can children write music when they don't know how to read notation and can hardly sing an entire song without errors? The answer is: They should not be asked to do so, unless the creative effort is structured and unless the teacher provides much help. Asking children to compose an entire song is one thing; asking them to manipulate a few sounds is quite another. So the basic principle for guiding creative activities in music is this: *Start with short, simple tasks in which the children have a limited number of options.* When they succeed in simple creative efforts, they can move on to more complicated tasks and eventually to complete songs.

One way to introduce creativity into music instruction is to add original ideas to songs the children already know. The creative increment is only a small part of the total piece. Suppose that the class has learned the song "Jump Down, Turn Around." Because it is short and simple, more children will be able to try out their ideas, without a sizable expenditure of time and effort.

JUMP DOWN, TURN AROUND

American Folk Song

Four distinct ways of varying the song coincide with the elements of music to be discussed in the next four chapters: rhythm, timbre, pitch, and dynamic level. Combinations of any of these four elements are also possible. Here is an example of how such changes might be introduced:

"For several days now, we've been singing 'Jump Down, Turn Around.' We've been careful to sing it exactly right, with no mistakes. But now I'm going to sing the song for you with some changes in it. Some of the notes will be higher or lower than we've been singing them. It won't be a mistake, because I'm making the change on purpose. Listen and tell me where I made the change." [The teacher sings the two notes on "cotton" one octave higher.]

[The children identify the word on which the changed notes appeared, and all sing the revised version.]

"Now see what *you* can do to make some changes in the song. The important thing about these changes is that they will be *your* ideas; they will come from inside your heads. Remember that you're going to change only how high or low *some* of the notes are. Change just a couple of notes and keep everything else the same, the way I did.

"I'll give you a minute or two to think through silently to yourself *one* change in the pitches of 'Jump Down, Turn Around' that you
would like to try. When you have your change in mind, you can sing it
to us and we'll all do it together. Okay, think of your change for a
minute." . . . "Jeremy, what change did you think up?" [Jeremy sings
"pick a bale of cotton" with all notes on the same pitch.]

The teacher should show enthusiasm for Jeremy's suggestion and
confirm it by replaying the phrase on the bells or piano to make sure
that everyone understands what is wanted. If the children can follow
notation, the new version can be written on the chalkboard. After hearing the changed version once or twice, the children can try to sing it
with the alterations.

The rhythm of "Jump Down, Turn Around" seems especially
suitable for a repeated pattern. Clapping the rhythm pattern of the
notes will probably suggest to the children a simple figure that they can
clap or play on instruments. A possible two-measure ostinato is:

$$\frac{2}{2} \; \downarrow \; \natural \; \downarrow \; \downarrow \; | \; \downarrow \; \natural \; \downarrow \; \natural \; :\|$$

The song can be repeated a sufficient number of times to accommodate the children's ideas for variations in loudness. Perhaps they will
want a gradual increase or decrease in the dynamic level, or a sudden
change in this aspect of the music.

Children should also be encouraged to experiment with instruments and to devise accompaniments for the songs. Suggestions for altering timbre are presented in Chapter 7.

The teacher should be prepared for a variety of responses when
children are asked to alter a song. Any response made in good faith
should be accepted, because participation is more important than ad-
herence to a compositional plan. For example, a child may suggest
sweeping changes that are unrelated to the original. In such a case, the
teacher can point out the different character of the new version, and
briefly discuss its merits with the class. Sometimes changes in rhythm
and pitch are proposed, when only a change in pitch has been requested.
The teacher can help the class discover that the changes are more extensive than the recommendation. Even though the changes exceed or
stray from what was requested, they should be treated as genuine efforts, because in no way does a teacher want to discourage creative
ideas.

In addition to altering one element or another in the music, the
class can also vary the words. Children in the primary grades enjoy doing this, especially if humorous words are encouraged, and they are sur-

prisingly good at it. One or two words may be changed, or an entire new set of words can be created. Here a teacher is trying to stimulate interest in the song by substituting humorous words.

> "There are songs that have silly words, songs that people sing just for the fun of it. 'Jump Down, Turn Around' is an enjoyable song that isn't serious, but it isn't funny either. Let's change the words at the end of the first line, 'pick a bale of cotton,' to something else—maybe something silly. Remember, the new words that you choose need to have six parts or syllables, just as 'pick a bale of cotton' does. I'll give you a minute to think of a new set of words that fit where 'pick a bale of cotton' is now. . . . Tom, what's your idea for new words?"
>
> "How about 'pet a noisy donkey'?"
>
> "All right, here's how the new words go: 'Jump down, turn around, pet a noisy donkey.' Let's sing them in the song to see if they work." [The class sings the song with the new words.]
>
> "Now we need to replace the last group of words: 'pick a bale a day.' We need five syllables. Take another minute now and think of a good ending for your song. . . . Bonnie, what are your new words?"
>
> "Pet it carefully." [The class sings the song with Bonnie's words.]

In addition to changing the words and altering the various musical elements, the children can think up short introductions, conclusions, and *ostinatos* (short repeated patterns). Actually, a one- or two-measure ostinato figure can be extended forward or backward to serve as an introduction or coda to the song.

INTEGRATING CREATIVE ACTIVITIES WITH OTHER ARTS

One way to stimulate creativity is to paint or draw to music. The point of this activity is to encourage the children to respond to what they hear by expressing their feelings visually—not necessarily in concrete images but in the liberal use of color, space, and motion. The teacher in this lesson has given each child two sheets of manila paper, and has provided a variety of colored chalk. The children are invited to sit on the floor to draw, or to use one of the available tables.

> "Today we're going to listen to two different pieces of music and just let our minds wander. Think how the music 'looks' to you. Don't begin using the chalk until after you've heard some of the music. When you're ready to put your thoughts and feelings on paper, just start

drawing. You don't need to make a picture of anything, although you may do that if you want to. Just try to show the feeling of the music you're hearing."

Two appropriate musical selections for this activity are the "Waltz" from *Swan Lake* by Tchaikowsky, and the "Hoe Down" from *Rodeo* by Copland. The two sets of drawings can be compared and discussed in terms of how they differ in style according to the qualities of the music they are expressing.

A second activity, explained more fully in Chapter 7, consists of adding sound effects to stories or poems.

Another way to encourage creativity is to have the children engage in interpretive bodily movement or interpretive dancing. The children try to express with their bodies what they think the music is "saying." This activity is more than just marching or keeping time with the music. Rather, after careful listening, the children make motions and adopt physical attitudes that to them reflect the music. Such bodily expression is an individual matter, not subject to a group decision-making process. Because younger children are usually less inhibited about such activities, the idea seems to work better with kindergarteners and first graders than with fourth or fifth graders.

Free rhythmic movement is generally more successful in a small group in which the teacher can observe the children easily. Large group efforts are sometimes dominated by one or two of the more aggressive or able children, and such a situation should be discouraged. Also, care must be taken so that the activity does not turn into a free-for-all with children bumping and pushing one another. The available space must be estimated realistically. Where floor space is limited, one solution is to have only a few children engage in free activity while the others sing, chant words, or clap. Another aid is to give the children "space-saving" ideas such as walking in place instead of moving around the room. They can even act out the motions of dancers with their hands on desktops.

Here is how a free movement activity might be introduced:

"Today we're going to move freely to music. So let's stand and spread out so that you have some distance between yourself and the person closest to you. Now, while you're standing quietly and listening to the music, think how you can show the idea of the music with *just your arms.* If the music seems fast and jumpy, then move your arms that way. If the music seems big and fluffy like a cloud, then move your arms like that and show us a cloud. Ready? Listen carefully. When you feel you have the motions in mind, show me with your arms." [The teacher plays a recording of *Pavane for a Dead Princess* by Ravel. The music is slow and flowing, suggesting movements that are expansive and graceful.]

Experience with expressive movement can be extended by involving more parts of the body than just the arms, by letting the children move about the room, and by providing music of a contrasting character. Children also enjoy impersonating animals and their actions. A direction such as "Gallop like a happy horse" or "Walk like a tired elephant" allows children to express a more specific idea in movement.

CREATING ORIGINAL MUSIC

Spontaneous singing

Many children, even before entering school, engage in spontaneous singing. A child playing alone may sometimes be heard humming or singing quietly. This improvised singing is a natural creative act and should be encouraged. Here is how this might be done.

> "Brad, I heard you singing about the rain that we're having today. It's a good idea to sing about things. Do you suppose you could sing your song about the rain for the whole class to hear?" [Brad agrees, but does not sing the same tune that the teacher heard. He does repeat the words sung before: "Wet rain, go away, I want to play."]
> "Thank you, Brad. That was a nice song. Does anyone else have a song about the rainy day we're having?"

The fact that Brad did not repeat his previous tune is typical. The previous singing was a fleeting musical expression that he didn't try to remember. But by asking him to sing it for the class, the teacher encouraged Brad and indicated to the other members of the class that creativity is valued.

Sound exploration

Children have a natural curiosity about their environment, including sounds. They should be encouraged to explore the classroom for the sound-making possibilities it offers. The children can devise games in which they identify what they hear without seeing it. They can rap pencils against flower pots, chair legs, and ventilator grillwork; they can crinkle paper, turn a noisy doorknob, hit chalk erasers together and the like. They should not overlook the possibilities for making sounds with their bodies—clapping hands, stomping feet, snapping fingers, clucking tongues on the roof of the mouth, hissing, whistling, slapping thighs, rapping knuckles on the elbow, and so on. Here is how such an exploration might be organized.

"There are all sorts of ways to make sounds right here in our room. I'll give you a couple of minutes to go around the room on your own and find three different ways to make sounds. Remember what your three ways are, then come back to your seats and we'll make a list of all those ways." [The children move about the room testing different ways of making sounds.]

"All right, now let's make that list of sounds. I'll ask each of you for one way to make sounds, then I'll go around again to find out your other sounds. Bethany, what was the first way that you found?" [Bethany suggests tapping on the table with a pencil, and the list grows, but none of the ideas involves making sounds with the body.]

"That's quite a list. But you know what? You forgot some ways of making sounds, maybe because they're as close as the nose on your face. Who can think of more ways that are here in this room right now?" [Eventually Jeff remembers that he can make sounds by clapping and snapping his fingers, and this unleashes a spate of body-sound suggestions from the class.]

Random sounds are not music, of course. To become music, they need to be organized. The distinction might be stressed to children in this way.

"Even though we have a good list of sounds, we still don't have music. If we're going to make them into music, we have to decide first which sounds we're going to use. They should be sounds that all of us can produce at our seats. Pick out your favorite Betsy?"

"Slapping your leg."

"Okay. Gary, what's your favorite?"

"Stomping my foot on the floor."

"Mark, how about you?"

"Hitting knuckles on the table."

"Good. Let's review the three sounds. First, all of you slap your leg, then stomp your foot, and hit your knuckles on the table.

"Now, how do you want to arrange the sounds? Keep it simple at first, to be sure we can all stay together on our three-sound composition." [Susan suggests performing the sounds, one after another, in an even rhythm.]

"All right, let's do Susan's pattern three times, ending with the first sound to finish off the piece. It will go 'One two three, one two three, one two three, one.' Got that? All together now, rea-dy go."

On subsequent days the three-sound composition may be expanded, as shown in this example.

"Do you remember the three sounds that you thought up yester-day? Today we'll try the sounds that some of the rest of you have in mind, but this time we'll try to make our piece a little fancier. What three sounds do you want?" [The children suggest a cluck of the tongue, a clap, and a hiss.]

"Three good sounds. Now think for a minute what we can do with them. We can make them more than once; we can make one of the sounds loud and others soft; we can make one sound longer than the others—yes, the hiss is the only sound we can lengthen—or we can make two of the sounds together, except a person can't do the cluck and the hiss at the same time. But we can do *almost* anything we want to with the sounds."

[The class decides to produce this familiar rhythm with the sounds indicated:]

As the children progress in their ability to organize simple sounds, they can begin to evaluate their pieces and to decide what can be done to make them better. The teacher can introduce certain compositional concepts, although the terms for the concepts need not be introduced in the primary grades.

[Frank's piece includes whistling, finger snapping, and a foot sliding on the floor. At his suggestion, each sound has been produced twice in succession.]

"What could we do to make Frank's piece more interesting? Cathy?"

"We could make each sound three times."

"All right, let's do each sound three times in a row. Here's the speed." [The teacher gives the tempo through three preparation beats, and the class performs the modified version of Frank's piece.]

"Did we make the piece more interesting by adding an extra sound each time?" [The class responds that the change didn't make a lot of difference.]

"That's true; we didn't change it very much by repeating the same sound more often. Maybe we need to mix up the order of the sounds. This will make some variety, or surprise, for the listener. Who can think of a way to do this?" [Frank volunteers to amend his original piece by proceeding "whistle-snap-slide-snap-whistle."]

"That's a good idea, Frank. It makes a balanced design that the listener can follow. Let's do the piece this new way, then describe the design that it makes." [The class performs the revised version, which the children describe as "going frontways and then turning around," and "going back and forth on a swing."]

"Good! Now let's work the opposite way. I'll describe a design first, then you figure out how to arrange the same three sounds to make that design. Are you ready? Okay: Make a *sandwich* piece of nine sounds—three for the bread, three for the peanut butter, and three for the bread again. The first three sounds and the last three sounds should match, because the slices of bread are just the same."

[The children offer various "sandwich" arrangements such as "whistle-snap-whistle, slide-slide-slide, whistle-snap-whistle."]

The same process can be followed to construct pieces of more complexity. The class can advance to more sounds, longer sections, more complex forms, and varied rhythms. With increased experience, children can devise rather sophisticated and interesting sound pieces.

Improvising

Another way to encourage creativity in music is to ask the children to improvise measures or short phrases in response to musical statements provided by the teacher or another child. Initially these efforts involve only rhythm, and the response is clapped or tapped. In this way the technical problems of performing are reduced to a minimum. The opening musical statement sets the tempo and style for the response. If asked to improvise without any idea of what is expected, a child is likely to feel bewildered. The process of improvising from musical statements can proceed in this way:

"I'll clap a short pattern. You 'answer' my pattern by clapping a pattern of your own, but do *not* clap my pattern over again. For example, I might clap

and you might answer

"See how it goes? The nice thing about this is that there aren't any wrong answers! So don't be afraid to clap whatever comes into your head. Try to make your answer last as long as the statement that I clap for for you.

"Let's start with you, Caroline. Here's the statement. I'll clap it for you twice. The second time you join in right after the statement is finished, so that your answer is connected to what I clap. Ready? Here we go."

[The teacher commends Caroline and lets other children improvise clapping "answers" to different statements.]

As the children become more proficient at improvising, they can work in pairs, with one child thinking up a statement and the other improvising an answer. The material can gradually be increased in length, and extended to include meters other than three or four beats to the measure. The activity can also be expanded into a game: A rhythmic statement is agreed on by the class. The first, third, and other odd-numbered members of the class clap it alone when their turn comes, while the second, fourth, and other even-numbered members of the class individually improvise responses. The object of the game is to keep the rhythm going without a break until everyone in the class has participated. The game can be made more complex, if the class is ready for it, by adding the stipulation that each improvised phrase must be different from any previously clapped. This is a particular challenge to the child who improvises last.

Rhythm compositions can also be created in which two or three parts occur at the same time. Again, the initial efforts should be simple, perhaps like this:

As the children demonstrate that they are able to perform easy pieces, they can create more difficult compositions with simultaneously sounding parts, such as this example in $\frac{3}{4}$ meter:

Other types of sounds can of course be substituted for the clapping.

The technique of providing the child with a musical statement can also be employed with melodic phrases. A musical statement like the following can be played or sung, and the child responds by singing or by playing on an instrument.

Orff-Schulwerk techniques

Many American music specialists have adopted various practices from the Orff-*Schulwerk*, a method of music instruction that was developed under the direction of the contemporary German composer Carl Orff and Gunild Keetman.[2] One aspect of the *Schulwerk* involves clapping, chanting, and other means of producing rhythm patterns. The *Schulwerk* also encourages children to improvise and create music. In effect, the method does what has been suggested earlier in this chapter: It permits the child a limited number of options in a highly structured situation. The structure is given in terms of meter, tempo, length of phrase, and a limited number of pitches. The initial efforts at making up a melody are sometimes restricted to only two pitches.

As the children demonstrate increasing competence, the number of available pitches is increased to three and then to five. The *pentatonic* or five-tone scale, which can be reproduced simply by playing the black keys of the piano, is found in the folk music of many cultures. This scale is well-suited to the improvisations of children because it eliminates two problems inherent in an eight-tone scale: (1) the possibility of dissonance caused by the clash between pitches a half step apart, and (2) the strong feeling of key center that makes certain note sequences seem more "correct" than others.

To make the initial efforts at improvisation even more foolproof, the Orff method utilizes instruments, such as the metallophone, that have removable bars. With the unwanted bars removed, the child cannot hit an "off limits" pitch. Music in two or more parts is encountered early in the *Schulwerk*, and ostinatos are featured prominently.

The use of Orff ideas for creating music requires teacher direction, because the efforts of several children must be coordinated if the composition is to be successful. Here is an example of how the improvisation might be introduced.

"Jason, here's an alto xylophone. As you can see, all the bars have been removed except for two. With those two tones, think up a part that is four beats long. When our composition is played, your part will be repeated over and over throughout the piece. Why don't you go to that end of the room and quietly work out a part."

"Sarah, here's a soprano glockenspiel with all the bars taken off except for two. You can make up the melody for our piece. Think of a tune that's two measures long—it should last for eight beats. You can take the instrument to that side of the room and work for a couple of minutes.

"We need one more part, not for another melody, but just for the interesting rhythm it can make. Let's use this hand drum. Doug, why don't you take it to that corner and quietly work out a part that lasts for eight beats."

Before trying to put the three parts together, the teacher should hear each one alone to make sure that it fits the pattern by having the correct number of measures and beats. (The pitches are sure to blend if the teacher made a careful selection before giving them to the children.) These limitations of rhythm and pitch are in no sense confining to the children's imaginations, because so many options are available even in the highly structured situation described in the example. One possibility is:

To the example above could be added a coda and contrasting sections of two measures each. The music can be made more complex by adding more instrumental parts, longer phrases, more pitches, and so on. But for most children, advanced improvisation can wait until fourth grade or later.

Creating melodies for texts

Another way to help children create music is to give them a short rhyme and ask them to set it to music. The pattern of the words provides a rhythmic structure, and the message of the text suggests a mood. Here is a stanza from a poem by Christina Rossetti:

The wind has such a rainy sound
Moaning through the town,
The sea has such a windy sound,—
Will the ships go down?

The teacher can focus the children's attention on the text by first asking them to add sound effects, a technique that was suggested earlier in this chapter.

To stimulate the children's musical ideas as the class is looking at the words, the teacher can play pentatonic tunes on the bells, on which only the notes C D E G A are available.

"There are lots of possibilities for tunes that fit the blowy, stormy quality of these words. There's this tune:

or this one, which has the same rhythm with different pitches:

or the same pitches with a different rhythm:

"Who'd like to try it? Lynn, here's the mallet. Experiment by playing the notes in any order you want. Sing or say the words along with your notes. When you find a tune you like for those words, we'll all sing your song."

Because a melody is being composed, not improvised, there should be an attempt to arrive at a "finished" melody that is musically satisfying. It is a good idea to have the child perform the melody twice to see if it is the same each time. Small discrepancies are not unusual, and the teacher should help the child to decide which of two options should be retained in the permanent version.

To ensure the permanence of the children's compositions, the teacher should write them down in notation, because almost no child in the primary grades is able to conceive a melody and then notate it accurately. Unless the youngster is another Mozart, this capability must be acquired through years of training. If the child can play the melodic phrases on a keyboard-like instrument, rather than rely on singing, the music is easier to put into notation because the interval relationships are visible, and inaccurate singing will not obscure the child's melodic intention.

When trying to motivate the class to compose, the teacher should not just write music on the board, perform it, and then ask, "Boys and girls, do you like that?" If they agree—and they usually do, because it is the teacher's suggested melody—the song is sometimes said to have been composed by the class, which of course is not an accurate description of what took place. The value of creative activity lies in the development and evaluation of music produced through the imagination of the children themselves.

Although creative efforts can occur in a class setting, each new idea is the product of an individual mind; music is not created by committee. Other people may react to and comment on what an individual creates, but the act of creating is the achievement of one person. That is its greatest value in the music education of children. Creating music is a learning experience as well as an enriching activity. For this reason, creative activities need to be included in the education of every child.

NOTES

1. J. P. Guilford, "Three Faces of Intellect," *American Psychologist*, Vol. 14 (1959), pp. 469-79.
2. Beth Landis and Polly Carder, *The Eclectic Curriculum in American Music Education: Contributions of Dalcroze, Kodály, and Orff* (Reston, Va.: Music Educators National Conference, 1972), pp. 69-107.

REVIEW QUESTIONS

1. What traits are believed by psychologists to be components of creativity?

2. What is the difference between composing and improvising?

3. Give three reasons for including creative activities in the music education of children.

4. What principles should teachers follow in helping students to create music?

5. Cite at least five ways to add creative aspects to a song that the children know.

6. a. Describe one way in which creative activity in art can be combined with music.
   b. Describe one way in which creative movement or dance can be combined with music.

7. Describe how a teacher can guide children to organize simple pieces of music composed of sounds available in the classroom.

8. In what ways does the Orff-*Schulwerk* method establish a structure for a child's initial effort at improvising?

9. What procedure might a teacher use in guiding children to create a short piece for glockenspiel, alto metallophone, and triangle?

10. Describe the teaching procedure by which a teacher might guide children to compose a song for lines of poetry.

ACTIVITIES

1. From one of the music series books for the primary grades, select a song to which you and other members of the methods class will add creative ideas.
   a. Make two or three changes in the pitches.
   b. Make two or three changes in the rhythm.
   c. Add a simple part for an instrument, one that contributes an appropriate rhythm pattern or tonal effect.
   d. Write a new set of words.

2. In class or elsewhere, make two drawings while listening to two contrasting pieces of music.

3. In class or elsewhere, develop a pattern of bodily movements expressing a piece of music. Demonstrate the movements to the class.

4. Discover six sound-making possibilities in the classroom. Then organize the six sounds into a composition. Determine the order of sounds, the rhythm, the dynamic level, and the manner in which two or more sounds will be handled if they occur simultaneously.

5. a. Develop two clapped rhythm patterns to which another class member can respond.

   b. Develop two melodic statements to which another class member can respond.

6. Develop an Orff-like composition using six classroom instruments. Determine the pitches, length of phrases, tempo, form, and content of introduction and coda if they are to be included.

7. Create a melody for these lines of William Shakespeare:

> Blow, blow, thou wind!
> Thou art not so unkind
> As man's ingratitude;
> Thy tooth is not so keen,
> Because thou art not seen,
>   Although thy breath be rude.

Music Exists in Time: Rhythm

As is true of all the components of music, rhythm is impossible to describe fully in words. One can define *rhythm* as "the ongoing sense of motion that occurs as music progresses in time," but even this description is inadequate unless it is given meaning through the experiencing of rhythm. Rhythm is more physical than intellectual. It is not a solution that one reaches at the conclusion of an exercise in logic. Rather, it is an experience as basic as life itself, as fundamental as a heartbeat. To overlook this elemental nature of rhythm is to miss its essential character.

Every sound has at least four aspects: tone quality, pitch (highness or lowness), loudness, and duration (called rhythm when consecutive sounds are involved). Because rhythm is intertwined with the other components of music, a music lesson cannot deal exclusively with rhythm, but it can highlight that aspect. The challenge for the teacher is to help the children to sense rhythm as a driving force in music, and to produce rhythms precisely but not mechanically.

Not only is rhythm interrelated with other aspects of music; it is itself made up of different components: beat, meter, tempo, and so on. Helping children to understand these components through experience is an important goal in teaching music, and is the basis for most of the teaching suggestions contained in this chapter.

RHYTHMIC MOVEMENT AND RESPONSE

At the early grade levels, music education somewhat parallels physical education in seeking to develop the children's coordination through fundamental movements such as waking, running, galloping, skipping, and simple dance movements. The music accompanying these activities need not be complicated. The teacher can merely tap regular sounds on a drum and encourage the children to move to that pulse. Or recordings designed especially for this purpose can be played on the phonograph. Piano playing or singing by the teacher also provides an appropriate background for children's movement.

Physical education teachers and music teachers see rhythmic movement as leading down different paths. Physical education teachers are trying to develop the physical coordination of the children. Music teachers—and that includes classroom teachers when they are teaching music—are trying to build musical skills and understandings on these early experiences.

There is disagreement among music specialists as to whether children should adapt to the speed of the music or the teacher should adjust the speed to the child's "natural" inclination. Adjusting the speed to suit the child is useful when helping an individual to find the beat. By matching the speed of a youngster's trot or walk, the teacher may be able to get the child's movements synchronized with a beat. The usual situation in a music class, however, is for the children to conform to the speed of the music. This is a more valuable skill because it requires them to recognize the recurrence of the beat and to adapt their responses accordingly.

EXPERIENCING THE BEAT

In music there are not many examples of inherently logical learning sequences that need to be followed if learning is to be successful. One of those exceptions, however, is the necessity for children to sense the beat first, because that ability is basic to learning other aspects of rhythm.

Children usually require many experiences with the beat before they can sense it consistently and accurately. This awareness is not a skill that can be acquired in a lesson or two; it must be reinforced over a span of months. The review can be brief, and it can be integrated with the learning of other aspects of rhythm, but it must be emphasized persistently.

The words "beat" and "rhythm" are not synonyms. The *beat* is the recurrent throb or pulse that makes a listener want to tap or clap, while rhythm is a more inclusive term referring to orderly motion as music progresses in terms of time.

Because the concept of a beat is so basic, the teacher should involve the children in discovering it. Here is one way in which this may be done.

> "How many of you have felt your own heartbeat or taken your own pulse? If you haven't, do it now. Touch your throat with your fingertips on one side of your voice box and your thumb on the other side, like this. . . .Then press backward gently until you can feel the strong pulse in your throat. . . .Can you feel it? . . .Notice that it's very even and steady: throb, throb, throb. The beat in music is like that: in fact, it can be called a pulse, too."

How can children be taught to feel the beat in music? Like feeling the heartbeat, it is done basically through physical actions rather than through academic procedures. Gaining a feel for the beat seems to happen best when one just "rides along" with the flow. It seems to happen more easily in a group situation than in an individual lesson. There is something captivating about a group of people clapping or dancing along with the music.

This fact has several implications for helping children discover the beat. One is that the teacher should establish situations in which the children who have difficulty in sensing the beat are caught up in expressing it along with their classmates. Another implication is the futility of trying to explain verbally what the beat is. When a child demonstrates that he or she is sensing the beat, *at that moment* the teacher should say, "There! Now you're feeling the beat of the music!" A third implication is the need for a relaxed atmosphere in the class. Tension and stress are impediments to feeling the beat.

Here is one way in which a sensing of the beat can be encouraged.

> "If you listen closely to a piece of music, you can sense a throb or beat that moves along very evenly. Let me show you. First, I'll play a recording of a march, and clap the beat for you." [The teacher demonstrates clapping the beat of the music.]
>
> "Now I'll do the same thing again. This time after you've listened carefully for a moment, and after you think you're feeling the beat, join with me in clapping to it. By the time we finish, I hope everyone will be clapping along on the beat."

Some music educators advocate starting children in kindergarten and the primary grades with rhythmic experiences that involve the use of large muscles. Recent research does not support this advice.[1] Marching in time to music is a seemingly simple large-muscle activity. Nevertheless, dancing or marching with the beat is a skill that some adults never acquire, so it is unrealistic to expect all children to be able to do this. Rather, it appears that children execute rhythms more easily through speech patterns or by smaller muscle movements such as hitting sticks together or clapping. The Orff-*Schulwerk*, Kodály-Hungarian Singing School, and Dalcroze methods have recognized this fact, and emphasize small muscle movements and the chanting of rhymes.

PERCEIVING THE STEADINESS OF THE BEAT

When children begin to sense the beat, they need to be made aware of its steady nature. Although the desire for beat regularity may appear to be a natural inclination, it probably is not. Like most human behavior, it must be learned. Much concentration is required to maintain a truly steady beat: some adults cannot seem to do this no matter how hard they try.

There are several ways to impress the steadiness of the beat on young children. It can be pointed out in the songs they sing and in the music to which they listen. It should be remembered, however, that listeners tend to take the beat for granted because they do not need to control it as does a performer.

The teacher may wish to bring a metronome into the classroom, preferably a wind-up model with a pendulum, because its movement can be seen. Clapping or chanting with the metronome will help children learn to maintain a steady beat. Youngsters may not believe they are rushing a tempo until they hear their deviations from the even ticks of the metronome. The simple routine of letting the children alternately listen to four ticks, then clap or tap four, is effective in helping them experience the steadiness of the beat.

Chanting short phrases is a further step toward establishing a feel of regular beat. Here are some examples.

One potato, two potato, three potato, four;

Five potato, six potato, seven potato, more.

Hickory dickory dock, (tick, tock)

The mouse ran up the clock; (tick, tock)

The clock struck one, the mouse ran down,

Hickory dickory dock, (tick, tock).

Phrases for chanting can be derived from many sources: school cheers, rhymes, verses of songs, and lines made up by the teacher or the class. As the children become accomplished at reciting them, the class can be divided in half, with different phrases being simultaneously recited, or with a particular rhythm being chanted in staggered order like a round.

Although there is little opportunity for creative effort in learning to sense a steady beat—one is either with the beat or not—some creative activity can be introduced by asking the children to make up their own chants and rhymes. Youngsters often devise their own rhymes when jumping rope or engaging in other play activity.

In these first experiences with group participation, the need for maintaining an even beat will be apparent to the children when they realize that an unstable beat creates confusion. A steady beat is necessary not only for the practical purpose of keeping the participants together, but also for the rhythmic drive that is required if the music is to sound vital and attractive. This sense of vitality and intensity is achieved not through harshness and strain but through attention to the underlying rhythm.

A pattern of chanted words can be introduced in this way:

"Do you all remember the rhyme about 'One potato'? I'm going to tap the beat and say the words at the same time, but I'm going to say some of the words louder than others. Listen and tell me which ones are louder: the words *on* the beat or *off* the beat." [The teacher says the rhyme, and Kent observes that the words on the beat are louder.]

"You're right, Kent! This time, class, say the rhyme with me, and make the words on the beat louder than the other words. Notice that the arrangement of loud and soft words makes the rhyme just swing along." [The class says the rhyme with encouragement from the teacher, who again taps the beat and emphasizes the louder syllables.]

"Good! Now let's add a motion to represent the beats. Slap your thigh for the beats and again speak extra loudly on the words that happen on the beat." [The class adds a thigh slap on the beat, producing an energetic and bouncy motion in response to the teacher's example.]

The following lesson shows how a teacher can help the children to feel the steadiness of the beat in a simple song. The actions suggested by the words add interest while reinforcing the feeling of the beat, particularly when the motions start with the two quarter notes in the second full measure.

"Here's a song that I'm sure you'll like. It's 'The Bus.' If you know it already, help me sing it." [The teacher sings the first verse and a few children join in.]

THE BUS

2. The wheels on the bus go 'round and 'round . . .

3. The horn on the bus goes "Toot, toot, toot" . . .

4. The money in the box goes "Ding, ding, ding" . . .

5. The wiper on the glass goes "Swish, swish, swish" . . .

"Good! Now, remember how you've been learning to feel the beat in music? Let's sing the song again and see if you can feel the steady beat. When you do, show us by doing the motions with lots of energy, right with the beat." [The class enthusiastically sings all verses.]

"Are the beats in the song even or uneven?" [Several students respond that the beats are even.] "Sure, they're even. To be really certain, clap the beats with me as we sing the first verse again. Rea-dy, go."

Other actions are possible with a song such as this. The children can walk to the beat if they have succeeded in clapping accurately. They can chant the words with special emphasis on the syllables that occur on the beat. The beat can be played on simple rhythm instruments such as drums or triangles.

It is important to emphasize the beats and to recite the lines vigorously. Energetic speaking should not be confused with shouting or forcing the voice in an unattractive manner. Rather, each word should be jabbed out decisively, especially the syllables that coincide with the beats. Rhythmic precision is aided by having the children tap or clap the beats as they say the rhyme.

TEMPO

When children can feel the beat and recognize its regular nature, they are ready to listen for the musical factor called *tempo*, which is the speed at which the beats recur one after another.

Tempo can be experienced by the children, with the help of a metronome, in the following manner.

"The other day you took your own pulses by putting your fingertips on one side of your voice boxes and your thumbs on the other. Do
the same thing today, only this time, check the speed of your pulse.

"Jill, move your free hand to show us each time your heart beats.
I'll measure the speed by adjusting this metronome to match it." [The
teacher and class count the movements of Jill's hand.] "Now we have
it: the speed measures 72 beats each minute. That's a nice, medium
speed.

"Now let's all stand up and run in place for about a minute. Pretend that we're jogging. Here we go!" [The class jogs in place.] "Okay,
sit down. *Now* check your heartbeat. Is it faster or slower than it was
before?" [The children report that their heartbeats are faster.]

"What does this have to do with music? Well, the speed of the
beats—how close they occur one after another—is called *tempo* in
music. I'll sing a song at two different tempos, and you tell me if the
second version is faster or slower than the first."

Judgments about tempo depend partly on how the listener perceives the music. In many songs, either a fast beat or a slow beat seems
to fit. As a general rule in concert and folk music, if the speed of the
beats is so fast that a conductor's motions would look frantic and fren-
zied, then the musicians' perception of the beat shifts so that it is felt
to be less frequent, and therefore the tempo is slower. Conversely, if
the beats occur so slowly that the elapsed time between them seems
unmoving, a shorter duration should be regarded as the beat. Some
performers in the popular music field prefer to think of the beat as
being very rapid. One can see their feet tapping furiously as they perform. In any case, some latitude is allowed in thinking of a piece as
being, for example, in two moderately slow beats per measure or in four
rapid beats per measure.

The most helpful factor in determining the correct tempo of a
song is to consider the mood or style of the music. A sprightly jig can
appropriately have more beats in it than are felt in a sacred hymn of the
same duration. In much folk music and in most of the songs that children encounter, the beat approximates the rate of a normal heartbeat,
or a moderate walking pace.

Several procedures can be employed to direct the children's attention to the speed of the beats. One is to sing the same song at different
tempos. The class can also listen to works of music that have different
tempos. For example, the slow second movement of Haydn's "Clock"
Symphony might be contrasted with the fourth movement, which has
a quick tempo.

When the children are secure in their ability to recognize a steady
beat, they can be introduced to music in which the tempos change noticeably during the course of one song or work. An example is the Hungarian *czardas*, in which the tempo of the music gradually increases

until the dancers are supposedly no longer able to keep up. Another work that effectively demonstrates tempo change is Villa-Lobos' imaginative "The Little Train of the Caipira." The train is standing still at the beginning, then it starts up slowly, rolls merrily along, and finally winds down at the end of the journey.

It is important to stress to the children that *the speed of the beat is not the same as the speed of the notes.* Music at a slow tempo can contain short note durations, and music at a fast tempo can consist of long, sustained sounds. Tempo refers to the span of time elapsing between the beats, not between the notes.

LONG AND SHORT NOTE DURATIONS

In the following lesson the teacher uses the rhythm pattern of a song to show the difference between the number of notes on a beat and the beat itself. In the process, the children can observe that notes are of varying durations, and that these durations are judged in relation to the beat. The important point to be learned is not that the length of sound or silence is referred to as "duration," but that the beat is the unit of time measurement in music.

"In some of the songs we've sung, you may have noticed that you sang more than one note on some of the beats. Remember 'The Bus'? Let's chant it together while we clap the beats, but instead of the real words, let's say 'ta' instead, like this: Ta tata tata ta ta ta ta ta—. Ready, chant."

[The children clap along with the teacher, and most of them say the neutral syllable accurately. To focus their attention on the relationship between the claps and the "ta's," the teacher invites individual responses to questions such as, "Were the beats all the same speed? Were the 'ta's all the same speed? Which 'ta's were faster: the ones at the beginning or at the end of the song? Was the last 'ta' longer or shorter than one beat?"]

"Now let's sing the song with the real words instead of 'ta's. Notice again that the notes are different in length, but the beats (your claps) are all the same length. The beats have to be even because that's how we measure the passing of time in music. The beat helps us decide how much time should go by on the long or short notes."

In a later lesson, in which "Are You Sleeping" is sung, the teacher emphasizes three common note/beat combinations: two notes lasting for one beat; one note lasting for one beat; and one note lasting for two beats.

"In music class on Monday you learned a new song, 'Are You Sleeping?' Today let's sing it again. This time, stand and try to step in time to the beat as you sing. Just mark time by walking on the same place." [The class sings the song while maintaining the beat.]

ARE YOU SLEEPING?

"This time, sit and just think the song in your head as you clap the rhythm of the *notes*. That's the same as the rhythm of the *words*. If it will help you, you may sing the song very softly as you clap the words." [The class claps the rhythm of the words. A few children are uncertain in their clapping, but they make an attempt to follow their classmates or the teacher.]

"Now I'll tap the beats as you clap the words." [The class's and the teacher's clapping are combined. The teacher then reviews with the children by asking, "Did your rhythm *always* sound the same as mine? Did your rhythm *sometimes* sound the same as my beat? What happens at the words 'Morning bells are'?" The teacher helps the class to find places where there are two or more notes to a beat.]

The song "Are You Sleeping?" can also be used to help the class discover similarities among various rhythm patterns. The children can find out for themselves that in this song there are identical rhythms for each pair of consecutive phrases: the first and second ("Are you sleeping, Are you sleeping") the third and fourth, and so on. A few observant children may notice that the rhythm for the lines "Brother John" and "Ding, dong, ding" is the same. The class can also be divided to demonstrate different patterns, with some of the children sounding the pattern of "Morning bells are ringing" while the others produce the rhythm for "Ding, dong, ding." They can sound the patterns by clapping, tapping on a drum, hitting rhythm sticks together, or playing other rhythm instruments.

An excellent technique for making children aware of rhythms is to help them discover the patterns of words and names. Children are curious to find out what rhythm patterns can be made from their own names. Here is one way in which this can be done.

"Did you know that the name of every person in this class has a rhythm pattern? David, let's use your name as an example. It goes:

Da - vid *Smith*

"The name 'David' seems to divide into two notes in one beat, just like the 'morning bells' in 'Are You Sleeping?' The word 'Smith' is just one note, which takes up one beat. Let's all say 'David Smith' in a rhythmic way, with lots of energy." [The class chants the name and David seems pleased. The teacher puts other children's names into patterns, pointing out that some names require three or four syllables within one beat,

Jen - ni - fer *Ar*- den   *Jer* - e - mi- ah *Hart* - man

and others require an "upbeat" because the first syllable is unaccented.

De - *nise*   *Rich* - ard -son.]

SOUND AND SILENCE

To a nonmusician, a *rest* (measured silence) might appear to be a void or a stopping place in the music. Actually, rests have musical significance. They help delineate the phrases and indicate aspects of performance style. Although there may be no sound for a particular moment in the music, the listener should feel that the flow of the music is continuing.

A good way to emphasize the continuity of the music is to let the children make decisive motions during rests. In the song "If You're Happy," the teacher introduces the children to rests by asking for silent action—moving the hands as if to clap, but not striking them together—during these intervals of "organized silence."

IF YOU'RE HAPPY

Traditional

Another technique is to sing a song in which portions of the melody are replaced with actions or silence. "Bingo" is an example of this type of song.

"The song 'Bingo' doesn't tell us much about the dog, but we can make the music interesting by playing a game with his name. As you can see, I've printed 'BINGO' five times on the board, not in a line but one above the other, like layers in a cake. Before we play the game, let's review the song by tapping the beat as we sing." . . .

BINGO

(For autoharp, transpose to F major)   American Folk Song

"Here comes the game! We'll sing the song five times. Each time, exchange a clap for one letter in Bingo's name. The first time, clap for the letter 'B,' the second time for 'B' and 'I,' and so on. I'll help you by circling the letter that you're going to replace with a clap." [The class sings the song five times.]

"Now let's make it more tricky. Sing 'Bingo' five more times, but instead of claps, just think the notes *silently*. When you think of the letters of Bingo's name, keep your thoughts moving at exactly the same speed as the music. Keep that beat going evenly in your head."

Echo-clapping is an excellent means of teaching children to listen carefully to the interplay between sound and silence. Here is an example of how a teacher may do this.

"I'll tap out a pattern on the drum, and you tap it back to me with your rhythm sticks. Listen carefully, and start tapping when I give you the signal by nodding my head."

As the children demonstrate increased competence in imitating rhythms and rests, the patterns can be lengthened and made more difficult.

METER

There is a human tendency to perceive a succession of beats in patterns, rather than as isolated, identical fragments. The ticks of a clock may be identical, but the human mind tends to organize them into "tick-tock." *Meter* is the organizing of beats into patterns according to the heaviness or lightness of each beat. Most metrical patterns are two, three, or four beats long, although other patterns are occasionally encountered. The beat that is heard and performed more strongly than the others is considered to be the first beat in each pattern. For example, a two-beat meter is: BEAT-beat, BEAT-beat, and so on. Each metrical pattern comprises one *measure*.

The phenomenon of meter is partly the result of human perception, and therefore it is somewhat subject to individual interpretation. For example, some measures can be thought of as containing two slow beats or four fast beats. This fact affects one's feeling of tempo as well as meter; earlier in this chapter it was pointed out that the speed of the beat can be perceived in various ways, depending on one's inclination and the style of the music.

Children should gain a concept of meter and develop the ability to recognize and perform various metrical patterns. When singing or playing, the performer should usually emphasize the notes on the first beat by making them a bit louder.

In the following lesson the teacher points out the pattern of strong and weak beats, and introduces the children to the term "meter."

"You've been learning about the beat in music for several weeks now. Can you clap the beat to 'Eency, Weency Spider' as we sing the song?" [The class sings the song, clapping with vigor.]

EENCY, WEENCY SPIDER

"You made your claps nice and even, so they all sounded alike. But did you know that in music some beats are stronger than others, so they're sounded louder? And those strong and weak beats happen in a pattern. Sing 'Eency, Weency Spider' again while I clap the beats. But this time, listen to my clapping to see which beats are stronger." [The class sings the song while the teacher claps the beat, emphasizing the first beat of each measure.]

"Did all the strong beats bunch together, one after another, or were they mixed in with weak beats?" ["Mixed in!" several children say with conviction.] "Did you hear a pattern to the STRONG-weak beats, so that after a while you knew what would happen next?" [The children's response is less certain, but a few class members acknowledge that there was a pattern.]

"This time sing 'Eency, Weency Spider' while you clap the beats. The pattern is STRONG-weak, STRONG-weak, so be sure to make a difference in the strength of your claps." [The class claps and sings the song, following the teacher's example by exaggerating the loudness and softness of alternating beats.]

"There's a word for the pattern of beats. It is *meter.* The meter of 'Eency, Weency Spider' is STRONG-weak, STRONG-weak. Each pattern has two beats in it, so we call it 'two-beat meter.' "

The following lesson shows how children can be made aware of the fact that the notes on the first beat of each pattern (measure) are emphasized.

"Yesterday you clapped the beats to 'Eency, Weency Spider,' and you did a good job of clapping the two-beat meter of STRONG-weak, STRONG-weak. Did you know that you can also show the meter just by the way you sing the song, without clapping? First we'll say just the words to 'Eency, Weency Spider,' all together, with a lot of energy." [The class says the words rhythmically.]

"Did you notice that the first time you said 'spider,' you didn't say the two parts of the word with the same loudness? You didn't go 'spi-der'; you said 'SPI-der,' because the beats on that word go STRONG-weak. In fact, you gave the first beat of *every* pattern more strength, and that's good. This time when we sing the song, keep on sounding the notes on the first beat a little stronger than the others. Notice that I said a *little* stronger. If you make too much difference, the song won't be smooth and musical."

In addition to reproducing various meters and recognizing those performed for them by the teacher, the children should learn to recognize the meter in music heard on recordings. The approach suggested for listening to a new song can also be employed for recorded music. The children can be directed to listen carefully and then tap or clap the beat lightly. As they sound the beats, they should try to determine what the metrical pattern is. Most marches feature two-beat meter, and minuets by Mozart and Haydn are clear examples of three-beat meter. Waltzes are usually not suitable for demonstrating three-beat meter because their rapid tempos cause them to be felt as one beat per measure instead of three, and tempo fluctuation (called *rubato*) is frequent.

Initially, the children should be introduced to only two- and three-beat meter. When they are consistently correct in differentiating between those two meters and performing them, they may move on to four-beat meter. Although music with complex and unusual meters may be sung by young children, the study of intricate meters should be delayed until the upper grades.

THE NOTATION OF RHYTHM

The experiences suggested so far in this chapter have involved the "doing" of rhythm, rather than the reading of its notation. This arrangement has been deliberate, because experience with rhythm must precede the symbolization of it. Especially in the primary grades, children should "ear" the music before they "eye" it, to cite an old maxim from music education.

One successful way to introduce the reading of rhythmic symbols is to use "stick" notation. The main virtue of stick notation is its simplicity; all distracting symbols are eliminated. At first the note values are limited to quarter and eighth notes, for which stems and beams are sufficient. In stick notation the quarter note is represented by a vertical line and the eighth note by a vertical line with a horizontal beam connecting it to another note. Note heads (the oval shapes found in standard notation) are unnecessary at this stage because both note values would require identical filled-in heads, and the absence of pitch eliminates the need for placing heads on a staff.

Often children are taught to say rhythmic syllables in conjunction with the stick notes. Although syllables can be introduced apart from notation of any kind, learning the two together enables children to "name" a note value and thereby reinforce the association between what they see and what they hear. (The advantage is possible only when different syllables are assigned to the different note values. A single syllable applied to all note values does not depict the relationship among various durations.) Rhythmic syllables have an additional benefit. Many children find it easier to perform rhythm patterns through speech or small-muscle activity rather than through large-muscle movements.

In fairness, it should be noted that some music teachers regard rhythmic syllables as being redundant, because the children are taught a word system that later will need to be replaced with standard terminology. Furthermore, the syllables are of nonsense construction and so they convey no inherent relationship among themselves. The conventional rhythm nomenclature ("two quarters equal a half," and so on) borrows from a number system that has its own logic.

There are several syllable systems, all of which work if taught consistently. The system most commonly used designates a quarter note with the sound "ta" and an eighth note with "ti" (pronounced "tee"). Here is an example:

Pattern in conventional notation:	♩ ♩ ♫♩
Pattern in stick notation:	| | ⊓ |
Rhythmic syllables for the pattern:	ta ta ti ti ta

In the following lesson the teacher presents quarter and eighth notes in stick notation. At this stage, the two types of notes are not mixed in the same pattern.

> "Today you'll learn a way to picture some rhythm patterns. First I'll draw a straight line that stands up. . . . This is a picture of a note that takes up one beat. Here's a pattern of four lines standing up. . . . This means beat-beat-beat-beat. Let's read what the picture tells us to do. For every note pictured by a line, say 'ta.' Rea-dy, go: 'Ta ta ta ta.'" [The class says the "ta"s with the teacher.]
>
> "Good! Now try to read the picture at a different speed, a little faster. The tempo this time is beat-beat. Rea-dy go: 'Ta ta ta ta.'"

The rhythm syllable "ti" is introduced in much the same way as the syllable and symbol for "ta." The mixing of the two types of notes begins only after each symbol has been learned. In the following example, the teacher asks the children to think and analyze before trying to perform what they see. Also, the teacher reviews previous learnings, providing a reinforcement that is often needed with children in primary grades.

> "Let's review what you've learned about stick notation and syllables for reading rhythm patterns." [The teacher draws the stick notation for two quarters, two eighths, and another quarter on the chalkboard. The class identifies the symbols as being three "ta"s and two "ti"s, and the children repeat the pattern after the teacher.]
>
> "Since you did so well on that pattern, I'll let you figure out the next one without my help. Here it is." [The teacher draws two eighth notes followed by three quarter notes.]

"Think about it before you raise your hand to answer. How many
'ta's and 'ti's does it have?" [The class figures out the rhythm and performs it by reciting the syllables aloud.]

The notation for rests can also be introduced in a simple form. A
quarter rest is represented by a zigzag line 𝄽. As was pointed out earlier
in this chapter, it is important to convey the idea of continued motion
in the music during a rest. Since the syllables are being spoken, it is
appropriate to have the silences also delineated by oral action, but not
vocalized. A short puff of air on each rest, as if one is blowing out a
candle, will help preserve the feeling of rhythmic continuity through
the rest, and yet will ensure that it is silent.

In the initial stages of rhythmic reading, only one more note
value is needed to complete a basic "vocabulary." It is the symbol for
a note lasting two beats, most often represented by the half note, 𝅗𝅥. It
can be the same in both stick and conventional notation. It is said
"ta-ah," with the "ah" occurring on the second beat of the note.

The transition from stick to conventional notation is easy because
of the similarity between the two types. All that is needed is the addition of heads to the quarter and eighth notes. When the children demonstrate that they understand stick notation, the change to conventional notation should be made.

There is a visual technique for helping children to understand the
relative durations of the various note and rest values. In conventional
notation every note and rest takes up approximately the same amount
of horizontal distance; in that sense, they all appear to be about equal
in length. To help the children associate the type of note or rest with
its appropriate length, the teacher can try the following technique,
which is an adaptation of the Cuisenaire rods used in teaching arithmetic. Essentially the technique consists of drawing notes and rests on
pieces of paper or cardboard of different lengths so that the piece of
paper for the quarter note is twice as long as the piece for the eighth
note, and the half-note piece is twice as long as the quarter-note piece.
Short exercises in reading or computing note values can be solved by
manipulating the slips of paper of various lengths. The technique is
described more fully on pages 213-14. Whatever system is used, the
rhythmic combinations that are seen should also be performed in some
manner, so that the children retain the association between symbol
and sound.

The children will of course encounter more notational symbols
than those introduced here. They will perform music involving compound meters, dotted notes, and more complex rhythms. In the primary grades their ability to hear and perform rhythm patterns will
greatly exceed their ability to read notation. For this reason, much
performance instruction is done by rote, and the children's inability
to read notation does not hinder their ability to perform music.

NOTE

1. Edward L. Rainbow and Diane Owen, "A Progress Report on a Three-Year In-vestigation of the Rhythmic Ability of Pre-School Aged Children," Council for Research in Music Education, Bulletin No. 59 (Summer 1979). See also Ana Lucia Frega, "Rhythmic Tasks with Three, Four, and Five Year Old Children," Council for Research in Music Education, Bulletin No. 59 (Summer 1979).

REVIEW QUESTIONS

1. Why is the experiencing of rhythm by students in the primary grades more important than a verbal definition of rhythm?

2. What are some teaching techniques for helping children to experience the beat in music?

3. How are chants and rhymes used in aiding children to become aware of the steady character of the beat in music?

4. Describe some teaching techniques for helping children to gain an understanding of tempo.

5. How can a teacher present a phrase of a song to help children understand the different durations of notes in relation to the beat?

6. How can a concept of meter be developed in children in the primary grades?

7. Why is it necessary for children to have adequate experiences in music before they attempt to read music notation?

8. What is the advantage of stick notation in teaching the reading of rhythms?

ACTIVITIES

1. Select a song with which to help your methods class become more aware of the beat. Decide the teaching procedures you will use to accomplish this.

2. Examine one of the music series books designed for first, second, or third grade. Select a song that illustrates the three commonly encountered rhythmic durations: one note per beat, two notes per beat, and one note for two beats. Teach a phrase of the song to the methods class and ask various class members to identify the different durations.

3. Set the names of some of the class members into rhythmic notation.

4. Make up four short phrases of rhythm patterns. Clap each phrase for the class so that the group can echo your patterns.

5. Make up a rhythm that includes the three kinds of note values described in activity 2. Clap it for the class so that each individual can write it in rhythmic notation.

6. Think up a new set of words and sounds for "If You're Happy." For example, "If you're happy and you know it, clack your teeth."

7. In the music series books, find three songs (other than those cited in this chapter) that would be especially good for teaching two-beat and three-beat meter to children.

8. List three songs that would be especially suitable for introducing young children to rests.

9. Create two rhythm phrases, each eight beats in length. Write them on the chalkboard in stick notation and lead the methods class in performing them by clapping and/or reciting them with rhythmic syllables.

Music Has Tone Quality: Timbre

Every sound, every person's voice, and every type of musical instrument has its own unique quality. The musical term for the quality of a sound is *timbre*, which is usually pronounced in the French manner as *tăm*-bur. Along with pitch, rhythm, and loudness, timbre is one of the four basic elements of music.

Chapter 5 contained suggestions for helping children create short "sound pieces," which are organized combinations of timbres. Although the term was not introduced at that time, the emphasis of that chapter was on creating music and manipulating different timbres as a means of composition. The emphasis in this chapter is on teaching children to become more aware of timbre and to appreciate it as a valid aspect of music.

TEACHING THE CONCEPT OF TIMBRE

Until they are made aware of the subtleties of tone quality, most children are only vaguely conscious of this element of music. One way to draw their attention to it is to compare timbres on a same-different basis. Here is how this can be done.

"Today let's notice the quality of the sounds we hear. We'll do it by
playing a game. On the table in the back of the room there are several
rhythm instruments. Todd, why don't you go back there by the table.
Look over the class to make sure no one is turning around and watching
you. Then play two different sounds, one after the other. You can play
them on different instruments or on the same instrument. Then call on
someone in the class to tell if the qualities of the two sounds were the
same or different." [Todd plays several pairs of sounds, each time calling on a different child to say whether the timbres were alike or not.]

The game can continue as other children take turns producing sounds
that are available around the classroom: tapping or scraping against
flower pots, window shades, radiators, the chalkboard, glass items, and
so on.

Children should learn to distinguish between sounds with different
timbres and sounds with the same timbre that are different in pitch.
When children first hear two different pitches on a melodic instrument,
they may respond that the sounds have different qualities. Here is how
a teacher might clarify the situation.

"I'm going to play two notes for you on the bells. Listen and tell
me if they have the same tone quality." [The teacher plays the notes G
and E descending.]

"Troy, was the tone quality the same each time, or was it different?"

"It was different."

"You heard that *something* was different between the notes.
Let's discover what it was. You heard these notes. . . ." [The teacher
repeats G E.] "It's the *pitch* that's different. Was the second note higher or lower than the first one, class?" [The class indicates it was lower.]
"Sure, it was lower. That means the pitch was different. But the tone
quality was the same. Here's a hint to help you the next time you want
to compare sounds: If different notes are played on the same instrument with the same sticks, the quality will be about the same."

Another way to stress the uniqueness of timbre is to ask the children to identify, without looking, the voice of a child who is speaking.
To prevent identification of the voice by its location rather than by its
timbre, the teacher can ask the children to stand in a circle but face
outward. The teacher then stands in the center of the circle and taps a
child on the shoulder to say a word or phrase in a normal manner. The
children should not try to fool one another by disguising their voices,
because that destroys the point of the activity.

"We're going to try to tell who is talking just by listening to that
person's voice. You're standing facing away from one another so that

person's voice. You're standing facing away from one another so that you won't be able to guess the voices on the basis of where the people sit in class.

"Each person will say the same thing. If I tap you on the shoulder, say 'Do you know my voice?' Don't try to change the way you normally speak. Let's practice the words together once, so you won't get mixed up if you have a turn. The words are 'Do you know my voice?' All together now, 'Do you know my voice?'"

[The teacher taps various children on the shoulder, and class members guess which child has spoken. The children return to their seats, and the teacher explains what has been demonstrated by the activity.]

"You see, you can recognize people just by hearing their voices, even though they're saying the same words. Why can you do that? Because each person in the whole human race has a somewhat different quality of voice. You don't get mixed up at home listening to your mother, father, brother, or sister speaking, even when they're in a different room, because they each have a quality all their own. The word for quality of sound is *timbre.*"

For a variation of this game, the children divide into teams. The winner is the first team to guess, without looking, the identity of every speaker on the other side.

EXPLORING SOUND PRODUCTION AND TIMBRES

Children can learn much about timbre by allowing their natural curiosity to function in exploring instruments. Because of its large size and easy availability, the piano is a logical instrument on which to begin exploring the nature of sound. Although variations in timbre are not likely on a single instrument, except perhaps at the two extremes of the pitch range, it is still possible to show on one instrument the motions that produce vibration and result in sound. Children can try the following:

1. They can feel the vibrations by putting their hands lightly on the piano's soundboard or on the strings after pitches have been sounded.

2. They can observe that the lower strings are thicker and longer than the shorter and higher strings.

3. They can watch the strings moving like a blur as they sound, especially the larger, lower strings that vibrate more widely. (String vibration can also be easily seen on a large string instrument such as a cello, string bass, or guitar.)

4. They can see that the felt hammer that strikes the string must immediately leave it if the string is to sound freely.

5. They can hold down the sustaining pedal—the one farthest to the right—while they tap the strings with different objects such as a pencil or a triangle beater.

6. They can hold down the sustaining pedal and then strike a low note forcefully. If the room is quiet, they can hear a faint ringing in certain other strings. After the experiment, the teacher can explain the phenomenon in this manner:

> "Did you notice that when Lisa played the low note loudly you could hear a soft ringing from some of the other strings? Sound it again, Lisa, so they can hear the ringing and remember it." [Lisa strikes the note again.]
>
> "Here's a puzzle: How is it possible to get faint sounds from the other strings when they aren't even connected with the low string that Lisa hit? Any ideas?" [The class can't guess why that happens.]
>
> "Well, here's the answer. When a note like that low string is sounded with enough force, it makes fast motions called *vibrations* that bump into the things around them. We can't see the vibrations traveling through the air, but we can tell when they hit other strings because they make the strings sound very softly."

The phenomenon of sympathetic vibration and the strength of various overtones in the vibrating agent form the basis for differences in timbre. That topic is generally too sophisticated for primary youngsters, but older children can benefit from a study of acoustics, which is usually undertaken in connection with science class.

BASIC INSTRUMENTS AND VOICE TYPES

Children in the primary grades should learn to recognize basic instruments and voice types. The process is not difficult, because they are likely to have some knowledge from their preschool experiences and from watching television. The basic instruments may be considered to be piano, violin, clarinet, trumpet, and snare drum; the basic voice types for this level are the male (bass-baritone) and female (soprano). The teacher should continue to stress that each instrument and voice has its unique timbre. The recognition game described earlier can be varied by playing recordings of instruments and asking the children to identify the instrument by name and picture. Instructional packages on musical instruments are available to assist teachers in this effort. (Appendix B contains a list of sources for these materials.)

At about the third-grade level, children can begin to compare families of instruments according to their methods of tone production. The most basic groupings are the winds, in which the player blows breath through the instrument; the strings, in which the player bows or plucks the desired note; and percussion instruments, which the player strikes or shakes. In addition to recognizing instrument families, children at this age should be able to identify such individual instruments as trombone, organ, cello, flute, oboe, and timpani.

Children need to understand that the way in which an instrument is played alters its timbre. They can discover this fact for themselves by experimenting with classroom instruments. Here is an example of how such experimentation might be conducted.

> "I'm going to pass out three different types of sticks for the metallophone. Karen, here's one that has a hard head. Dan, this one is medium, and Melissa, here's a soft one. The three of you go to to the metallophone and take turns striking any bars that you wish. The rest of us will compare the tone qualities that we hear when the different types of sticks are used."

Similar changes can be observed on the autoharp when the children play with different picks—one that is felt and another that is plastic, for example. There is even a difference in sound when the angle of the pick strumming the strings is altered. Drums produce a slight change of timbre when struck at different places on the drumheads, or with different parts of the hands.

A good way to encourage children to investigate timbres and types of instruments is to ask them to make simple instruments at home from inexpensive articles they find around the house: a piece of old garden hose, empty cereal cartons, tin cans, bottles, pie pans, combs, and so on. A few guidelines should be given to prevent the experience from becoming an exercise in junk collecting. If the instrument is of the percussion type, it should have a clear and easily heard tone, plus the capability of withstanding repeated striking or shaking. If the instrument is of the wind or string type, it should be capable of producing at least three distinct pitches with a reasonably clear timbre.

Here is a list of simple instruments that can be constructed with the help of a teacher or parent.

> DRUM — Remove both ends of a gallon can and paint the can. Cut two circles from a tire inner tube, making them somewhat larger than the ends of the can. With a paper punch, make holes about 2½ inches apart around the edges of the rubber circles. With leather strips, lace the heads onto the drum by running the strips back and forth between the two circles.

TRIANGLE — On a steel rod about 18 inches long, measure 6 inches from each end and bend the rod in a vice until the ends nearly touch, forming a triangular shape. Attach a cord to one corner of the triangle, and hold the instrument by the cord when playing. Use a large nail for a beater.

SAND BLOCKS — Cut two wood blocks about 3″ x 5″ x 1″. Attach a knob to the large side of each block and paint. Cut two pieces of heavy sandpaper large enough to cover the side of each block opposite the knob, and long enough to fold over onto the ends of the block. Attach the sandpaper with thumbtacks or staples. To play, hold each block by its knob and scrape the rough sides together to produce a brushing sound.

MARACAS — Paint two empty half-pint milk, yogurt, or cream cartons. Place dried beans or metal nuts inside and staple the top closed.

RHYTHM STICKS — Cut dowel rods, about 3/8-inch thick, into lengths of about 14 inches and paint.

The children should be prepared to answer questions about the instruments they make.

1. Can the instrument produce both high and low sounds? If its pitch is limited, is the range basically high or low?
2. Does the sound tend to be loud or soft? How much variation in loudness is possible on the instrument?
3. Can one sound be held for a while if desired?
4. Can notes be played on the instrument one right after another in rapid succession?
5. Does the sound have a "ring" or is it dull?
6. Is the timbre especially suitable for a certain type of song?
7. Is the instrument more appropriate for playing a tune or for accompanying?

Children should also learn that a given song may call for a particular voice quality. Songs in the music series books, for example, sometimes require the youngsters to imitate animal sounds ("peep, peep") or other tonal effects such as the howling of the wind ("oo-oo-oo"). These words or sounds are attempts to infuse a special timbre or tonal effect into the music.

Songs about instruments are helpful because they imply certain tonal characteristics. The "German Instrument Song" concludes with a simple instrumental part of four pitches. Of the five instruments men-

GERMAN INSTRUMENT SONG

English words by Tulla Statler   German Folk Song

1. If I had a bell to play a tune on, If I had a bell, oh, how I'd *ring.*

(Instrumental)

2. If I had a fiddle, fiddle, fiddle,
   If I had a fiddle, how I'd *bow.*

3. If I had a pipe to play a tune on,
   If I had a pipe, oh, how I'd *blow.*

4. If I had an Autoharp to play on,
   If I had an Autoharp, I'd *strum.*

5. If I had a drum that I could play on,
   If I had a drum, oh, how I'd *beat.*

6. Now we have a tune to play together,
   Now we have a tune, oh, how we'll *play.*

From Bennett Reimer et al., *Music*, Book 3. Words copyright © 1974 by Silver Burdett Company.

tioned in the song, a set of bells can play the notes of the instrumental part in the first verse. The next two instruments can also play their respective verses as written, with the recorder assuming the role of "pipe." Chords are suggested for the fourth instrument—the autoharp—which is not at its best when played melodically. The drum, which cannot play pitches at all, is given an independent rhythmic part to add interest to the song. If no instruments are available, the children can make up sounds and words for those parts, as the teacher has them do in this class.

> "We don't have all the instruments mentioned in the song, so we'll just have to make the instrument sounds ourselves. What would be a good sound or word for the bell? Matthew?" [Matthew suggests "ding," and that seems acceptable to the other children.]
>
> "All right, let's say 'ding' for the bell. Who has an idea for the fiddle? Vicki?" [Vicki suggests "zing," which seems to satisfy the other children.]
>
> "That's a good sound, and it rhymes with 'ding' for the bell. Now, what about the pipe to blow on? Michael?" [Michael suggests "toot," which doesn't please some of the other class members.] "What other sound might work for the pipe? Cheryl?" [Cheryl suggests whistling the notes for the pipe.] "How many of you prefer 'toot'? . . . How many prefer whistling?" . . . [The class favors whistling.]
>
> "Okay, let's sing the first verse with 'ding' for each note of the bell, the second with 'zing' for each note of the fiddle, and the third with whistling for each note of the pipe."

SOUND EFFECTS IN STORIES

Children in the primary grades like to add sound effects to stories that they know, and this helps to increase their consciousness of timbres. For example, "Jack and the Beanstalk" could be "orchestrated" in the following way:

Jack climbing up	— ascending pattern on bells
Jack climbing down	— descending pattern on bells
Giant	— large drum or low notes on piano
Hen cackling	— castanet
Harp	— autoharp
Chopping beanstalk	— woodblock
Beanstalk falling	— cymbals and drums

As the children gain experience in associating "effects" with a story, the teacher can move on to more sophisticated music.

Many compositions feature timbres by associating them with a story. Prokofiev's *Peter and the Wolf* includes a part for a narrator, who tells how a boy with the help of some animal friends captures an angry wolf. Various instruments play tunes specifically associated with the characters: Peter, Grandfather, a duck, a cat, a bird, some hunters, and of course the wolf. The music is imaginative and charming. On the first hearing the children can concentrate on the story, because they will be interested in the outcome. On subsequent hearings they should concentrate on the tonal qualities of the instruments that are associated with the characters—the clarinet with the cat, the bassoon with Grandfather, the strings with Peter. The oboe, which represents the duck, has a nasal quality that somewhat resembles the sound of that animal. The oboe also has a plaintive quality, which Prokofiev must have thought appropriate for the story, since the duck gets eaten by the wolf.

Timbres are not always associated with objects, animals, and personalities, of course. Children should also experience abstract music that consists of tonal effects. Otto Luening's "Sonic Contours" is a composition of flute sounds recorded on tape and then manipulated in several different ways to create an interesting musical work. It is not performed in the usual sense of the word, with musicians re-creating and interpreting the composer's ideas. Instead, the final tape is heard exactly as he created the different sounds. Luening's short piece contains no meter or other conventional characteristics of music, but it is fascinating to hear, with tune fragments and reverberations that are attractive and enjoyable. If music truly is organized sound, such works qualify as music.

A good combination of tonal effects and conventional music is Carlos Chavez's *Toccata for Percussion*. The percussion family is a large one in which the instruments can be played in various ways to produce many timbres. In this work, Chavez successfully exploits rhythms and the possibilities offered by the variety of percussion instruments.

Timbre is an important component of music. To help children appreciate its potential, the teacher needs to employ a variety of procedures through which they can discover and experience timbre in music.

REVIEW QUESTIONS

1. Why is the same-different comparison a good teaching procedure for children in the early grades of elementary school?

2. How can children be taught to discriminate between differences in timbre and differences in pitch?

3. Describe a game that can be played to encourage children to listen for differences in timbre.

4. What aspects of sound can children learn from exploring a piano?

5. Name four basic instruments that children in the primary grades should learn to recognize by sight and sound.

6. How can children learn that the manner in which an instrument is played often affects its timbre?

7. Describe two instruments and explain how they can be constructed by the children and/or the teacher.

8. What are four questions that can be asked about the timbre of an instrument, especially one that is homemade?

9. In what ways can the activity of singing contribute to children's increased awareness of timbre?

10. Name three works that are especially effective in encouraging youngsters to listen for timbre.

ACTIVITIES

1. Try out the same-different listening game in class by having various class members strike objects around the room.

2. Select an instrument, other than the piano, that is often available in the elementary classroom, and explain what can be learned about sound and timbre with that instrument.

3. Develop a lesson in which the children learn about the basic groups or families of instruments. Encourage the children to discover for themselves the basis for the groupings.

4. a. Make an instrument and bring it to class.
   b. Explain how your instrument could best be used in an elementary school music class.

5. In an elementary music series book, find a song that is especially suitable for helping children become aware of timbre. Describe how you would teach the song to help the children understand this aspect of music.

6. Listen either to Luening's "Sonic Contours" or to a movement of Chavez's *Toccata for Percussion*. Plan how you would teach about the timbres and tonal effects in the musical work you have selected.

Pitch:
The High and Low of
Music

Pitch in music is the impression the hearer has about the relative highness or lowness of a sound. In music, a high pitch has little to do with height in the usual spatial sense, nor with loudness, despite the fact that a loud record player invites the comment, "The volume's too high! Turn it down!" In some cultures, words associated with masculine and feminine also describe the extremes of pitch, and this has a certain logic in terms of male and female voice ranges. However, like it or not, the words "high" and "low" are the accepted terms in the English language for describing pitch levels.

Pitch is determined by the number of vibrations of the sounding medium. In acoustics this is known as *frequency*. A string vibrating 880 times each second sounds higher than one vibrating 600 times each second. Some factors influence the hearing of frequency, so that the pitch the listener perceives is not always exactly the same as the actual frequency, but it is usually closely related. The string, vocal cord, or other vibrating medium sets the molecules of the air in motion. They bump into one another like a chain reaction through a lineup of billiard balls. This bumping continues until the energy of the vibration is dissipated or the molecules strike an object.

Pitch is extremely important in music. While there can be musical works without recognizable pitch levels, almost all music does involve pitch differences. This aspect of music forms the basis of melody and harmony.

CONCEPT OF HIGH AND LOW

A concept of high and low must take into account the relative nature of the terms. A certain pitch is not automatically high or low; it is higher or lower than another pitch. In this music lesson the teacher stresses the comparative nature of pitch discrimination.

"For the past few music classes, we've been calling sounds 'high' or 'low' or 'about the middle.' Now here's a problem for you to solve. I'm going to play some notes on the piano, and you tell me how high or low they are. What should we call this sound: high, low, or medium?"

[The class responds that the note is high.]

"What about this sound: high, low, or medium?"

[The class says that the sound is low.]

"That was pretty easy. The first sound was much higher than the second. Now you'll hear two more sounds. Here's the first one: high, low, or medium?"

[The class, guessing the answer ahead of time, enthusiastically replies, "Medium!"]

"Now the next one. High, low, or medium?"

[The class hesitates, then a few children propose that the sound is medium.]

"Scott, the class says both sounds are medium. Does that mean those two sounds are the same?" . . . [If Scott answers incorrectly, the teacher plays the interval again and asks another child to compare the two sounds.]

"One sound is higher and one is lower, even though both of them are in the medium range. When we decide how high or low a sound is, our answer depends on the other sounds around it. A tall person doesn't seem so tall when he stands with other tall people. But when he stands with short people, he seems even taller. Sounds are like that, when we judge how high or low they are."

The echo-singing of two-note pitch patterns is one way to help children concentrate on pitch. The "cuckoo" interval, which in musical terms is referred to as a "descending minor third," is found in children's chants and games around the world, including the taunt, "Johnny has a girlfriend." It is the first interval introduced in the Kodály program, and is often utilized in the Orff-*Schulwerk* instruction. In the following lesson, the children imitate the "cuckoo" interval sung to them by the teacher.

"Today we're going to sing bits of songs back and forth. Listen carefully as I sing, then you sing the notes back to me. Do all of you know about the cuckoo? It's a bird that sings a short two-note call. Let's start by imitating the sound of a cuckoo. Listen to me first; I'll sing the cuckoo call two times."

Cuck-oo,   cuck-oo

"Now all of you sing the call twice." [The class sings the pattern.] "Good! I think some of you are ready to sing the cuckoo song back to me all by yourself. I'll go around the class and give a chance to as many of you as I can. Michelle, let's start with you. Listen carefully and sing back what I sing."

If the interval is being repeated many times in succession, the teacher should change the pitch level occasionally. The continual use of the same pitches is tiring for both the teacher and the children.

The teacher can try other intervals on subsequent days. Intervals smaller than the "cuckoo" pattern are somewhat more difficult for children who have trouble discerning pitch differences. Intervals in which the notes are quite far apart are also difficult, not so much because they are hard to hear, but because children with a narrow singing range simply have trouble reproducing widely separated pitches. For variety, the teacher can play the pitch patterns on an instrument.

Simple games can be devised to help children become more aware of pitch levels. The teacher may:

1. Play or sing pairs of pitches and ask individuals to tell which pitch is higher.

2. Invite various children to "play teacher" by sounding the pairs of pitches and deciding whether the responses of their classmates are correct.

3. Sound an interval twice in succession. For the first hearing, the children should notice which sound is higher and which is lower. When the interval is repeated, they should show with their hands or other bodily movement which pitch is which. For example, for the low pitch in the second pair they might crouch or put their hands on their toes, and for the high pitch they might put their hands above their heads. Asking the children to close their eyes during this game encourages careful listening and discourages the copying of another child's motions.

4. Pass out six or eight bells (one to each child) in random pitch order, then invite the children to discover the relative pitch of each bell and arrange themselves in order from low to high.

Some songs are especially good for aiding children in developing a sense of pitch. In the song "Tony Chestnut," the opening four notes outline a chord, and the second portion of the first line is a descending scale. The actions that accompany the singing emphasize the play on words that is apparent in the construction of the boy's name: on the syllable "To(e)," bend over and touch the toes; on "-ny," touch the knees; on "chest," straighten up and touch the chest; and on "nut," touch the top of the head. On the words "Touch your fingers to the ground," wiggle the fingers while moving the arms and hands to the toes for the beginning of the next line.

The indexes in the teacher's editions of some of the music series books suggest other songs that reinforce the concept of pitch level through actions.

TONY CHESTNUT

It is only a short extension of the high-low concept to the notion of melodic lines ascending or descending ("going up" or "going down"). In "Tony Chestnut," the children can discover that the first four notes ascend and the next several notes descend. Simple pictures can be drawn and posted to provide visual reinforcement for the idea of pitch direction.

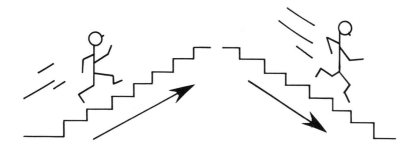

MELODY

Children in the primary grades should be introduced to the standard terms for basic aspects of music, like *melody*. A verbal definition such as, "A melody is a cohesive series of pitches" is largely a waste of time for children at this age level, partly because the definition itself contains words that need to be defined. A knowledge of basic terms is valuable, however, because a word can say something more precisely and clearly than a description like "the bunch of notes that seem to belong together."

Here is how a teacher might help a class to understand what the word "melody" means.

"The other day you learned a song called 'Tony Chestnut.' Let's stand up and sing it again, with the actions." [The class sings the song.]

"Did you notice the direction in which your hands moved on the first four notes? You made them go higher because that's the way the notes sound at the beginning of this song. In what direction do the notes move on 'Touch your fingers to the ground'? Sing it and show me." [The class members move their hands in a downward direction.]

"That's right, the notes get lower; they go down.

"Since you're listening to the music so well, I think I'd better ask you to do something harder. Sing the song on the sound 'loo,' without the words. Then tell me if it's still the same tune. Think what your answer is going to be as you sing." [The class sings the song on "loo."]

"Okay now. Did you still sing the tune for 'Tony Chestnut' when you didn't sing the words and just sang on 'loo'?" . . . [The class responds, with some disagreement among the children about whether or not they did.]

"You're both right, in a way. The words are needed if someone wants to know how the whole song goes. But a person who already knows the song would recognize what you were singing just from hearing the *melody* you sang on 'loo.'

"That word 'melody' is an important word in music. Every song has its own melody—its own special combination of high, medium, and low notes, with certain places where the tune gets higher, or lower, or stays the same. A string of pitches and its rhythm, when they seem to belong together, make a melody. The melody for 'Tony Chestnut' is what you sang on 'loo,' and it's the same no matter what words you put with it."

In the following lesson the teacher applies the concept of melody to instrumental music.

"Today we'll listen to music that features a very clear melody. But instead of being a song, it's a piece for four string instruments: two violins, a viola, and a cello. The melody is like a song, though, and it's sometimes played under the name 'serenade,' which is a certain type of song. Listen to it, then tell me whether the melody is in a higher or lower instrument." [The class listens to the second movement of the Op. 3 No. 5 string quartet attributed to Haydn.]

"Who can tell me in which part the melody is played? Is it near the top, bottom, or middle of the pitch range?" [The class notices that the melody is in a high range.]

"So that you can see for yourselves how song-like this melody is, I'll play a little bit of the recording again so you can learn the tune, and then we'll sing the first few notes of it. Listen." [The teacher plays about a minute of the work.]

"There, now. Can you remember that tune? Let's sing the melody on 'loo.' Here's the starting pitch. Rea-dy, sing." [The class sings the first two measures of the quartet theme.]

Here is one way in which a teacher can emphasize the sense of cohesiveness that is necessary if successive pitches are to be perceived as a melody.

"I'm going to sound some pitches on the bells, but I'll do it without looking or thinking." [The teacher strikes random bars in no recognizable rhythmic or melodic pattern.]

"Is that the kind of melody you'd like to sing?" [The consensus is "no."] "No, because the notes don't seem to fit together. It's a bit like this class right here. You belong together; you do things together. You're not just 25 children who got thrown into a room to ignore one another. The notes in a melody have something to do with one another, and that's what makes a melody sound good, instead of just being a bunch of scattered notes."

PITCH AND INSTRUMENTS

Most of the melodic instruments that are played by children in the primary grades are of the simple keyboard type. Although they do not have keys to be depressed as on a piano, the bars on the xylophone, metallophone, and similar instruments are arranged with the pitches in the same horizontal pattern. This creates a problem for many children. After getting accustomed to describing pitches with "high-low" words and actions, they are now told that "high" is to their right on the instrument they have in front of them. In other words, the terms for vertical alignment are now employed for horizontal alignment.

One aid in overcoming this inconsistency is a simple xylophone instrument called the Step Bells. The pitches on it follow the horizontal keyboard arrangement and ascend from left to right, but they do so with each pitch raised in stair-step fashion. In this way, children are better able to relate the vertical and horizontal aspects of pitch arrangement. If Step Bells are not available, a metallophone or other xylophone-like instrument can be propped up on a table or hung on the wall so that the bars are viewed vertically.

In this lesson the teacher encourages the children to notice certain facts about pitch and the instruments.

> "Julie, would you please take the mallet and strike each bar on the Step Bells? Go from the one nearest the table up to the one that's highest off the table." [Julie plays the bells in ascending order.]
> "Class, what was the order of the pitches that Julie played? Did they move from high to low, or low to high?" [The class reports hearing the low-to-high direction.]
> "That's right: low to high. Kevin, you try the bells this time. Start with the bar highest off the table and play them in order moving toward the table top." [Kevin plays the Step Bells in descending order, and the class notices the high-to-low direction.]

When the children understand pitch relationships on the Step Bells or on a vertically positioned instrument, they can move on to instruments that have the keyboard arrangement on a horizontal plane. The transition can be aided by having the children discover that high and low pitches can be determined by their placement to the right or left, and by the relative length of the bars, with the longer bars being lower.

Children enjoy preparing water bottles to produce different pitches. Thin-sided glass containers, such as ordinary drinking glasses, produce a clear tone, but using them increases the risk of spilling and breaking. Bottles with caps are safer and better for preventing evaporation. The set should be matched in size and construction so that the orderly gradations in water levels can be observed.

To prepare the set, the children can fill the bottles to varying levels of water, tapping them frequently to be sure each pitch relates properly to others in the lineup. (The teacher may prepare the bottles ahead of time, or may just experiment to find the appropriate water levels and then mark each bottle with a line to aid the children when they fill the bottle later. Either type of help reduces the amount of mess and confusion.) There may be as few as three bottles—tuned to *do, re, mi* or to *sol mi la*, depending on the songs being sung by the class—or as many as eight, tuned to the steps of a major scale. It is visually helpful to add different food colorings to designate bottles. This helps the children locate specific notes as they play, and points out any melodic pattern the teacher may want to emphasize.

As an outcome of their work with water bottles, the class should observe that more water in a bottle produces a lower pitch when the container is tapped. Older children can learn that this happens because the water, by touching the glass, keeps it from vibrating as fast as it would if empty. The opposite situation prevails if someone blows across the top of a water bottle: only the air column is vibrating, so more water makes a shorter air column, which produces a higher pitch.

Some of the songs in the music series books have optional parts for instruments. These can contribute to the children's understanding of pitch and melody, but they should not be allowed to consume too much class time. The children's singing should have first priority, and classroom instruments are limited in their ability to enhance this skill. Bell-like instruments are pitched in a higher octave than the voice, and their percussive tones do not provide as good a model for singing as do instruments like the flute or violin, which can sustain sounds. Although classroom instruments are not the best aids for developing pitch discrimination and vocal tone, they do provide variety within the music class, and introduce the children to the vast and rewarding world of instrumental music.

MELODIC STEPS AND LEAPS

As children grow in their understanding of melody, they should begin to notice the relative closeness of pitches to one another. Intervals of a whole or a half step are referred to as being a *step* apart. Larger intervals are described as *leaps*. In the following lesson, the teacher helps the class to decide whether an interval is a step or a leap. The song is shown on the following page.

"Last week you learned a song called 'The Little Chickens.' Let's sing it again today to see how well you remember it. Here's the starting note. Rea-dy, sing." [The class sings the song.]

"That's good. Now we're going to find out how far one note is from the next one. Listen to the first five notes of 'The Little Chickens' as I sing them slowly. As you listen, decide if the notes are 'next door' to each other, which is a *step,* or if they're farther apart than that, which is a *leap.*" [The teacher sings the first five notes, then helps the class to discover that they move up by step.]

"So we have five notes, each one a step away from its neighbor. What about the notes on the words 'chicks say'?" [The teacher sings the two notes, which happen to be the "cuckoo" interval or descending minor third. The class discovers that the interval is a leap.]

The teacher can proceed through the song, asking the children to decide whether various intervals form a step or a leap. Variations of this procedure include playing the intervals on an instrument, asking the children to sing or play the intervals, and showing the relative distance between steps and leaps through hand motions.

LOS POLLITOS ("The Little Chickens")

Mexican Children's Song

Los pol - li - tos   di - cen: pi - o, pi - o,   pi - o,
Hear the lit - tle chick - ens   peep - ing, peep - ing,   peep - ing,

cuan - do tie - nen   ham - bre,   cuan - do tie - nen   fri - o.
when___ they are   hun - gry,   when___ they are   cold.___

PHRASES

Phrases in music are like phrases in language: They are a grouping of sounds or words that are intended to stand together as a single idea. On a printed page of language, phrases are marked off by commas, semicolons, and periods. In music, stopping places are also delineated with varying degrees of finality, primarily through the choice of notes and chords at the phrase endings. If a song is well written, the phrase points of the text and the music will coincide.

Here is one way to help children become aware of logical groupings in music. (The song "All Night, All Day" is presented on p. 57.)

"I don't know if any of you have tried it, but it is nearly impossible to sing a whole song without stopping to take a breath. Even if you could do it, it wouldn't be worth it, because you'd have to race through the song with no expression at all. Let's sing 'All Night, All Day' all on one breath. Sing as far as you can, and then drop out. Take just one breath at the beginning, now: 'All night, all day . . .'" [All sing the song as far as possible on one breath.]

"We didn't sound too good, did we? And it wasn't very comfortable to feel as if we were going to pass out near the end. Music has places where it seems right to take a breath at that moment. The music and the words just seem to make more sense if you pause at certain places.

"See if you can find those places that seem right for taking a breath. I'll sing a bit of 'All Night, All Day' and stop for a breath, and you tell me if I stopped in the right place." [The teacher stops after the first note, to the amusement of the class. Later pauses occur after "night," "day," "watching," "my," and so on, while the children indicate whether each spot seems like the right place for a pause.]

"You're getting good at noticing where music has sensible places for a short break. In music, the sections that should *not* be split up are called *phrases.* When you pause or breathe only at the logical breaks between sections, you are *phrasing* the music, and that makes it sound better."

Noting the similarity of phrasing in speaking and in singing helps to reinforce the concept.

"Phrases in music are like phrases in speech. You've been phrasing ever since you learned to talk—and you didn't even know you were so talented! When you talk, you don't run all your words together or say them all in the same way. Remember when you learned about patterns in rhythm? You discovered that people don't talk like a machine 'with-all-sounds-ex-act-ly-a-like.' You make certain sounds stronger or lighter, and you group them in certain ways so that other people will understand what you mean."

Another way to make children more aware of musical segments is to print the words on the board and mark off the phrases with over-arching lines:

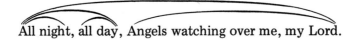

All night, all day, Angels watching over me, my Lord.

The options available in even this short example indicate that judgments about phrase length are subjective and open to interpretation. There is no single right way to analyze every phrase.

When the children have had experience in analyzing phrases in vocal music (which has words to provide clues), they can try to identify the exclusively musical phrases in instrumental works such as the Haydn string quartet discussed on page 122.

Children in the primary grades should learn to notice whether phrases are alike or different. In the song "Tony Chestnut" (p. 120) the children can sing the song and then decide how many phrases there are and whether the phrases are the same or different. If the children hear two long phrases, further analysis should elicit the observation that the two phrases are identical until the halfway point, and then they differ.

Children should also begin to sense the statement-answer phrase pattern that appears in so many songs. In this construction, one phrase seems to present the first half of a musical statement, and the second phrase seems to respond to it with a certain degree of conclusiveness. This pattern is apparent in "All Night, All Day" and "Tony Chestnut." Sometimes the statement-answer idea is a bit more difficult to find, as in "The Little Chickens." In the first two measures the pitch level quickly ascends five notes, while for the last six measures it gradually descends in an overall stepwise manner that can be traced by examining the first pitch of each measure from 3 through 8. In fact, the class can capitalize on this basic descending line by turning it into a counter-melody to be sung along with the main tune:

Peep, peep, (etc.)

The important point for the children to learn in comparing phrases is that there is a *musical* logic that undergirds the organizing of musical ideas.

ROUNDS

Children in the primary grades generally do not sing in parts. They may, however, occasionally sing songs in which the same music is sung in strict imitation by different sections of the class starting at different times. These songs are called *canons* or, more commonly, *rounds*. Only certain songs can be sung as rounds, but several are included in the music series books. A round is notated like any other song, except for the inclusion of numbers indicating when the second and subsequent groups of singers should start in relation to the progress of the first group. A round can be repeated as often as desired, but traditionally the melody is sung as many times as there are sections participating.

"Good Night" is a typical round. It has three lines, so it will sound best when performed by three groups of singers. The second group starts at the beginning of the song when the first group starts the second line, and the third group begins when the first group gets to the third line. The rendition of a round is balanced, with the first group singing the first line alone at the beginning, and the last group singing the last line alone at the end.

GOOD NIGHT

Old English Round

1. Good night to you all, and sweet be your sleep,

2. May an - gels a - round you their si - lent watch keep,

3. Good night, good night, good night, good night.

The techniques for teaching a round are similar to those for teaching any other song. Three points should be kept in mind by the teacher, however. First, the children must know the song thoroughly in unison, and be able to sing it without teacher help, before they attempt it as a round. Second, the youngsters must hold the tempo steady when they sing it as a round. Despite the potential distraction caused by different entrances and exits, the experience is not a race to see who can sing fastest. Third, the children should not cover their ears in an effort to eliminate the sound of other groups. The musical appeal of a round is the harmony that is created automatically as the groups proceed through different portions of the song at the same time. Blocking out the singing of other people negates the point of the class effort, and makes it harder for those children to stay together with their respective groups.

If the class has little experience in singing rounds, the teacher may sing the second part alone while the entire class sings the first part. Or the teacher may sing one part while playing another on the piano with the children. (The teacher may have to practice this double skill alone before the class, and then remind the children to "match the piano part, not my voice.") When the class is first divided, it is better to try only two parts at a time, even on a three-part round. As their experience increases, the children will be able to handle more parts.

The children assigned to begin a round must be especially stable and independent so that they can keep singing as the teacher directs the entrance of the second group. Generally the teacher should assign a larger proportion of reliable singers to the first group, because a round is most likely to break down as the first group enters its second section unaided. Once the round is underway, with the first two groups singing steadily, success is more likely.

TEACHING THE NOTATION OF PITCH

As in the learning of rhythm, the children's understanding of pitch can be furthered through the use of visual symbolization, if the instruction is based on prior aural experience. The teacher should introduce the reading of music symbols only after the students have demonstrated a solid aural comprehension of pitch.

The initial efforts to teach pitch symbolization need not start with conventional notation. Rather, the use of one- and two-line staffs, with notes placed in relative positions around those lines, has been found to be a successful introductory system. Here are two examples of simplified pitch notation.

The first example utilizes a one-line staff, which is sufficient for melodies that have only a three-note range. A two-line staff is preferable if the melody contains five adjacent pitch levels. The clef sign, bar lines, and meter and key signatures are missing because they are not necessary at this point, and their absence reduces the number of distractions. Here is how a teacher might introduce the graphic symbolization of pitch.

"You've been reading pictures of rhythms for quite a while. I think you're ready to look at drawings of different pitches. First, let's start by putting down two lines that run along together sideways. They're like railroad tracks, because they're the same distance apart from one end to the other. One step is the distance from a line to the next space, or from a space to the next line. With two lines, we can show five steps."

"Now I'll put some notes on the lines and spaces, and you tell me how far apart the notes are, and whether the sound moves higher or lower. Here's an example." [The teacher draws a note head under the bottom line and another slightly to the right, on the bottom line.]

"This interval moves up a step, doesn't it? It will sound like this." [The teacher sings an ascending whole step on a neutral syllable, establishing the pitch according to the first two notes of a major scale.

Another note is added in the space above the second note, and the class observes that it is higher by one step.]

"Very good reading! The hard test is to see if you can play on the bells the notes that I put on the board." [The teacher draws two more notes: one on the upper line and another on the space above it.]

"Tim, here are five bells, arranged by step from lowest to highest. That means the bell on your left is the sound for the lowest space note on the board. First play all your notes in order from low to high as I point to them on the board." [Tim plays the notes.] "Good. Now I'll point to two notes on the board and you play them on the bells."

The children should sing each pattern after hearing it on the bells, then they should try to sing directly from the notation, which is more difficult than singing by imitation or playing the pattern on an instrument. The children may be invited to come to the board individually to draw or point to notes for the class to perform.

At this point, no attempt should be made to combine rhythm and pitch in the notation exercises. The children may be seeing complete notation in the songs they sing from their books, but they are not trying to sightread that music. As they become more proficient at reading, the stick notation discussed in Chapter 6 can be presented in conjunction with a two-line staff. Note heads are necessary, of course, if pitch is to be reproduced accurately from the printed symbols.

PITCH SYLLABLES

It is a well-known fact that certain syllables traditionally are applied to pitches in music. The song "Do Re Mi," which is from the musical *The Sound of Music*, is an attractive piece that is based on this aspect of music. The reason for pitch syllables is not so well understood, however.

There are two systems that use the same syllables. One is called *fixed do*, and it establishes a specific syllable for a specific pitch. That is, C is always *do*, D is always *re*, and so on. The other system is called *movable do*. It transfers a single order of syllables to any desired key: *do* refers to E in E major, to A♭ in A♭ major, and so on; *sol* refers to step 5 of any major scale, no matter what the note may be. The two systems share one thing in common, in addition to the actual syllable names. The size of the interval is the same; for example, *do* to *re* is always a whole step, and *mi* to *fa* is always a half step. The fixed system, known as *solfège* in French or *solfeggio* in Italian, is favored in France and Italy; movable *do* is preferred in Hungary, Germany, England, and the United States. The syllables show their Italian heritage by being pronounced as they are in Italian: The "e"s are pronounced "ay" as in "hay," and the "i"s as "ee."

Although the fixed *do* method has the advantage of associating every pitch with a constant syllable, it is more difficult to learn. As soon as music appears in a key other than C major, syllables for sharped and flatted notes must be introduced. This means that instead of seven syllables to learn, there will be twelve from which to choose as one ascends through the sharped notes within an octave: *do, di, re, ri, mi, fa, fi, sol, si, la, li, ti.* In addition, five different syllables are required for the flatted notes in the twelve-note descending pattern: *do, ti, te, la, le, sol, se, fa, mi, me, re, rah.* The benefit of easily recognized relationships within a key is largely lost. The interval represented by the ascending *sol-do* is the same as that of the ascending *di-fi,* the descending *le-rah,* and several other combinations.

The movable system also presents problems, however. When music changes key, the pitch of the original *do* is no longer the key center. There are ways to indicate a different *do,* but they add an element of complexity to the process of assigning syllables. Then there is the matter of what to do about songs in minor keys. After trying to establish in the children's thinking that *do* is always the keynote syllable (representing the note on which the scale is built), the music teacher must either introduce chromatic syllables or say that *la* is the keynote in a minor key. Neither option works very well.

Assigning consecutive numbers to the scale steps is a method similar to the movable *do* approach, except that numbers cannot in themselves indicate whole and half steps. There is not much tradition for using the number system, but because children already understand ordinal relationships among numbers, it may seem more sensible to them than a system based on syllables.

The basic function of pitch syllables is to aid in the reading of music; they are a means, not an end. They are like a cane for a person who has an injured leg. When the cane is needed, it can be used with benefit; but when it is no longer needed, it becomes a nuisance and is put away. Syllables help children when they are first learning to "walk," musically speaking. When youngsters can read the pitches with letter names and sing them accurately, the syllables can be discontinued.

Regardless of the system that is employed, a familiarity with syllables eventually does aid in the reading of music. Persons who know the relative pitch pattern for *do-mi-sol* can more easily read:

Persons skilled in the fixed method can just as easily read the same pattern, but they will be thinking of different syllables:

Do   mi   sol   Re   fi   la   Mi   si   ti

The extent to which syllables aid in reading is a question that is debated among music educators. Some maintain that knowing the syllable name helps children to sing the right pitch, while others suspect that the singer first senses the correct pitch and then figures out which syllable should be assigned to it. Perhaps the reading process works both ways, depending on the melodic pattern and the experience of the singer.

ORFF AND KODÁLY TECHNIQUES

As was mentioned in Chapter 2, the Orff-*Schulwerk* and the Kodály-Hungarian Singing School methods are educational approaches that have been undertaken by many American music specialists. To be implemented fully, each system requires specialized knowledge and training. An introduction to these methods is warranted, however, because classroom teachers should be prepared to follow up the activities and procedures previously started by music specialists, and to give the children additional practice in the techniques.

Both Orff and Kodály use the movable *do* system and begin the work on pitch with the "cuckoo" interval—the descending minor third. Songs are selected to feature this interval, and children practice specifically to sing it accurately. Often the pitches are assigned the syllable names of *sol* for the higher pitch and *mi* for the lower. Numbers may also be used for this purpose, but they are not advocated by specialists in either of these methods.

The next syllable to be taught is *la*. With just these three pitches it is possible to create a surprising number of simple songs. The pattern is featured in many songs such as "A Tisket, a Tasket." (See next page.) The children can sing the song while the teacher points to the three notes that have previously been put on the board. If the children have access to the complete notation of the song, they can find the three special notes in the longer version.

A TISKET, A TASKET

Singing Game

The next pitch to be added is *do*, which greatly expands the song possibilities. The addition of *re* completes the pentatonic scale that is featured in both the Orff and Kodály approaches. The syllables *fa* and *ti* do not appear until later because each creates a half step with neighboring notes of the scale, and this sets up a more rigid expectation of key center.

The Kodály method employs hand signs, in which a different hand position represents each syllable. The signs for the most frequent syllables are shown here. The syllables *fi*, *si*, and *ta* are chromatic alterations that sometimes occur in a key. They are indicated by accidentals in the notation because they represent a departure from the prevailing key signature.

The purpose of the hand signs is to provide a physical, kinesthetic reinforcement of the relationship among various pitches. Many music specialists, however, adequately indicate pitch level by simply moving a horizontal hand either up or down, without changing its appearance. This procedure is helpful to the children and easier for the teacher, because much time needs to be invested in learning the hand signs before a person feels fluent and comfortable with them.

In the following lesson, the teacher integrates practice on the melodic pattern *sol-mi-la-sol-mi* with a phrase from "A Tisket, a Tasket."

"Now that you've been singing the syllables *sol, mi,* and *la* for a while, you can make them into a phrase of five syllables going in this order: *sol, mi, la, sol, mi.* I'll sing *sol* again. Just follow my hand so we can all stay together on our tune." [The teacher leads the class in singing the five pitches.]

"Good! Have you sung a song in the past week that uses those syllables just as we sang them?" [The children discover that the pattern appears three times in "A Tisket, a Tasket."]

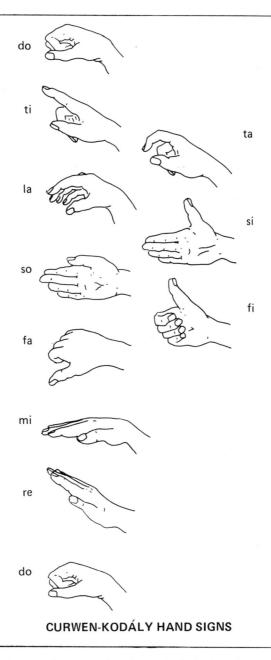

do

ti

ta

la

si

so

fi

fa

mi

re

do

CURWEN-KODÁLY HAND SIGNS

"Let's sing that song, but instead of singing the regular words when you get to those three places, sing the syllables. I'll sing it for you once. Notice that I'm singing syllables for these three sets of words: first, 'A Tisket, a tasket,' then 'a green and yellow basket,' and finally 'I dropped it, I dropped it.'" [The teacher sings the song with syllables through the word "basket," with text through the first "I dropped it" phrases, and with regular text to the end.]

The procedures in the foregoing lesson may vary depending on the musical experience of the children and the preferences of the teacher. Hand signs can be presented, notation can be drawn on the board, and syllable songs can be created by the class. It is important, however, that the children realize that the pattern on which they are focusing is not just an isolated exercise. Attention to melodic patterns should derive from, and revert to, actual music.

REVIEW QUESTIONS

1. Why are definitions of words like "pitch," and "high" of limited value to young children?

2. Describe four teaching procedures for helping children to gain a better understanding of high and low pitch.

3. How can a teacher help children to transfer their vertical high-low concept to the horizontal high-low arrangement found on keyboard-type instruments?

4. Suppose that several first-graders are having trouble telling the difference between steps and leaps. Describe a teaching procedure that might improve their ability to do this.

5. Describe three techniques for helping children to become aware of phrases in music.

6. What special steps may be helpful for teaching a round?

7. Suppose that a class has trouble singing a round in three parts. What might a teacher do to help the class sing the round better?

8. What are the advantages of a one- or two-line staff in the initial stages of reading music notation?

9. a. What are the strengths and weaknesses of the fixed *do* method of reading music?
   b. What are the strengths and weaknesses of the movable *do* method of reading music?
   c. What are the strengths and weaknesses of numbers instead of syllables in reading music?

10. (True or false?) Learning to sing with syllables is an important objective in music education.

11. With what syllables do both the Orff and Kodály approaches begin?

ACTIVITIES

1. a. Plan a three-minute lesson in which you help the class to gain a better idea of high and low pitch.

   b. Plan another three-minute lesson to help the class apply an understanding of high and low pitch to a simple instrument such as the bells or xylophone.

2. From one of the music series books, select two songs—one that contains melodic movement primarily by step, and one that contains many leaps. Plan how you would use the songs to help the children gain a better understanding of steps and leaps.

3. Referring to the two songs you selected for the preceding project, decide how you would help children in a primary class to recognize the phrases in these songs. Identify the aspects of phrasing that you would point out to the class.

4. Select a round from one of the music series books and list the steps by which you would teach it. If time is available, teach the round to the methods class.

5. Get together with another class member and practice sight-singing short and simple melodic patterns, with syllables, from songs selected at random from music series books.

Loudness and
the Combining of
Musical Elements

In music, the relative strength of a sound is referred to as its *loudness*. Although radios and television sets are regulated by a knob to control "volume," that is not the preferred term in music. It has been replaced by *dynamic level*, which refers to the degree of loudness.

LOUD-SOFT CONCEPT

The difference between loud and soft music is perhaps the element most easily recognized by children in the primary grades. They may have trouble sensing the beat or discerning differences among pitches, but seldom do they find it difficult to distinguish between contrasting dynamic levels.

Although loud-soft differences may appear to be the most obvious element of music, and therefore the least interesting, this aspect of music can be very subtle. It is largely responsible for the nuances that create effective phrasing and convey the performer's musicianship. It is true that children approach loudness in music in a more basic way. But the more they notice changes in dynamic level, the more they will understand and enjoy music.

Even in kindergarten, the children's attention can be directed to this element of music. For example, the youngsters can perform simple rhythm patterns at different dynamic levels. If the class is clapping a series of quarter notes, the children might be told to clap four of them loudly, four softly, and four loudly again. To ensure that differences in dynamic level are achieved, the children can be asked to use the entire hand for loud clapping and one finger against the palm of the other hand for soft clapping.

As they become more adept in their ability to switch levels, the youngsters can change from loud to soft more frequently: two loud and two soft, then one loud and one soft. They can also learn to achieve gradual changes, even if the terminology for gradual changes has not been introduced. A clapping game might be devised by asking the children to get gradually softer by clapping four times with four fingers in the other palm, four times with three fingers, then with two fingers, and finally with one finger. The pattern can also be reversed, of course. One side of the class can listen, without looking, to determine by the loudness how many fingers are involved in the clapping produced by the other team. The clapping patterns presented in Chapter 6 are appropriate for games and exercises that develop the children's control of dynamic level.

It is not necessary to introduce the traditional dynamic markings in the primary grades; that can be done later. In fact, songs in the music series books for younger children often do not contain dynamic markings. They may include an oblique reference to loud-soft considerations by proposing that a song be sung "gently" or "vigorously," but these terms have as much to do with style as they do with dynamic level.

Some songs by their nature suggest certain treatments of dynamic level. The "Echo Carol" (p. 140) contains repeated phrases that sound more effective when the second phrase of each pair is sung softly, like an echo. To ensure that the echo portions will be softer than the rest of the song, the teacher can choose two or three reliable singers to perform the echo part. The echo effect is more apparent if the small group is positioned away from the rest of the class.

Here are other techniques that can be tried to help children become more sensitive to dynamic level.

1. Ask the children to determine which classroom instruments are essentially loud and which are soft. For example, the rhythm sticks and maracas may be considered to be soft, while the drum is loud. The children should experiment with different ways of playing the instruments, to learn the extent to which each can produce loud and soft sounds. They will discover, for example, that hitting a drum with a wire brush produces a softer sound than hitting it with a stick.

ECHO CAROL

German Song

1. While I my sheep did watch one night, Lo, there appeared an an - gel bright. O sing with joy! Sing with joy!
He is born! He is born! Glo - ry to God who
reigns on high! Glo - ry to God who reigns on high!

2. Born is the Child, in manger small,
   Whom God hath sent to save us all.
   O sing with joy, etc.

3. Go you this night, and you will find
   God's Son so pure, so sweet and kind.
   O sing with joy, etc.

4. He has been sent from God above;
   He brings to man the gift of love.
   O sing with joy, etc.

5. If you will keep him in your heart,
   Never will joy from you depart!
   O sing with joy, etc.

2. Say chants or rhymes at different dynamic levels. The following rhyme describes an echo.

> I sometimes wonder where he lives,
> This Echo that I never see.
> I hear his voice now in the hedge,
> Then down behind the willow tree.
>
> And when I call, "Oh, please come out,"
> "Come out," he always quick replies.
> "Hello, hello," again I say;
> "Hello, hello," he softly cries.

He must be jolly, Echo must,
For when I laugh, "Ho, ho, ho, ho,"
Like any other friendly boy,
He answers me with "Ho, ho, ho."

I think perhaps he'd like to play;
I know some splendid things to do,
He must be lonely hiding there;
I wouldn't like it. Now, would you?
                                                      —Anonymous

3. Suggest that the children find and display pictures of things that produce loud noises and things that are soft in sound. A diesel railroad engine and a large dog barking are examples of loud noisemakers, while a cricket and a small bird make soft sounds.

GRADUAL CHANGES IN DYNAMIC LEVEL

It may be premature to introduce the musical terms for gradually louder and gradually softer (*crescendo* and *decrescendo*) before the third grade. The musical experience and ability of the class will determine the proper time for this. But gradual change in dynamic level can certainly be introduced, and children can learn to accomplish such gradations effectively.

Although few songs in the music series books include dynamic markings, subtle changes in level can be noticed when the music is performed expressively. Most music would be quite uninteresting if performed at the same dynamic level from beginning to end, and the phrasing would be less effective. To determine where nuances might be appropriate in a song, the class should examine not only the words but the melodic line. The highest notes in a phrase are often the most important and are approached with more intensity. Conversely, notes that dip especially low tend to convey a sense of relaxation and can be sung a little more gently, if the words of the text support this interpretation.

"There's a Little Wheel" (p. 142) contains crescendo and decrescendo marks. The children can easily guess from the appearance of these signs what effect is indicated for the dynamic level. The signs are pictorial in that the crescendo expands as the music progresses, while the decrescendo decreases in size. As with other elements of music, the symbols should be introduced only after the children have had experience in hearing and manipulating this aspect of musical sound.

THERE'S A LITTLE WHEEL

3. Oh, I feel so very happy in my heart,
   Oh, I feel so very happy in my heart,
   In my heart, In my heart,
   Oh, I feel so very happy in my heart.

There are numerous examples of gradual changes in dynamic level in recorded instrumental music that can be played for the class. Villa-Lobos' "The Little Train of the Caipira," mentioned in Chapter 6, is a good example. Another is the "Bydlo" ("Peasant Cart") from Mussorgsky's *Pictures at an Exhibition.* The ponderous sounds of the cart increase in loudness over a long span of time, then subside in the same way.

ACCENTS

Some notes tend to be stressed slightly because they occur on the first beat of the measure, as explained in Chapter 6. But other notes can also be emphasized. An accent is the technique by which this emphasis is most often accomplished.

On a page of music, the accent mark looks like the letter "v" turned counterclockwise on its side. Although it resembles a decrescendo in shape, it applies to only one note; it is not elongated to span several notes in succession. The shape of the accent shows how it should be performed: The beginning of the accented note is abruptly loud, with an immediate decrease of loudness. The effect is a quick "jab" of sound.

The song "Boom Dali Da" contains several accented notes. Here is how the teacher might introduce them.

"Listen while I sing you a new song. Don't worry about the strange words; just listen to the way I sing the *music* differently on some of the notes. When I finish, tell me in what way those notes were different." [The teacher sings "Boom Dali Da," performing the accents with exaggerated emphasis. The children observe that certain notes are punched out more than others.]

"Good for you! I really gave those notes a poke. It's called an *accent* in music. The song is in your books. Let's look at it. . . . Do you see a sign we haven't talked about before?" [Some class members notice the unfamiliar marks.]

BOOM DALI DA

"Right; those signs that look like a 'v' on its side are the accent marks. As we sing the song and you come to an accent mark, give that note a quick punch with your voice. Here's a hint to help you: Keep the other notes smooth and whispery. Then when you come to the accent, the sound will seem to pop out without a lot of effort. Pretend you're trying to scare someone on that note, like a surprise on Halloween."

On another day the teacher might review the learning of accented notes in this manner.

"In music yesterday we learned 'Boom Dali Da.' Let's sing it again today to make sure that you know it. Show me, by your singing, how much you remember about accented notes." [The class sings the song, observing an occasional accent.]

"Is it coming back to you now? We'd better sing it again, because I missed hearing the Halloween effect. You didn't scare me! Maybe Halloween isn't your favorite holiday. What other holiday might fit the loud surprise notes?" [Greg suggests the Fourth of July, and the class sings the accents more explosively.]

"Much better! Now is there some way we can make these notes even stronger than we can with our voices alone?" [Shauna suggests clapping or playing a percussion instrument on the accented notes.]

"Good idea, Shauna. Let's all clap *once* on each accented note. Don't forget to sing as you clap; we shouldn't let a clap take the place of singing."

DYNAMIC LEVEL AND TONE QUALITY

Although children do not have strong enough voices to produce a wide range of dynamic levels, they can still make small differences and perform music expressively. They should try to make a difference not only between a vigorous song and a lullaby, but also between various phrases within a song. This is called *expression*, or *interpretation*, and even slight nuances help to make the music more effective.

Children should learn from their earliest school music experiences that loudness in itself is not an indication of vocal mastery. Because of contemporary performance practices in some popular music, children tend to equate loudness with musical sophistication. In an effort to duplicate a popular style, they sometimes force their voices, resulting in a tone that is strained and unnatural.

Some children (and teachers) seem to regard boisterous singing as evidence of youthful exuberance and enjoyment. While it is true that one of the objectives of a music class is to get all of the children to sing with enthusiasm, sheer loudness is not the best measure of their interest. In fact, their enjoyment in their music-making will increase as they learn to appreciate musical nuance and realize that they can contribute in less obvious ways to a musically satisfying result.

Occasionally a teacher will encounter particular children who sing noticeably louder than the rest of the class. These individuals may not realize they are louder, either because they are not listening or because they are overly zealous in wanting to demonstrate their singing abilities or their familiarity with the song. An occasional child will even appear to be singing more loudly than the others to get attention, sometimes with a conspicuous lack of pitch accuracy. Whatever the reason for this disparity in individual levels of loudness within the group, the teacher should take steps to correct it. This should be done not by criticizing the child who is louder but by emphasizing the need for a blended quality within the group, to make the music sound better.

Children may need to be reminded that soft singing should not result in diminished mental alertness. When the music is soft, inexperienced singers sometimes relax to the point of inattention and lose a certain amount of vocal control, to the detriment of the tone quality. A feeling of energy (not strain) must be maintained through the soft passages so that the music conveys a sense of direction and optimum tone quality at every dynamic level.

PUTTING THE MUSICAL ELEMENTS TOGETHER: PERFORMING

Now that methods for teaching the basic elements of music have been introduced, the principles presented in Chapter 3 can be expanded and applied in more detail. Study of the various aspects of music is important, but it is in putting them together that such learning pays off.

"Boom Dali Da" (p. 143) contains several features that represent an integration of musical elements.

1. The tempo changes from slow to fast, creating the effect of a meter change from three beats per measure to one beat per measure. In fact, the quarter-note beat speed in the first six measures can be regarded as the dotted half-note beat speed from measure 7 to the end. This triples the pace of the song while keeping the beat speed constant. The children can observe this by tapping at one rate from beginning to end.

2. The rhythm pattern created by the dotted-eighth- and -sixteenth-note figure requires a sensing of a subdivided beat if it is to be performed accurately. Although youngsters may never have seen the pattern in notation, nor heard of the 3:1 ratio that exists between the dotted eighth and the sixteenth, the figure appears frequently in the songs they sing. For example, "There's a Little Wheel" (p. 142) contains several such figures. By learning words to go with various sixteenth-note combinations, the children can reproduce the combinations more accurately because they are more likely to feel the beat subdivisions in passages of a song.

3. The melody is interesting, partly because the song is in a minor key and the seventh step of the scale is raised. In the faster section, one-measure patterns are repeated a step lower, giving the music a feeling of continuity and drive.

4. The phrases are of unequal length, creating a feeling of imbalance and surprise. The slow segment consists of three measures that are repeated exactly. The fast section presents phrases of four measures, then three, then six. The total of nineteen measures is an unusual length for a song.

5. The text of repeated nonsense syllables is of little interest, so new words can be created by the class. The sudden tempo change may suggest a twist within narratives invented by the children for this tune.

6. The absence of story-telling words, the shifts of mood, and the inclusion of accents only on the strong first beat of a measure suggest that this is a dance tune. The children can make up their own steps and motions to convey their interpretation of the music.

7. The song is an excellent one for adding simple instrumental accompaniments. There is the "boom" sound to suggest a timbre, and the tempo change is extreme enough to divide the song into two segments, each of which can have a different instrumental treatment. On a melodic instrument, the note C will blend with every measure of the

song except at the first dotted half note; the D♭ and C will clash there momentarily, but the dissonance will resolve in the next measure. By considering the note F as an option, in addition to the C, the children can devise their own two-note harmonizing part.

8. The fact that the song is an Israeli folk tune makes it a useful bridge to the study of another culture.

Seldom is a teacher likely to cover all eight features of this song with a class. Such instruction would require several class periods, and while "Boom Dali Da" is a nice song, enough is enough. The ideas can be pursued in other songs that are equally good. The purpose of the endeavor is to help children see that rhythm, pitch, timbre, and dynamic level all combine to form a unique musical work.

PUTTING THE MUSICAL ELEMENTS TOGETHER: LISTENING

Although children should consider what happens in the music when they are learning to perform it, they should think even more analytically when they listen. Listening is not simply immersing oneself in a cascade of sound, much as one lets water pour over the body during a shower; rather, it means noticing every aural feature that contributes to the musical effect. Often people turn on a radio or record player and insist that they are "listening" to it as they study or talk to friends. Providing oneself with music as a sonic background for other activities is not listening as musicians use that word. Listening means giving the music undivided attention, keen concentration, and contemplative thought. For this reason, music instruction in the elementary school should include experiences that help children listen to music in a more mentally active and analytical way.

Unfortunately, several factors in American society actually work against the idea of careful listening. First, music is so pervasive in our culture that no one can pay careful attention to all of it. The sounds emanating steadily from business establishments, radio, television sets, and record players provide so many aural stimuli that people find it hard to listen selectively. They simply fall into the habit of "tuning out" many of the sounds that they hear every day. Second, popular songs are generally short and simple. Art music (or what is often called "classical music") tends to be longer and more complex, requiring more concentration. Third, people expect much of today's popular music to be performed loudly. They are not accustomed to focusing attention on music that does not capture their interest through sheer strength of sound. Fourth, much popular music does not present the sophisticated manipulation of sound that is a feature of art music. For these reasons, the idea of listening analytically is foreign to most children and adults.

It is not possible to change society and significantly reduce the amount of music that people hear each day. What is practical, however, is to teach children to listen to different types of music in different ways. Much of the music they hear on the radio or in the supermarket can be given only cursory attention because it does not contain subtle or sophisticated organization. To appreciate music that is carefully crafted, however, the listener needs to give undivided and concentrated attention to the sounds, because there is a depth of expression and compositional skill that cannot be encompassed in one hearing. Such music has a quality that invites examination and discloses new facets with repeated hearings.

Listening is a skill that is developed. That is why children in a music class should be given many opportunities to listen as well as to perform and create music. In fact, the ability to listen is basic if the experiences with performing and creating are to be musically satisfying for the children.

How can children be helped to listen more effectively?

1. Direct them to listen for something specific in the music. Asking youngsters simply to "listen" is too vague a request. They should know ahead of time what features they are expected to notice, as in this example:

> "Here's a piece of music written a long time ago by a man named George Frideric Handel. He composed it for the king of England to listen to as he sailed on the river near his castle in London. The musicians floated along nearby on boats and played the music 'live' for the king to enjoy. That's why the music is known to this day as the 'Water Music.'
>
> "First listen to the music straight through, so that you'll get an idea of how it goes. At the end, be ready to tell how fast you'd say the music is." [The teacher plays the "Allegro deciso" or thirteenth movement of the *Water Music Suite.* After hearing it the class decides that the tempo was fast.]
>
> "That's right. The name of this section has 'allegro' in it, which means fairly fast. I'll play the opening part again so that you can learn the opening theme." [The teacher plays the first 20 seconds of the piece twice.]
>
> "This time I'll let the music go to the end. Close your eyes and listen to whether or not that opening theme comes back. When we're through, I'll ask you if it came back."

The above example consumes probably the maximum amount of time that should be spent on listening in any one period. On subsequent days the children can discover the syncopated rhythmic figure in several measures of the melody, the fact that sections of the orchestra seem to answer one another, and so on.

2. Limit the number of features that the children are expected to notice in a single hearing. It is better to select fewer aspects and examine them more thoroughly. Kindergarten children may be able to attend to only one feature at a time. It is good teaching procedure, however, to present the music again and ask the youngsters to notice one or two additional characteristics.

3. Direct the children's attention to musical features. Programmatic music—instrumental music that has nonmusical ideas associated with it—is attractive to children because it suggests images that are familiar to them. However, like salt and pepper on food, it should be used sparingly. Children need to realize that instrumental music cannot truly "tell a story." Only words, which can be sung in a song, have the capability to relate a specific message. Instrumental music can offer only general impressions. They are so general, in fact, that almost any story can be made to fit a particular instrumental work. When children become preoccupied with attempting to identify certain events in the music with the story or program, it is likely that they are not listening to the work as a piece of music. Furthermore, they are apt to assume that all instrumental music is incomplete, and therefore uninteresting, unless it serves as a backup for song words or narrative events.

If programmatic music is to be played for the class, the teacher might present it with an explanation similar to this one.

> "Today we're going to hear a short piece called 'Circus Polka.' This piece, written by Igor Stravinsky, is not trying to tell us any details about the clowns and animals and trapeze artists. Instead, Stravinsky is giving us his impressions of a circus. The piece may remind you of a circus, but you won't be able to say, 'Now he's telling us about the lion trainer,' or 'There's the music about cotton candy.' Let's listen to the meter of the music. Is it in twos or threes?"

In the preceding example, the teacher has encouraged the children to listen to a programmatic work for its musical qualities, and not for its "story."

4. Play a particular work enough times so that the children become familiar with it. Think of it not only as a means of illustrating compositional features to the class, but also as an artistic experience in itself. The children should hear it often enough to recognize it, remember it, and enjoy it as one of "their" pieces. This is not to say that a work should be repeated until the children tire of it. Rather, the listening repertoire should be varied in number of selections and frequency of appearance. In this way, each listening event will reflect a balance between freshness and familiarity.

What musical selections are best for listening experiences in the primary grades? In general, the pieces should be short enough to be heard within a class period. Extending the listening over several days is possible but not as effective. Children at this age level respond more favorably when the music presents a feature that they can hear rather easily: the second movement of Haydn's "Clock" Symphony, Stravinsky's "Circus Polka," Bach's "Sheep May Safely Graze" from the *Birthday Cantata*, and similar works. Teachers should not assume that twentieth-century works are too difficult or too dissonant for children. Youngsters are in fact receptive to electronic music and other contemporary styles. Most of the music series books designed for use with the primary grades suggest several selections that are appropriate for listening.

Many children have record-playing equipment of high quality in their homes. For this reason, and also so that the music may be rendered adequately, recordings should not be played on inferior equipment at school. Cheap record players and equipment in disrepair are worse than nothing. Each elementary school should purchase one quality set of components that can be attached to a cart, rolled from room to room, and locked up when not in use.

Experiences with rhythm, pitch, timbre, and dynamic level, as well as with the skills of performing and listening to music, are all necessary if children in the early grades of elementary school are to establish a solid foundation for their further education in music. Unless they receive a comprehensive introduction to these understandings and skills, their musical future is limited in both breadth and depth. For this reason, the quality and amount of music instruction in the primary grades are extremely important.

REVIEW QUESTIONS

1. (True or False?) Songs in the elementary music series books usually recommend specific dynamic levels.

2. What instruction can be given to help the children exaggerate the difference between loud and soft clapping?

3. When the class is singing a song with echo effects, what can be done to ensure that the echo phrases will indeed be softer than the rest of the song?

4. Describe three techniques to help the children notice differences in dynamic levels.

5. Describe how an accented note should be performed.

6. Why is it difficult for children in the early grades of elementary school to produce extreme differences in dynamic level when they sing?

7. What are some of the causes for the habit of not listening carefully?

8. List four guidelines that should be followed to help children learn to listen to music more fully and accurately.

9. Why should the "program" or "story" associated with program-matic music be de-emphasized when children are learning to listen to music?

10. What are some characteristics of musical works that are especially appropriate for listening by children in the primary grades?

ACTIVITIES

1. From one of the music series books, select a song that would be especially suitable for making children more aware of dynamic level, and decide what teaching procedures would be effective in presenting the song.

2. Using twelve consecutive quarter notes, plan two clapping patterns —one simple and another more advanced—that emphasize changes in dynamic level.

3. Find a song that contains some accented notes and is appropriate for children in the lower grades of elementary school. Plan how you would teach the children to notice the accents and to observe them in performance.

4. Referring to the song you selected for either activity 1 or activity 3, select at least two other aspects of music that could be taught through that song.

5. Select a recording of an instrumental work that would be enjoyed by children in the early elementary grades, and prepare to present it as a listening lesson.
   a. Decide which features of the music you want the children to notice.
   b. Decide the steps by which you would present the music to the class.
   c. Estimate how much time would be needed to teach the features you have selected.

THREE

TEACHING MUSIC IN THE UPPER ELEMENTARY GRADES

Although this book discusses music teaching in only two broad categories—primary and upper elementary grades—there is no clear line distinguishing the musical development of children at either level. The changes that occur as students progress through school are gradual and individual, and they are affected in large part by the child's previous experience and education in the subject.

Much of what students do in music in the upper grades is a refinement of skills and information started at the primary level. The main difference, especially in skills such as singing and reading music, is that older children can perform more accurately and easily than they could in the earlier grades. They can relate to pieces of music that are longer and more complex, and they can perform them more impressively.

A number of new topics are best introduced in the upper grades. For example, playing the recorder is more effectively taught in about the fourth grade, or in a few cases in the third grade. Not all of the new course content deals with specific performance skills. Other topics, such as form and harmony, are more abstract in nature, and so are best emphasized in the upper grades because of the conceptualization required in these areas. Similarly, aspects of music previously introduced can now be examined in more depth.

Musical experiences at this level can be especially rewarding for both teacher and students.

Re-creating Music
in the Upper Grades

Every child should be encouraged to re-create music. Specifically, this activity implies singing and playing instruments, and often it involves the reading of music notation. Making music is important because it turns the learning experience into one of active participation rather than passive acceptance. Students learn the music better when they can perform it.

IMPROVING SINGING SKILLS

If children in the upper grades of elementary school have had a solid experience of singing in the earlier grades, with prior instruction of sufficient quality and amount, they should be able to sing on pitch with a clear and pleasant tone quality. The singing experience should continue to emphasize deep breathing and the erect posture described in Chapter 4. Singing is a skill, and skills are developed over a period of time, so continued work does not at all imply that the children's earlier instruction was faulty.

Voice quality

As children mature, their voices become gradually stronger. A ten-year-old's singing voice does not sound like an adult's, but it is noticeably more vibrant than it was at the age of five. The bigger vocal quality permits a greater range of loudness, which in turn permits more expressiveness in singing. The pitch range gradually increases, also. The average usable top note for first-graders is A on the second space of the treble staff, and the range appears to increase by about one note per year, so that by sixth grade the upper limit is about F on the top line of the treble staff. The range also expands slightly below the middle C cited for first-grade children to about A below the staff. Many children can force their voices higher or lower than their comfortable range, but the singing quality suffers when this is done.

The singing range seldom differs between boys and girls until after grade six. A small percentage of boys will begin to show signs of voice change in the sixth grade, especially if the average age of the group is higher than usual. The first indications of change are likely to be a characteristic huskiness and signs of strain when singing higher pitches. By the sixth grade, but prior to the voice change, it is not unusual for some of the boys' voices to acquire a brilliance and power that is not found in the girls' voices. This is the age of the boy soprano and boy choirs, a tradition more familiar in European churches than in America. A fine boy choir can achieve a quality of singing that is unique in the world of music.

Elementary music series books expect that the boys and girls will sing the same music on almost all songs. If there is more than one part, no indications are given as to who should sing the various lines. In a few instances, songs in the sixth-grade books have parts designated for boys, as in the Spanish carol "Fum, Fum, Fum" on page 156. The range for the boys' part is one octave, extending from A below the treble staff to A on the staff, while the range for the girls' parts is from D below the treble staff to D on the staff. The boys' part is also very simple. The opening interval is a fifth, which is rather easy to sing; the same interval also introduces the new section that begins in the third set of combined staffs, or what is called a *score*. Almost all of the remaining pitches in this part are approached in descending order by step, except for the phrase of the melody in the sixth score.

Diction

Another aspect of singing that should continue to be stressed in the upper grades is the clear enunciation of words. Although "Fum, Fum, Fum" has only a brief message, it should be communicated clearly. One cause of poor diction is laziness in adding the final consonants, especially on words that end with "d" or "t." A teacher should listen carefully for the final "d" on "child" in "Fum, Fum, Fum."

FUM, FUM, FUM

Another diction problem is the mispronunciation of words, which is often the result of regional speech patterns that characterize the children's environment. Sometimes portions of words are not pronounced, or an incorrect vowel sound is employed, as when "mountain" is pronounced as a nasal "meow-tin." While it is not possible to change such ingrained habits completely, they can be reduced by persistent effort and attention.

Part singing

The most noticeable change from primary to upper grades in terms of singing is the addition of songs in parts. In a sense, work on part singing begins when the children first sing a round. Starting with a few songs in third or fourth grade, the teacher can introduce music with additional parts until about half of the songs at the sixth-grade level are of this type, sometimes with as many as three parts. In this way, part singing is introduced gradually over a period of years.

A sequence of difficulty should be developed for teaching part singing. An effective first step has already been mentioned: singing rounds. A second step is the "echo" song, in which one part answers the other. "Follow Me" is such a song. It is like a round, but instead of a continuous melody, it features short statements or fragments. Simultaneously sounded pitches appear halfway through the song and at the end, but for only four beats each time.

A third step in teaching part singing is to present a song in which the second part is sung on one note or chanted. Such a part is easier to learn and to maintain than a second melody. "Chicka-Hanka" (p. 160) contains a line consisting of only one pitch. The words "chicka-hanka" are probably intended to imitate the sounds of an old steam engine puffing. The second part presents a rhythmic challenge, but if the singers start each phrase at the right time and accent the syllable "hank," they can sing it successfully. A few people can also perform the line on appropriate rhythm instruments such as sandblocks, woodblocks, or maracas.

The interval most often found between parts or in chords is the third, or its inversion, the sixth. An *inversion* is produced when either the upper or lower note of the pair is moved to a different octave, making it appear that the original interval has been inverted or turned upside-down. For example, C up to E is a third,

but E up to C (its inversion) is a sixth:

Many times a second part will move parallel to the melody at the interval of a third or sixth for much of the song. If the second part proceeds

FOLLOW ME

Traditional

Come a - long, Sing a song,

Come a - long, Sing a

Fol - low me; It is eas - y, you can

song, Fol - low me; It is

see. Ev - ery day, In this way,

eas - y, you can see. Ev - ery day, In this

Just re - peat 'Til the tune's com - plete.

way, Just re - peat, com - plete.

CHICKA-HANKA

Track Laborer's Song

Melody: Cap-tain, go side-track your train,

Chant: Chick-a-hank-a, chick-a-hank-a, chick-a-hank-a, chick-a-

Cap-tain, go side-track your train,

hank-a; Chick-a-hank-a, chick-a-hank-a, chick-a-hank-a, chick-a-

Num-ber three in line A-com-in' in on time

hank-a; Chick-a-hank-a, chick-a-hank-a, Chick-a-hank-a, chick-a-

Cap tain, go side-track your train.

hank-a; Chick-a-hank-a, chick-a-hank-a, chick-a-hank-a.

parallel to the melody and also has the same rhythm, it is relatively easy to learn. Initially, it may be wise to introduce a part in thirds or sixths for only a short portion of a song.

In "Marianina" (p. 162), the last few measures provide an optional part in small notes. Historically, phrase endings in music have been more ornamented than the rest of the phrase, and this remains a good way to inject part singing into a song. The part singing should follow a unison passage rather than precede it, so that the unison portion will not sound thin by comparison.

The first and third lines of "Marianina" are identical, and the second and fourth are similar. Several phrases appear in *sequence*; that is, the same melodic pattern recurs at a different pitch level. Sequence is discussed more fully in Chapter 14.

To teach the added part in the seventh line of "Marianina", the teacher might use this procedure:

> "Can you see the small notes in the last line of the song? What are those notes for? Kim?"
>
> "They're another part we can sing," Kim responds.
>
> "Right. Are they supposed to substitute for the notes in the melody, or should they be sung along with the melody?"
>
> "I think they're supposed to go along with the melody," Kim guesses.
>
> "Right again. The large note and the small note above it are to be sung at the same time. To sing the small notes, all you need to do is go up one note from the word 'like,' instead of down, as the melody does. Let's sing the last line with the small notes in place of the regular melody notes. I'll sing it once for you, then all of you can try it." [The teacher sings the last line, and the class imitates what was sung.]
>
> "Good try. Now keep singing that part on the last line and I'll sing the melody. Don't let me throw you off! Here's the pitch. . . . Rea-dy sing." [The class sings the last line with the small notes while the teacher sings the melody.]
>
> "Good! Now we'll trade. You sing the melody and I'll sing the part with the small notes. This time we'll start at the refrain." [The teacher and class sing the refrain of the song, with the teacher singing the small notes in the last line.]

When the class is comfortable singing the last few notes of "Marianina" in thirds, they can be invited to sing the first five lines entirely in thirds, with the exception of the last note of line 2, where a fourth sounds better. A simple two-note part throughout most of lines 6 and 7 completes an attractive two-part song. When the class is ready, a three-part ending, incorporating the small notes of the first version, will sound good (see p. 163).

MARIANINA

Words adapted by Mary Val Marsh

Italian Folk Song

1. Ma - ria - ni - na is a maid so rare,

2. With her spark - ling eyes and rav - en hair;

3. Though her smiles on you she may be - stow,

4. She is mine a - lone, I know.

Refrain

5. Ma - ri - a - ni - na, tra, la, la, Ma - ri - a - ni - na, tra, la, la.

6. Oh, Ma - ria - ni - na, Oh, Ma - ria - ni - na,

7. You make me feel like sing - ing all the day. day.

From Mary Val Marsh et al., *Spectrum of Music,* Book 4. Words copyright © 1980 Macmillan Publishing Co., Inc.

MARIANINA

Words adapted by Mary Val Marsh

Italian Folk Song

From Mary Val Marsh et al., *Spectrum of Music*, Book 4. Words copyright © 1980 Macmillan Publishing Co., Inc.

The second part of "Wonderful Copenhagen" basically contributes parallel thirds and a few sixths. It is rather easy to maintain when singing, because the rhythm of every syllable conforms exactly to the melody in the two-part passages. A slight emphasis on the first note of each measure will convey a feeling of rhythmic energy. The music is a waltz, and should "swing" with only one beat per measure.

WONDERFUL COPENHAGEN

Arranged by William Stickles   Words and Music by Frank Loesser queen of the sea._____

queen of the sea._____ Once I sailed a - way, but I'm

Sing - ing Co - pen - ha - gen, won - der - ful,

home to - day, Sing - ing Co - pen - ha - gen, won - der - ful,

won - der - ful Co - pen - ha - gen for me._____

won - der - ful Co - pen - ha - gen for me._____

 Because there are only slight differences among children's voices in the upper elementary grades, all class members should learn both parts of a song, then trade parts occasionally. The only time when parts should be assigned on a more or less permanent basis is when the song will be sung in public. In that case, the children can still learn both parts initially, but they should soon be assigned to a specific part so that they can learn it more thoroughly.

 The melody is usually learned first because it is musically the more important line. But if the children then become reluctant to learn an additional unfamiliar part, the order of presentation can be changed, for variety and extra challenge. It is even possible to teach both parts together by alternating between them, one phrase at a time, but this tends to interrupt the melodic flow of the music.

 When the children are first experiencing two-part singing, the teacher can lend support by singing or playing one part on the piano while the entire class sings the other part. This gives them the solidarity and confidence of participating with a large group, and yet acquaints them with the total sound.

 The children should learn to notice when the second part is parallel to the melody and when it is not. The teacher might instruct them as follows:

"Often in music a second part runs parallel to the melody. It goes in exactly the same direction to it, just as one rail of a railroad track runs parallel to the other. Where does parallel motion happen in 'Wonderful Copenhagen'?" [The students discover that most of the motion is parallel.]

"So the second part moves parallel to the melody most of the time in this song, but not always. Where does it move in *contrary* motion—not parallel—to the melody? Ken?"

'Um . . . wait . . . Around the last part of the song, like on the words 'singing Copenhagen,'" Ken finally answers.

'Right, Ken. Are there other places where the parts are not parallel?" [The class goes on to find more instances of contrary motion.]

Next in the general progression of difficulty are songs with a second part that is somewhat different from the melody. Perhaps its rhythmic patterns differ, or the words of the text. A *descant* is one such type of contrasting line. It is usually pitched above the melody, although the simple descant for "Sandy Land," shown here, lies within the range of the melody. The similarity of range makes this song especially appropriate for the recommended procedure of letting the entire class learn both parts, then asking them to trade occasionally.

SANDY LAND

Oklahoma Folk Song

1. Make my liv - in' in san - dy land, Make my liv - in' in san - dy land,
2. Hoe - in' ta - ters in san - dy land, Hoe - in' ta - ters in san - dy land,
3. One more riv - er I'm bound to cross, One more riv - er I'm bound to cross,

Make my liv - in' in san - dy land, La - dies, fare you well.
Hoe - in' ta - ters in san - dy land, La - dies, fare you well.
One more riv - er I'm bound to cross, 'Till I meet my hon - ey.

Descant

San - dy land, San - dy land, San - dy land, Fare you— well.

The song, which may have been sung at square dances, contains frequent repetition of melodic, rhythmic, and text patterns. Similarly, the descant repeats a rhythm of its own: The dotted quarter-, eighth-, and half-note pattern occurs three times. The pitch pattern of measures 1 and 2 appears again in measures 5 and 6, and the third and fourth measures maintain that pattern, except at a lower pitch level. The first pitch of the first three phrases matches in both parts, which is a further help to young singers. The descant for "Sandy Land" is simple, which is to its credit.

DECK THE HALLS

Descant by Beatrice and Max Krone

Reprinted from *Descants for Christmas* by Beatrice and Max Krone, © 1949 Neil A. Kjos Music Company, San Diego. Used by Permission.

The descant for "Deck the Halls" (p. 167) is somewhat more difficult because it is not so similar to the melody, and it begins on a different note. It is still suitable for elementary school children, however, because it has a strong melodic character, and three of its four lines are identical.

The teacher should be aware that parts are sometimes added to a song simply to provide a chordal background. Such parts are likely to be more difficult to learn than a descant or countermelody, because they lack melodic character of their own. They are more easily remembered in the context of the harmony than as an independent melody. Hearing the parts as harmony requires musical experience, which the children in elementary school are just acquiring. The subject of teaching harmony is developed more fully in Chapter 15.

The song "Joyful, Joyful, We Adore Thee" is the famous theme from the fourth movement of Beethoven's Ninth Symphony. The words are not a translation of Johann Schiller's text for which Beethoven originally wrote the music; they were added later when the music was adapted to serve as a church hymn. The melody itself seems to defy descriptions of good melodic writing: Its first 12 notes are all of the same duration, it moves by step within a range of only five pitches, and three of its four phrases are almost identical. Yet there is something intriguing about it—a quality that people have found fascinating for more than a century and a half.

The two harmony parts follow the persistent rhythm of the melody. A lack of melodic character can be observed in the lowest part, on the lower staff; for the first five measures it contains predominantly the note D. Yet the music conveys an impression of strength and vitality, and the frequent repetition of notes is an aid to inexperienced singers.

The more parts a class sings, of course, the fewer singers are available for each part. If a class of 28 divides into two parts, there will be 14 in each section. If it divides into three parts, there will be only 9 in each section, with an extra singer for one of the parts. There is a feeling of security when more singers are assigned to a part, but this can lead to mental laziness and may slow the development of independent singing.

In the following example, the teacher is trying to develop the children's part-singing skills while increasing their understanding of the music.

[The class has tried unsuccessfully to sing "Joyful, Joyful, We Adore Thee" in three parts.]

"You tried—good for you! I heard mostly melody, though—not much second or third part. You people on the lower parts seemed to 'run out of gas' as we went along. Try your two sections together without the words; just sing the notes on 'la.' Here are your pitches . . . . Rea-dy, sing." [The students on the second and third parts sing through

JOYFUL, JOYFUL, WE ADORE THEE

Words by Henry van Dyke

Music Arranged from Ludwig van Beethoven

1. Joy-ful, joy-ful, we a-dore thee, God of glo-ry, Lord of love,
2. All thy works with joy sur-round thee; Earth and heaven re-flect thy rays,

Hearts un-fold like flowers be-fore thee, Open-ing to the sun a-bove.
Stars and an-gels sing a-round thee, Cen-ter of un-brok-en praise.

Melt the clouds of sin and_ sad-ness, drive the_ dark of doubt a-way.
Field and for-est, vale and_ moun-tain, flow-ing_ mead-ow, flash-ing sea,

Giv-er of im-mor-tal glad-ness, Fill us with the light of day.
Chant-ing bird and flow-ing foun-tain, Call us to re-joice in Thee.

the song on a neutral syllable without the melody. The portion in the fourth score with the D♯ and D♮ sounds insecure.]

"You're having some trouble on the words 'drive the dark of doubt away.' I'm not surprised; it gets tricky there. I'll play the song for you again. As you listen, concentrate on the parts below the melody, *not* on the melody itself. There's a certain logic to what Beethoven composed for the music at that phrase. He's suggesting a different key center—writing different harmony—to make the piece sound uncertain and more interesting at that spot. Listen." [The teacher plays the first verse of "Joyful, Joyful, We Adore Thee" on the record player, or on the piano.]

"Now let's have all three parts sing the two measures for 'drive the dark of doubt away.' We'll do it slowly so that you can notice how the music sounds. Here are your notes." [The teacher plays each starting note, then proceeds slowly, playing all parts at the piano as the children sing.]

"That's better. Now sing it again, this time a little faster and without the piano. Here are your notes . . . . Rea-dy, go."

There are other techniques for helping young singers learn music in three parts. The melody can be hummed while the other parts are sung with the words or a neutral syllable. Each part can be sung alone with piano accompaniment or with a recording. Various combinations of two of the parts can be tried at the same time. If the melody seems secure, more singers can be assigned to double the second or third parts, to give them more support.

INCREASED UNDERSTANDING OF MUSIC

Certain aspects of music performance are more successfully introduced in the upper grades because a mastery of the concepts requires more maturity than most primary grade children possess. The teaching of specific understandings will be discussed in the following chapters. In this chapter, only three points related to the performance of music are presented: expressive singing, phrasing, and songs as music literature.

Performing music expressively

The idea that not all songs should be sung in the same way begins more appropriately in the primary grades, but efforts at furthering this notion should continue throughout elementary school. The point to

emphasize in the upper grades is that the music and the text are combined to project ideas and feelings. The performers' role is to get "inside" the song and convey its intent.

A certain amount of sophistication is required to project the mood
of "A Scottish Lullaby."

A SCOTTISH LULLABY

Scottish Folk Song

The Scottish words may need to be translated for the class. "Bairn"
means "child," "greets" means "cries," "ken" means "know," "fu'" is
the dialect sound for "full," and "saut" means "salt." Actually, the
text of the song may be more profound than children can fully comprehend. The mother is thinking about the routines and hardships of
life—the sewing of cushions and sheets, the rocking of a restless infant,
and the long waiting when the father is away at sea. Even if the children
do not understand the text fully, they can enjoy its beautiful melody
and gain insight into one aspect of human experience.

Since the song is a lullaby, it should be sung tenderly and smoothly. The children's ability to control the flow of vocal tone will be challenged when they sing up a sixth to the syllable "baw" in the third
line. The contour of the melody seems to require a moderate rise and
fall of dynamic level within each line. The word "hush" suggests the
gentle treatment that should permeate the entire song.

By contrast, "Wonderful Copenhagen" (p. 164) is a more boisterous, jovial song. Although it is like "A Scottish Lullaby" in meter
and key, the two songs differ unmistakably in spirit, and the children's
singing should reflect this.

Phrasing

The phrasing and interpretation of a song are influenced significantly by the singers' willingness to breathe together at certain places
in the music. Students in the upper elementary grades should begin to
notice where these moments occur, during which time it makes musical
sense to breathe. First, however, they need to recognize the phrase as a
logical unit of music and text.

> "Some of you are singing, 'Wonderful, wonderful Co- (breath)
> penhagen (breath).' What's wrong with that, Laird?"
> "It splits up the word?" Laird ventures, while his neighbor com-
> ments that "It sounds jerky."
> "Exactly. It breaks up the flow of the song. We should keep the
> melody flowing along until—where, Kirsten?"
> "Maybe after 'town,'" Kirsten replies.
> "Right. Why?"
> "Well, the word 'town' and the music sort of end a thought
> there," Kirsten continues.
> "Good, Kirsten. But that's a long way from the beginning. Some
> people may not be able to sing that long without a breath. If they can't,
> where would be the next best place to breathe? Heidi?
> "I think it would be after 'Copenhagen,'" Heidi answers.
> "I agree. But let's try it, class, all the way to 'town' without
> taking a breath. Remember, don't waste air when you sing; we want
> sound, not air. All right, good breath, now. Rea-dy, sing." [The class
> tries singing to "town" in a single breath.]

Music literature

Students in the upper grades of elementary school should learn
to recognize different types of songs. For example, "Wonderful Copenhagen" is from a motion picture about the Danish storyteller Hans
Christian Andersen; "Marianina" is an Italian folk song; "Joyful, Joyful, We Adore Thee" is the melody from the fourth movement of
Beethoven's Ninth Symphony; and "Sandy Land" is a folk song from
the western United States. Whether performing or listening, students
should be aware of the source of the song and the type of music with

which they are involved. In time, they can develop a sense of how Italian songs sound and how they differ from Irish songs, which in turn differ from Mexican songs. Children of this age can rather easily learn to identify different types of music, however—hymns and chorales, art songs, marches, waltzes.

Information should be provided to the students when they perform the music of a well-known composer. The process should not involve detailed biographical data; it is enough to mention some background about the times in which the composer lived, and perhaps pertinent information about the composing of the piece. The teacher's editions of the music series books usually provide such information. In short, the students should begin to acquire an understanding of the literature of music.

IMPROVING INSTRUMENT PLAYING

Piano

Some elementary classrooms have a piano available to enrich the music experiences of the class. Classroom acquaintance with the instrument is in no way intended to replace private piano lessons for interested students. It will not equip them to play piano solos. Besides, most children whose families want them to engage in serious piano study have already started private lessons by the fourth grade. Children should perceive the classroom piano neither as a toy nor as a quick means to soloistic skill.

The value of a classroom piano lies rather in the fact that its keyboard is a fine visual tool for teaching pitch relationships. Because the pattern of black and white keys is tactile and clearly visible, it is easy to see and feel where the half and whole steps occur. By experimenting at the piano, the students can gain a greater awareness of how pitches are arranged in a song and on the keyboard. It does not matter if the children play the pitch pattern with one or two or more fingers; what matters is that they experience the pattern more fully when they hear, see, and feel it than when they only hear it.

"The Inch Worm" (p. 174) contains several patterns that can be understood better if they are played on the piano or on a xylophone-like instrument. Here is how the teacher might involve the children with piano as they learn the song:

> "In 'The Inch Worm,' the notes of the melody are exactly the same the first time we sing 'two and two are four' and 'four and four are eight.' But the next two times we sing those words, they're changed

THE INCH WORM

Words and Music by Frank Loesser

Two and two are four, four and four are eight; That's all you have on your busi-ness-like mind. Two and two are four, four and four are eight; How can you be so blind?

Refrain

Two and two are four, Four and four are eight,

Inch worm, inch worm, mea-sur-ing the mar-i-golds,

Eight and eight are six-teen, Six-teen and six-teen are thir-ty two.

You and your a-rith-me-tic, you'll prob-a-bly go far.

Two and two are four, Four and four are eight,

Inch worm, inch worm, mea-sur-ing the mar-i-golds,

Eight and eight are six-teen, Six-teen and six-teen are thir-ty two.

Seems to me you'd stop and see how beau-ti-ful they are.

so that the word 'are' is higher each time. Eric, come to the piano and help me play the note that changes each time." [Eric comes to the piano and is shown the notes B♭ and A. He practices them on cue, in the rhythm of the song, while the teacher sings softly with him, ". . . are four." The brief rehearsal continues with the same notes but with the teacher singing ". . . are eight."]

"Good, Eric! Now help us, class, by singing only 'Two and two (rest rest rest), four and four (rest rest rest).' Be really silent on the rest so you can hear Eric's part. He's playing a *half step,* where the notes are close together. Here's your starting note, class. . . . Rea-dy, sing."

[The class sings measure 1, the teacher and Eric perform measure 2, the class resumes at measure 3, and the teacher and Eric perform measure 4. The class participation is good, so the teacher decides to continue with measures 5-8.]

"Not bad! Now, Eric, play '. . . are four' on the notes C A, and '. . . are eight' on the notes D A, just as they occur in the song. Class, as Eric practices, notice that each set of notes gets farther apart than the half step he started with. Show them, Eric." [Eric plays the new notes on cue as the teacher points to them and sings them.]

"Okay, class, it's your turn to sing just 'Two and two (rest rest rest), four and four (rest rest rest)' as you did before. Start at the beginning, sing to the refrain, and listen to Eric's part as it changes during the 'resting' measures." . . .

"Thanks, Eric. Stay here a moment, though. Someone else take a turn at the piano, now. Okay, Lori, come on up. Eric, teach her the pairs of notes. While you're doing that, you people by the windows come up and watch. Stand so that everyone can see the keyboard— that's better. Those pairs of notes are called *intervals,* and they get wider as they go along in this song. . . . Nice going, Lori!"

Another interesting interval pattern in "The Inch Worm" occurs in the refrain on the words "eight are sixteen, six-." The pattern of E flat, D natural, D flat, and C creates a descending chromatic line that the children should start to recognize as a series of half steps. The repeated D in the chromatic segment can be omitted for purposes of this exercise so that the half-step series will proceed at an even pace. Or the teacher can make a game of the note series by adding a repeated note to any of the tones in the chromatic fragment; the class will have to listen carefully to determine whether the teacher is playing E♭-E♭-D-D♭-C or E♭-D-D♭-D♭-C or some other combination of descending half steps with one note duplicated.

In addition to melodic phrases, students can also play simple one-hand chords on the piano. Many songs in the series books contain symbols indicating chords. Even an inexperienced player can play the three notes of a triad. Here the class is learning a simple song in the key of G major.

"How many different chord symbols do you see in the song, class, and what are they?"

"Two: G and D," answers Darlene. "Right! Keith, come to the piano and find the notes G, B, D, which make up the G chord. I'll help you . . . . Good. Stay right here, Keith. Marcus, come to the piano and find the notes D, F♯, and A, which make up the D chord." [The teacher helps the players find their respective triads so that the roots lie in the octave above middle C.]

"Here's a music book for you. When you see the symbol for your chord in the music, play the chord and hold the keys down for one measure. If you see no new symbol, then play your chord again for the next measure. Be sure to move your hand away to let the other player have a chance when it comes his turn. Practice the entire piano part, now. I'll help you by pointing to you when your turn comes." [Keith and Marcus practice the part.] "Good. The accompaniment's ready to put with the singing now, class. Here's your starting note . . . . Rea-dy, sing." [The class sings the song with the block chord accompaniment played on the piano.]

It is suggested that the chords first be played within the children's singing range, for two reasons. The youngsters are accustomed to hearing and producing musical sounds at that level, so their aural pitch discrimination will be more acute within that range. Further, if the chord tones are written out on staff paper for the "pianists," or are written on the board for the class to see, the notation will look more familiar, just like the notes the children have been seeing in their books.

For variety of pitch level, however, it is good to let the piano-playing students occasionally move their chords to the octave below or above the central range, remaining at the new location for perhaps one verse of the song. This acquaints them with the "geography" of the keyboard and provides the class with an opportunity to make musical judgments as to the accompaniment range that sounds best with a particular song.

The chords recommended by the teacher may be in *root position* (with the tones ascending in normal order: root, skip a note, skip a note) or they may be *inverted* (with the chord tones rearranged so that the root sounds anywhere except on the bottom). Or a series of chords may contain some chords in root position and others in inversion. As the children become more adept at playing chords at the piano, they can learn to handle all the chords of a song without a partner's help, and can make more decisions as to what chord arrangement feels best under their hand and sounds most appropriate with the song.

Most activities that can be done with the piano can also be performed on the bells and similar keyboard instruments. Even chords can be performed by using mallets in both hands or by involving additional players in the activity.

Recorder

The recorder is introduced in many upper elementary classrooms. It is especially well suited for music instruction because it can be inexpensive, is simple to play, and can sound most of the pitches that the students sing. (Its notes sound an octave higher, but they are notated within the children's singing range.) The recorder also possesses a light and gentle tone quality; if a player blows too hard on it, no sound will be emitted. Its sustained tone is more like singing than are the diminishing sounds produced by the piano and bell-type instruments.

Although not difficult to play, the recorder takes time to learn; it cannot be mastered in a couple of minutes as an incidental music activity. Some of the music series books devote a few pages to learning the recorder, and inexpensive method books for the instrument are available commercially.

The recorder is played by inserting it slightly between the lips, holding it at a 45-degree angle to the body, and with the tongue against the back of the upper teeth, starting the sound gently with the syllable "doo." The first note learned is usually B in the middle of the treble staff. It is followed by A and then G. This pattern logically leads to the song "Hot Cross Buns" as one of the first pieces learned on the recorder.

The most frequently encountered problems in teaching the recorder are:

1. Failing to cover the holes completely. This allows air to leak out, causing a wrong note or no sound at all.

2. Placing the right hand instead of the left on the upper portion of the instrument. Except for the first few notes, it is not possible to play the recorder "cross-handed."

3. Puffing out the sounds instead of starting them with the tongue. Puffing, which is like blowing out a candle, is tiring for the player and does not produce a clean start or "attack" to the sound.

4. Failing to learn the names of the notes. Sometimes children associate the notated pitch with a particular finger pattern, without realizing what note they are playing. While they can play simple music this way, they will be limited in what they can do when more difficult music is encountered. For example, the recorder player, like a pianist, must consciously observe sharps and flats—a consideration that is rather much taken care of when singing.

When the students have learned several notes on the recorder and have mastered the essentials of tone production on the instrument, they will be able to play as well as sing most of their songs, especially those that are in easy keys such as G, F, and C. Recorders sound especially good on descants and other types of added parts.

There are a few practical obstacles to overcome in teaching the recorder. The children will learn more effectively when the class is not too large, say over 20. Storing and keeping track of instruments may present a problem. If the children keep the instruments with their other school materials in the classroom, there is more risk of breakage and loss. But if the teacher keeps them, the children are less likely to practice and improve their playing skills outside of class time. If possible, they should buy their own recorders. This increases the children's sense of responsibility, and they can keep the recorders when they are through using them in school. If the school owns them, the instruments need to be cleaned before they are passed on to other children.

The autoharp is discussed in Chapter 15. Further suggestions on the enrichment of songs through the use of instruments are also offered in that chapter.

MUSIC READING

Music reading is a skill in the sense that eye movement must be coordinated with physiological reactions to produce the sounds specified on the page of music. As is true of so many skills, appropriate physical response to visual stimuli depends on knowledge as well as on successful past experience in similar situations. So in addition to continued practice at responding to the symbols on a page of music, students in the upper elementary grades can apply their increasingly greater understanding of music. For this reason, the topic of music reading is also discussed in this book with rhythm and other aspects of music.

If the children are directed to look at the song "Sandy Land" (p. 166), and if they have been taught to recognize patterns in music, they will notice that the same rhythmic pattern is repeated three times, and so is the basic pitch pattern, except that the second pattern is lower. They will see that the descant contains the same amount of repetition, and that the two-word phrase "Sandy land" repeats itself. If they have been taught to look for chord patterns, their awareness of harmonic change will make their reading of the music easier.

In the case of "Wonderful Copenhagen" (p. 164), the students will read more accurately if they understand the accidentals in the music. Here is one way in which the teacher might help them apply what they have learned.

[The class is looking at "Wonderful Copenhagen" for the first time.]

"Before you try to sightread this song, you should be prepared for some of its features. Who can find some measures that are alike? Better use measure numbers. Marcie?"

"Measures 1 and 2 are alike, and . . . um . . . 5 and 6 . . . (pause). . . . And later it goes like the beginning again."

"Right, Marcie. Now, are there some measures that are a lot alike but not exactly? Adam?"

"It seems like 'With her harbor light' and 'that she wears at night' are nearly the same," Adam volunteers.

"Yes, they are. Later in the song, the same is true for the words 'Once I sailed away' and 'but I'm home to stay.' What about the musical symbol on the second note of the song? Meg?"

"That's a sharp, I think," answers Meg, a bit unsure of herself.

"Good thinking, Meg. What does a sharp mean?"

"It says to make the note a little higher than it was," Meg replies.

"That's the idea. It's not just a little higher, but exactly one half step higher. All right, we have several repeated places and a number of sharps. Be on the lookout for them as we sing through the song with all of us on the top line of each staff, which is the melody. Since this is the first time, we'll sing it without the words. Sing it on 'loo.' Here's the starting note . . . Rea-dy, sing." [The class sings through "Wonderful Copenhagen" on a neutral syllable.]

The amount of help the teacher needs to give a class in reading a song of the difficulty of "Wonderful Copenhagen" varies depending on the previous experience of the children. Sounding a note here and there at the beginning of a new phrase or at the more tricky passages is often all that is needed. The teacher should not habitually sing or play the entire melody along with the class. If this is done consistently, the students, instead of reading, will merely become adept at following what they hear someone else doing. In this version of "Wonderful Copenhagen," in the seventh line, the melody is briefly given to the second part. If the entire class is singing the top part, the children can simply count out the measures silently. While this practice breaks the flow of the melody, it is good training for the children because it makes them more conscious of the beat.

The words need not always be omitted on the first reading of a song, but it does make the task of music reading easier because there is one less factor requiring attention. Also, it relieves the singer of having to coordinate an up-down motion of the eyes to read the two lines of words and music, in addition to the left-right motion normally required for reading.

Reading music is a complex skill involving not only mental comprehension but also prompt and finely developed physical responses. If children are going to learn to read music, they need to do it often, and in an organized sequence of difficulty. They need to practice to develop the mental comprehension and the muscle responses that transform a printed code—music notation—into sound. In the upper grades it is a good idea to provide this practice by encouraging the children to sight-sing most of their new songs. Music-reading exercise material is also useful. Some of the music series books contain short reading exercises, and there is at least one graded music reading program available commercially.*

Opinions differ among music teachers as to the value in the upper grades of pitch syllables and numbers (which were discussed in Chapter 8). If the students are well-grounded in these systems and seem to profit from them, the use of syllables or numbers may be continued. Older children, however, should gradually begin to discard these reading aids. For example, in the song "Wonderful Copenhagen," teaching the chromatic syllables for the sharped notes would probably be of minimal help to the children. They can sing the affected note one half step higher without attempting to memorize *sol-fi-sol* for the first measure and *mi-ri-mi* for the fifth measure. By the sixth grade, the level at which this song appears in some of the music series books, syllables or numbers are likely to be more of a hindrance than a help.

If students can understand notation and read it with some degree of fluency and accuracy, they can learn a piece of music faster, and music will be more enjoyable for them. Although the enjoyment of music does not depend on the ability to read music, this skill enables a person to grow as a performer. Performing, or re-creating music, is not absolutely essential to a person's enjoyment of music as an appreciative listener. But children in the upper elementary grades want and need the active and varied musical experiences that are possible through music-making.

REVIEW QUESTIONS

1. How do the quality and range of children's voices change during the elementary school years?

2. What differences, if any, exist between boys' and girls' voices in the upper elementary grades?

*Joseph S. Curatilo, Richard C. Berg, and Marjorie Farmer, *The Sight and Sound of Music* (Delaware Water Gap, Pa.: Shawnee Press, 1972.)

3. What aspects of enunciation and diction in singing often require special attention?

4. a. How may part singing be introduced to elementary school children?
   b. What order of difficulty is recommended in presenting the various types of part songs?
   c. What is a descant?

5. Suppose that you are teaching a three-part song. The children singing the second and third parts are experiencing trouble with their parts when the entire class sings. What teaching procedures might help them?

6. What steps can a teacher take to encourage the class to sing more expressively?

7. What factors in the music and the text guide singers as they determine where a breath should be taken?

8. What are the benefits of including the piano as an aid in the teaching of music?

9. What are the problems encountered most commonly when teaching the recorder to children?

10. To what extent should pitch syllables or numbers continue to be used in the upper grades as an aid to reading music?

11. What are some effective ways to help students increase their music-reading skills?

ACTIVITIES

1. Examine one of the music series books designed for fourth, fifth, or sixth grade. Randomly select six songs and study each for the following features:
   a. What is the pitch range?
   b. Is the song written in parts, and if so, how many parts are indicated?
   c. Are any of the parts specifically designated for boys or girls?
   d. How would you rate each part song as to difficulty? Give reasons for your ratings.

2. From the six songs studied for the previous activity, or from another source if necessary, select a part song and prepare to teach it to the class. Consider the following steps in your preparation:

a. Learn the song thoroughly, both the text and all vocal parts.
b. Determine what expressive qualities should be projected in the song.
c. Decide what the singers should do with the tone quality, dynamic level, tempo, and style to help bring out the expressiveness of the music.
d. Anticipate the phrases that may cause difficulty for the singers.
e. Notice any repeated melodic or rhythmic patterns.
f. Decide on the places where a breath will create the most effective phrasing.
g. Decide what you can teach the class about the song as a work of music literature.

3. Learn to play an accompaniment of three-note triads on the piano for one of the songs in the elementary music series books.

4. Learn to play two simple melodies on the recorder.

Creative Experiences in Music

The principles for guiding music classes in creative experiences at the upper grade levels are generally the same as those discussed in Chapter 5 for children in the lower grades. Usually it is individuals, not classes or committees, who think up musical ideas. Every successful effort to manipulate sound contributes to the child's musical growth and feeling of competence.

ALTERING EXISTING MUSIC

An easy introduction to creative efforts is to take a piece of music that already exists and modify or alter it. The existing music provides a structure from which the children can work, and the number of options is less bewildering than when they start from scratch. They can change the music in several ways.

Instrumentations

A good way to encourage creative thought about music is to devise instrumental accompaniments to songs the children know. They need to decide which instruments will be used and in what way. The type of song often suggests appropriate instruments, as it does in "La Conga."

LA CONGA

1. When you hear ma - ra - cas_ "boom-chick, boom-chick, boom - chick!"
2. When you hear this rhy - thm_ played up - on a bon - go,—

And you hear the cla - ves_ tap - ping "click - a - click - click!"
Then you know it's time for_ all to do La Con - ga!_

One, two, three, kick!_ That's the way you do it!__

One, two, three, kick!_ There is noth - ing to it.__

"Which instruments would be good for accompanying 'La Conga'? Joy, you can write down all the suggestions on the chalkboard. Does the song suggest any instruments? Bill?"

"It talks about maracas at the beginning," Bill offers.

"And in the second verse it has a bongo," Glen adds.

"Claves," Tricia volunteers. [The class seems satisfied with the three instruments mentioned in the text of the song.]

"Those seem like good choices to me. Why don't the three of you get the maracas, bongo, and claves and take them into a corner by yourselves for a minute. Think up a simple pattern that's two measures long to go with 'La Conga.' Practice softly so that the rest of us won't know what you're going to play."

Sometimes it is helpful to give the players a few ideas for an accompanying pattern. They certainly should not feel required to use another person's suggestions, but many children appreciate an idea or two. The song often contains a rhythmic or melodic pattern that seems especially adaptable for an instrumental part.

"The three people who have the instruments may want an idea or two about what can go into the part they're thinking up for us. Does anyone have a suggestion that's inspired by the song? Rick?"

"Well, the same rhythm comes up in every other measure, the one that goes 'Dah-da-ah,'" Rick replies, attempting to demonstrate the tied and syncopated figure, to the amusement of the class.

"Very good, Rick! Did you get that, instrumentalists? You're welcome to use that rhythm unless you have a better idea."

Before the instrumentalists attempt to play their parts with the song, they should perform alone once to make sure that their rhythmic patterns fit well with "La Conga." The parts the students develop might be:

After the players have tried their parts, the class can evaluate each rhythm as to its appropriateness for the song. In that way, the entire class can share in the creative efforts.

"Arirang" (p. 186) is a Korean folk song. If the children are sensitive to the qualities of this music, they will choose accompanying instruments and rhythms quite different from those they selected for "La Conga." The teacher might guide the class in this way:

"You know 'Arirang' well enough now so that you can add instruments to it. Gwen, could you go over to the table and name off some of the instruments that we have there? Point to one thing at a time and name it, then call on someone to tell us whether they think it would sound appropriate for an oriental song like 'Arirang.' They have to give you a reason for their answer, too, Gwen."

[Gwen begins her instrument identification.] "Claves. Maureen?"

"Um . . . no. Claves always sound Mexican or some country like that."

"Finger cymbals. Valerie."

"They seem sort of gentle and I think they might be nice with an oriental song," Valerie decides.

"Bongo. Randy."

ARIRANG

Korean Folk Song

1. A - ri - rang,_ A - ri - rang,_ A - ri - rang,_ A - ri - rang,_
2. A - ri - rang,_ A - ri - rang,_ A - ri - rang,_ A - ri - rang,_

A - ri - rang,_ A - ri - rang,_ A - ri - rang fair.
A - ri - rang,_ A - ri - rang,_ A - ri - rang fair.

Through the pass___ I watch you___ go___ there.___
Here I wait for you, wait, wait___ and___ stare.___

A - ri - rang,_ A - ri - rang,_ A - ri - rang fair.
A - ri - rang,_ A - ri - rang,_ A - ri - rang fair.

"Nah. Too loud." [The selection process continues, and the following instruments are chosen: temple blocks, gong, small drum, triangle, and finger cymbals.]

During this decision-making process the teacher should be sensitive to the reactions of any students who appear to be in disagreement with a friend's judgment. The merits of a particular instrument can be discussed briefly to hasten consensus.

Chants

Another way to use an existing piece of music as a springboard for creative effort is to add a *chant*—a rhythmic line with little variation in pitch, so that the style resembles speech. "This Old Hammer" suggests the relentless monotony of tools, machinery, and hard work—an appropriate setting for a repetitious chant. Here is one way to help the children develop a chant:

THIS OLD HAMMER

American Folk Song

This old ham-mer___ killed John Hen-ry,___ This old ham-mer___ killed John Hen-ry,___ This old ham-mer___ killed John Hen-ry,___ but it won't kill me, won't kill me.

"You may have noticed that 'This Old Hammer' has a persistent, machine-like quality about it. Here's an assignment for you: make up a chant that a few of you can repeat over and over while others sing the melody. Your chant doesn't need to have a pitch to it at first—just a strong rhythm and a word or two. Keep it short. We'll sing through the song again, so you can get ideas for a short phrase that might make a good chant for this song. Here's the pitch. Rea-dy, sing." [The class sings "This Old Hammer."]

"Who has an idea for a chant? When you have one, say it for us in a rhythmic, energetic style. Tony?"

"How about '*Ham*-mer, *ham*-mer, *ham*-mer," Tony suggests, illustrating with steady eighth notes and a nod of his head on each beat.

"Sounds good. Let's try it: you six people closest to Tony, say his chant with him. The rest of you sing the song. Here's your pitch . . . Rea-dy, go." [The class divides and sings the song with the suggested chant, to the obvious pleasure of Tony.]

The teacher, after a few subtle hints to the class, may be able to elicit from the group another chant, spoken at first, then pitched as follows:

This old ham - mer, ___ This old ham - mer, ___

The pitch D is a good choice because all phrases of the song begin and end on that pitch, so the one-note chant is likely to be successful. The momentary dissonance between the chanted D and the E in the next-to-last measure of the song is not offensive. In fact, it gives good emphasis to an important word, and can well be accented for dramatic effect.

Chants seem more effective when the song is not fast and when the melody contains a few long notes during which a listener's attention can pass to the chant for a moment. The main problem in performing a chant is that young singers tend to rush the tempo. They must maintain a steady beat if the chant is to be convincing.

A chant, performed alone at the beginning and end of the song, makes a fitting introduction and coda. It sets the mood at the beginning of the song and reinforces it at the end. When combined with well-controlled changes in dynamic level, the chant has a dramatic effect.

Ostinato parts

A chant must be spoken or vocalized in some manner, but an ostinato can either be played on an instrument or sung. Its characteristic feature is its persistent repeating of a rhythmic or melodic pattern. (The word "ostinato" in Italian literally means "obstinate" or "stubborn.") An ostinato can be created in the same way as other accompanying parts. A simple figure derived from the song is effective, and choosing a pitch level is easy if the harmonic structure is straightforward and uncomplicated. In "Swing Low, Sweet Chariot," the note C is selected to predominate in the ostinato because in the key of F major, C is common to both the tonic chord (F A C) and the dominant chord (C E G). The fleeting implication of the subdominant chord (Bb D F) does not clash because it is so brief.

SWING LOW, SWEET CHARIOT

Black Spiritual

I looked o-ver Jor-dan, and what did I see,— Com-in' for to car-ry me home?

A band_ of an-gels com-in' af-ter me,— Com-in' for to car-ry me home.

Although an ostinato must be limited in pitch range to minimize dissonance with the chord changes in the song, this restriction is helpful in guaranteeing that the part will be easy to sing or to play on an instrument. An ostinato, like a chant, can serve as an introduction and coda to the song. The last repetition of the ostinato may be altered, if desired, to sound more final. In "Swing Low, Sweet Chariot," for example, the part can conclude in any of the following ways: "Swing low, chariot, swing____," or "Swing____ swing____ low____," or "Comin' to take me home____," ending on the tonic note.

Variations

The theme and variation technique has a long history in music. For centuries, composers have been intrigued by the possibilities of devising variations on a melody. Students will find that simple, familiar songs are the easiest to vary. Here is how a teacher might help a class create variations on "Yankee Doodle."

"You all know 'Yankee Doodle.' Well, now it's time for you to change it some to make it truly *your* song. How can you change it? Let's list some of the ways here on the board." [The teacher explains each point while writing "Change pitches in the melody. . . . Decorate the melody. . . . Change the rhythm. . . . Combine two or more of the above techniques. . . ."]

"For now, we're going to change only one feature of the song. Don't try to do a combination yet! Now, people sitting by the windows, you try to vary 'Yankee Doodle' by changing just a few pitches. Each one of you by yourself think of a few changes, but not too many, please.

"You people here in the center of the room, try to make a few changes in the rhythm, like lengthening some notes and shortening others. You people by the door, think of some decorative notes that you can work into the melody of 'Yankee Doodle.'" [The teacher gives an example of decorative or ornamental notes.]

"We'd better sing the song together once, in case someone has forgotten how it goes." [The class sings the song.]

"Okay, take a couple of minutes to think quietly. Decide how you want to demonstrate your ideas. You can play your variation on an instrument or sing it. Don't worry about the words. Just sing with any syllable you want. Ready? Start planning your variation."

It is helpful to have the music for "Yankee Doodle" written on the chalkboard or on large sheets of paper, so that the children can see the notation as they plan, and so that their changes can be added later with colored chalk or felt marker. If the teacher cannot notate what the students perform, a tape recorder can be used to preserve their creative efforts.

Some of the changes that knowledgeable students might propose are like the following examples:

"Make it sound like minor instead of major."

"Add a repeating note at the start of every beat."

"Fill in the skips between notes that are far apart."

"Change the meter so it sounds like a waltz."

Some of the students' variations will probably contain ambiguities of rhythm and key. But the children are learning from the experience of manipulating musical sounds, and the teacher should be supportive of every child's effort.

[Joe has just played his "Yankee Doodle" variation on the bells, but his creative intention is unclear because he hesitates frequently and seems unsure of the notes on the instrument.]

"Thanks, Joe. Stay right here for a minute, please. You notice, class, that Joe repeated several notes, and took a slower tempo. I like that idea. Joe, let's both hold the beater and I'll play a variation that may be like the one you were trying." [The teacher, with one hand over Joe's, plays the following variation, then joins the class in clapping for Joe as he takes his seat, looking pleased.]

The teacher should encourage the class to sing each child's variation. This will have to be undertaken on a neutral syllable, since the original song words will not accommodate the addition or deletion of notes, or the shifted accents caused by a change of meter. Obvious mistakes can be smoothed over as the creative effort is reproduced by the class. The group participation involves everyone in supporting the novice "composer," and is a means of keeping performance alive in an area that can quickly become merely an intellectual exercise. Finally, the composing project requires the class to think about sounds and their organization, which is the essence of music.

New words

There are hundreds of melodies that have been associated with more than one set of words. Many patriotic songs and church hymns originally had words other than the ones to which they are sung today. At the upper grade levels, students can progress beyond simply substituting humorous words as suggested in Chapter 5, although the occasional writing of a nonsensical text is certainly acceptable.

The value of writing new words for a song is that the activity makes the child notice heavy and light beats, and it requires attention to the way in which word patterns are arranged to conform to those beats. Simply stated, stressed syllables should occur on the beat. When words are written to accommodate the music, the arranger should experiment until the language is as natural as possible, while at the same time supporting the nuances of each musical phrase. Fortunately, older children are generally sensitive to rhythm in both music and language, and they will know when their arranging efforts are comfortable to sing.

Children often assume that song words must rhyme at the end of each line. In fact, however, rhyme is one of the least relevant considerations in selecting words for a song. Rhyme, with its similar-sounding words, may to some extent reinforce the similar-sounding notes at phrase endings in the music. And children can learn about language from the experience of manipulating words to fit a rhyme scheme. But rhyme is essentially an artificial contrivance that too often leads to trite expression and garbled syntax. Since the purpose of song words is to convey ideas and feelings, children should be encouraged to write with a natural flow of language so that they can communicate more fully and accurately in their music.

CREATING NEW MUSIC

Changing someone else's melody does not require the degree of originality that is demonstrated when a composer creates an entirely new piece of music. It is more difficult to develop the original work, because the composer must choose from among so many options of procedure and content. The teacher will need to provide discreet guidance so that the children do not feel overwhelmed by their own inexperience and the array of choices before them.

Providing structure

When students first attempt to create original music, the teacher should provide structure by specifying rather fully the conditions and requirements of the project. Initially the students can be asked to compose a piece involving only the element of rhythm (perhaps a pattern for drum or a one-pitch pattern on some other instrument) or the element of tone quality (probably a series of sounds derived from various vibrating objects). Rather than limiting the students' creativity, such restrictions seem to inspire inventiveness. In San Francisco, for example, contests have been held by cable car bell ringers. The single bell is sounded only when the rope is pulled, so the sounds can be manipulated in no other way. Despite this apparently severe limitation, the bell ringers devise interesting patterns, and a winner is selected. The restrictions provide a structure, and the contest has encouraged creative musical thought.

When children in the upper grades are successful in developing one-element pieces, they can begin using more than one element at a time. The specifications can be more varied, like the following:

1. Write a melody eight measures long, in $\frac{2}{4}$ meter.
2. Use only quarter, eighth, and half notes, and end with a half note.
3. Begin and end on the same pitch.
4. Indicate two changes of loudness.
5. Make the music smooth and songlike.

As the children gain experience in writing according to specifications, the amount of such structure can be reduced for the next creative effort.

The work on composition assignments need not be done in class, although it can be. Children should be encouraged to work on their melodies outside of school time, and they should be reminded that they can try out their music by singing it or by playing it on any instrument they wish. The performing media most likely to be chosen are the more familiar classroom resources: bells, piano, recorder, and voice.

Many children do not know notation well enough to transcribe what they sing or play into music notation. In such cases, if the school has a music specialist, they can perform their melodies for him or her to write down, or they can record them on tape, either at home or at school, for playback at a later time. The inexpensive cassette tape machines that many children own do not adequately convey the clarity and tone quality of a good music performance, but they are satisfactory for the purpose of preserving the children's compositional ideas.

Another solution to the notation problem is for the teacher to accept "homemade" notation systems. That is, the child can devise any set of symbols that serves as a personal reminder of the previously constructed melody. Such a system may not be intelligible to another individual, but it is commendable because it represents the child's ingenuity in solving a problem. Of course, a child can simply remember a melody that has already been thought out, and render it whenever invited to do so. But for accuracy and permanence, conventional notation is the best way of encoding musical sounds.

Setting poetry to music

For many centuries, people have been setting poems and other texts to music. That is generally what happens when a composer writes an art song or opera: the literary aspects are developed first, then music is composed to enrich and enhance the words.

Some children in the upper grades of elementary school can devise music to express a text. Such an activity should be attempted only if and when they have succeeded in the creative activities cited earlier in this chapter. Straightforward poems with clear imagery or distinctive moods are best for the initial efforts at writing music for a particular text. "Who?" by Edith Savage is such a poem. Its first verse is:

With great yellow eyes
Staring through the night
The dark owl watches . . . watches . . .
All night he cries
Who? Who?
I wish I knew.

The teacher might introduce the creative effort like this:

"All the words of 'Who?' are important, but some seem to require more attention than others. For instance, in the first line, which
is more important, 'with' or 'great'? Nancy?"

"'Great,' it seems like," Nancy answers.

"Yes. And what about 'staring' and 'through'? Andy?"

"'Staring' is more important," Andy decides.

[The class continues to look for the more significant words. The
teacher concludes as follows.]

"This poem isn't strongly rhythmic like some we've read. It
doesn't make you want to tap your foot. But there's a kind of rhythm
to it. Imagine that you're going to mark the words or syllables that
receive more emphasis. Let's read the poem through together, so you
can notice the places that you should mark for emphasis."

Determing the rhythm of the words is important, but it is only
one step in preparing a musical setting. The mood of the words is also
significant.

"Let's read the first verse of 'Who?' together again. This time,
think about the expression, the feeling projected by the words. The
poet is trying to communicate something to you." [The class reads
through the verse together expressively.]

"What kind of music should go with that poem? For now, don't
try to decide if your ideas are good or not. Just 'brainstorm.' Brian?"

"Since it's sort of moody and talks about night, I don't think
the music should go very fast," Brian comments.

Holly adds, "You could make 'watches, watches' more important
by having a little silence after each one."

"If the owl 'cries,' then you could make that word special" Wen-
dy suggests. "You could make it louder than the other words, and
maybe higher, too."

"And when an owl says 'Whooo, whooo,' he makes it long and
smooth, sort of slide-y," Roger offers, enhancing his bird call by putting
his hands in his armpits and flapping his elbows, while looking around
at his neighbors for encouragement.

After the class has exchanged ideas and considered suggestions, individuals can begin to set the poem to music. When sufficient time has elapsed, they can present their finished songs in front of the class. As was pointed out in Chapter 5, the process is *not* one in which the group is asked to approve or disapprove of phrases as the teacher puts them on the chalkboard. Consensus is unnecessary because there is not going to be a final amalgamated version that supposedly has been composed by the class. Instead, there should be several compositions, each valued because it represents individual creative effort. The class should listen attentively to each version and comment on the following factors:

Does the music reinforce the mood of the poem?

Does the beat of the music fit easily with the rhythm of the words?

Do the phrases of music seem to belong together, so that the song sounds unified?

Is the song attractive and interesting?

Because the children's musical inventiveness may exceed their ability to write down their ideas, this is a good opportunity for the teacher to extend their understanding of notation. They will see a need for learning the written symbols, and they will be able to use this knowledge immediately, in a personal way, as they try to preserve their compositions.

Composing with tape recorders

This technique, in which taped sounds are manipulated to form a composition, is discussed in Chapter 13. Such compositions present fewer problems in terms of notation and performance, but require the necessary equipment.

Improvisation

The line between composing and improvising is by no means clear. Essentially the difference is that composing takes place over a period of time, during which revisions and trial-and-error procedures are expected. *Improvisation* means making variations on a melody or on certain chord tones, with the music performed spontaneously so that it appears to be made up on the spot.

Improvising is a dual skill, then, because the improviser must be a competent performer as well as an inventive arranger. Both talents are woven together during performance. It is rare to find a student in elementary school who can effectively demonstrate this combination of musical abilities, but many children in the upper grades are intrigued by the process.

Class members who thought up variations on "Yankee Doodle," and were able to sing or play their altered arrangements, have had an initial experience with improvisation, especially if there was minimal time lapse between the idea and the child's performance of it. Most students in the upper grades of elementary school cannot go much beyond that level of improvisational competence, however, unless they receive outside help. There is just not enough time in the typical twice-a-week music class to teach the necessary skills, among which is a good knowledge of harmony.

But all children, even those who were uncertain in their modifying of "Yankee Doodle," can experience the feeling of improvisation by participating in the statement-answer technique suggested in Chapter 5. Although this is not sophisticated improvisation, the use of a short rhythmic or melodic pattern as a statement provides a structure for which the answering child can provide an immediate response. In addition, the temporary nature of the answer—if it is not notated, recorded, or previously planned—may help to put at ease those children who are uncomfortable with the more formal creative activities. They will probably enjoy spontaneously completing a musical phrase like the following:

Comments on a child's musical "answer" might discuss how well it matched the style of the opening phrase, contrasted with it in contour or dynamics, and had a sense of finality.

If children enjoy the experience of creating music, the benefits will be both psychological and practical. Their self-esteem will be enhanced, they will be motivated to improve their musical skills, and they will understand music better.

REVIEW QUESTIONS

1. When children have had little previous experience in creating music, what are the advantages of asking them to add their own ideas to existing pieces of music, in contrast to composing entirely original works?

2. Name a factor that a class should consider in deciding which instruments to assign to a song accompaniment.

3. What qualities in a song make it a good choice for the addition of a chanted part?

4. What is an ostinato?

5. Describe how children can be guided to create variatons on a melody that they already know.

6. What words or syllables in the text of a song should coincide with the beats in the music?

7. How can structure be provided for children in the initial efforts to create original music?

8. a. How can children be helped to discover the more important words in a poem they are setting to music?
   b. How can a class be encouraged to become more aware of the mood of a poem?

9. Many children cannot put their musical thoughts into notation. What are some ways of overcoming this problem?

10. How can improvisation experience be introduced and implemented in a school music class?

ACTIVITIES

1. Examine one or more of the music series books designed for grades 4, 5, or 6. Select a song for which you can create a simple accompaniment involving two instruments. Either tape record your instrumental parts or write them in music notation.

2. Make a few melodic variations in the song you selected for activity 1. Then make a few variations in the rhythm of the song.

3. Write a different set of words for the song you selected, keeping the music in its original form.

4. Select four lines of a poem you find in a music series book, and create a melody that expresses the text. Evaluate your efforts according to the questions raised on page 195. Either tape record your song or put it into notation.

Teaching Rhythm in the Upper Grades

The musical education of children in the primary grades is important because it forms the foundation on which subsequent learning is built. This fact is especially true of rhythm. Few of the aspects of rhythm described in this chapter will be understood by upper elementary level children unless they have a prior understanding of the topics presented in Chapter 6.

Actually, during each year of elementary school there should be some review of fundamental aspects of rhythm such as the feeling of the beat, its subdivisions, and the relative durations of sound and silence. Children tend to forget during vacations, and some never learn the material sufficiently the first time they are taught it. Also, changes of schools, music teachers, and music curricula are inevitable for the many children in America who move from one place to another. The need for review is evident, and is acknowledged by experienced teachers as well as by almost all of the music series books designed for use in elementary schools.

The difference between rhythm instruction in the primary grades and in the upper grades is revealed in the greater complexity of the music studied at the upper levels, and in the increased role of notation. Older children do not outgrow their need for physical experiences with rhythm, however. Trying to learn notation without a sense of what the symbols mean in terms of actual sound and physical sensations—like clapping—is largely a wasted effort.

Chapter 6 emphasized the order in which the basic aspects of rhythm should be taught to young children. For expanding on these ideas with older students, however, the order is not significant. No pedagogical sequence is implied, therefore, by the order in which topics are presented in this chapter.

SIXTEENTH NOTES

Sixteenth notes are a logical extension of the 2:1 ratio of note and rest values presented in the earlier grades. If the children can sense the division of a note into two equal durations, they can sense sixteenth notes as subdivisions of eighth notes. Here is how a teacher might approach the teaching of sixteenth notes, while referring to the song "Clear the Tracks."

CLEAR THE TRACKS

"If you look at 'Clear the Tracks' in your books, you'll see some notes that we haven't talked about before, even though you've sung them in songs already. Bob, what do the new notes look like?"

"I don't know, but I've got a different question," says Bob. "What's a 'bullgine'?"

"It's a short way of saying 'bull engine,'" answers the teacher. "It's the engine of a steam locomotive. Now, back to our unfinished business, Bob, what do the new notes look like in this song?"

"Um . . . they have two bars over them?" Bob guesses.

"That's right. We call them 'beams.' Do you know what those two-beam notes are called, Tina?" [Tina shakes her head.]

"Does anyone know? Sally?"

"Well, in piano they're 'sixteenth notes,'" Sally answers.

"Yes, and they're sixteenth notes in singing, too. They're so short that it takes two of them to last as long as an eighth note. Look at the second measure of the second line of 'Clear the Tracks.' Here's how the pattern should sound." [The teacher claps the pattern of two eighths and four sixteenths, then says in the tempo of the music, while continuing to clap: "Clap-it-with me, here-we-go." The class joins in the pattern clapped by the teacher.]

"Now say the words of the whole song in rhythm, but this time, let your hands clap the *beat* instead of the rhythm of the words. How many claps should we have per measure, Cindy?"

"Six?" guesses Cindy.

"No, that's how many individual sounds are in the measure we just did. To find out the number of beats in each measure, look at the beginning of the song."

"Oh, yeah—two," Cindy corrects herself.

"Of course! Clap the beat with me at this tempo, class, then say the words when I cue you." [All clap together at a moderate tempo, then the teacher says, "Rea-dy, go" in the rhythm of two eighths and a quarter note, and the class recites the words in rhythm.]

After several experiences with a pattern, most children will be able to figure it out when they see it in notation, and not rely on imitation. Again, experience must precede symbolization. It may be helpful to post the following representation of sixteenth-note combinations that occur within the span of a quarter note. A class member can be invited to prepare a similar chart of different patterns in notation that sound the same.

is the same as

is the same as

is the same as

DOTTED NOTES

Although children in primary grades look at music containing dotted notes, they usually have little understanding of what the dot to the right of a note means. A simple approach for teaching dotted notes is to consider the dot as an abbreviation for an additional note value that is half as long as the printed note. Here is one way a teacher, referring to the song "Come, Follow Me," might introduce dotted notes.

COME, FOLLOW ME

"All of us come across shortened words every day in what we read. We see S T for 'street' and M R for 'mister.' We have shortcuts in written music, too. You all know the round 'Come, Follow Me.' Think of the last part that goes 'To the greenwood' three times. As you can see in your books, each word 'to' is a quarter note with a dot after it. The composer could have written the dotted quarter note as two tied notes, like this."

[The teacher draws on the chalkboard.]

Instead, he abbreviates the eighth note into a dot. This particular dot adds half of a beat to the quarter, just as the tied eighth note added that amount.

"The thing to remember is that the dot *to the right* of a note always adds half again as much duration as the note has by itself. Here's another problem for you to figure out." [The teacher writes a dotted half note on the chalkboard.] "Assume that the half note gets two beats, which it usually does. How much does the dot add to it? Jenny?"

"Half a beat," Jenny answers quickly but incorrectly.

"Jenny, you're still thinking of the dot that's beside a quarter note. The value of a dot changes, remember, depending on the note beside it. This one's next to a two-beat note. Half of two beats is . . ."

"One beat," Jenny responds correctly, then whispers "I goofed" to her neighbor.

A few students may be willing to make posters illustrating the effect of a dot on various note values, and these can be displayed in the room as a reminder of the "shorthand dot."

COMPOUND METER

Meter with a beat that divides into twos or multiples of two is called *simple*, and meter with a beat that divides into threes is called *compound*. Compound meters are no more difficult to perform than simple meters, despite the misleading terminology. Several familiar songs are in compound meter—"Pop Goes the Weasel," "When Johnny Comes Marching Home," and "We Three Kings of Orient Are"—and children perform them easily.

"Git Along, Little Dogies" is another song in which each beat divides into threes. When the children can sing it fluently, the teacher can direct their attention to the way in which the rhythm is notated. They may need help in perceiving a fundamental fact about compound meter: the beat is represented by a dotted note.

GIT ALONG, LITTLE DOGIES

American Cowboy Song

1. As I was a - walk - ing one morn - ing for pleas - ure,
2. Now ear - ly in spring - time we round up the do - gies,
3. It's whoop - ing and yell - ing and driv - ing the do - gies,

I spied a cow - punch - er a - rid - ing a - long;
We mark them and brand them and bob off their tails;
Oh, how I wish you___ would go right a - long;

His hat was thrown back and his spurs were a - jing - lin',
We drive up our hors - es and load the chuck wag - on,
It's whoop - ing and punch - ing, git on, lit - tle do - gies,

And as he ap - proached he was sing - ing this song.
Then throw___ the do - gies out on - to the trail.
You know that Wy - o - ming will be your new home.

Refrain

Whoop - ee ti - yi - yo, git a - long, lit - tle do - gies.

It's your mis - for - tune and none of my own;

Whoop - ee ti - yi - yo, git a - long, lit - tle do - gies,

You know that Wy - o - ming will be your new home.

[The teacher writes two sets of three-beamed eighth notes on the board.] "This is the basic rhythm of our song. Clap the beat with me as I point to the first eighth note in each group, and say 'One-and-a, two-and-a' for the eighths. Rea-dy-now, here-we-go." [The class performs the rhythm several times.]

"That's the way. Now, what note value should we assign to the beat? It can't be a quarter note, because that divides into only two eighth notes. The beat can't be a half note, either, because that divides into four eighths. So the beat will have to be the note value that's between a quarter and a half note in duration. What note is that?"

[The room is silent. The teacher finally gives a hint by suggesting that a dotted note can represent a beat.]

"Oh, I know!" Nathan suddenly calls out, beaming broadly. "A dotted quarter note!"

"Good, Nathan! Are there any dotted quarter notes in this song, Melinda?"

"I can't find any," Melinda answers after a moment.

"You're right; there don't happen to be any. It's interesting that we know all about the beat note by hearing this piece and seeing the notation, but it never once occurs in the song."

"Git Along, Little Dogies" contains several of the patterns that typically occur within a beat in ⁶⁄₈ meter:

These can be written on the board and read rhythmically by the class, while a steady beat is maintained and the teacher points to the patterns in random order.

An observant student may notice a discrepancy between the two beats actually felt in a measure of ⁶⁄₈ and the number "6" in the meter signature, which seems to promise six beats in each measure. The teacher can explain the discrepancy by pointing out that there is no provision for indicating a dotted note in the bottom number of a meter signature. So in compound meter the two numbers describe the subdivision of the beats, not the main beats.

Sometimes the tempo of a song in compound meter is so slow that it is in fact performed so that each subdivision serves as the regular beat. In such a situation, the meter signature accurately describes the meter that is actually felt in the music. The tempo determines whether the measure has two or six beats.

Songs in compound meter produce a different effect from those in simple meter. Compound meter gives a feeling of swinging or skipping, while simple meter suggests the balance that occurs when motion alternates between two conditions such as "right-left" or "up-down." The familiar "Wassail Song" contains both types of meters. Changes of meter are encountered occasionally within a song, but they almost always involve merely a change in the number of beats per measure, moving perhaps from $\frac{4}{4}$ to $\frac{2}{4}$ to $\frac{3}{4}$. The "Wassail Song" retains the feel of two-beats-per-measure throughout, but there is a distinct difference in mood between the waltz-like $\frac{6}{8}$ and the march-like $\frac{2}{2}$ sections.

WASSAIL SONG

Traditional English

1. Here we come a - was - sail - ing A - mong the leaves so green,—
2. We are not dai - ly beg - gars That beg from door to door,—

Here we come a - wan - d'ring So fair___ to be seen.
But we are neigh-bors' chil - dren Whom you have seen be - fore.

Love and joy come to you and to you your was - sail too,

And God bless you and send__ you a Hap - py New Year,

And God send you a Hap - py New Year.

BORROWED NOTES

Although most songs maintain standard note proportions, a few pieces of music exhibit rhythmic features that depart from the norm. They are called "borrowed" notes. A common borrowed pattern occurs when a three-note figure is inserted into a beat where a two-note background is expected. This pattern carries the logical name *triplet*. To indicate that three equal notes are being inserted into a time span that would normally contain only two, the music must include the number 3 written over or under the triplet, to indicate the unusual division of the beat. The round "Ev'rybody Loves Saturday Night" contains two triplet figures.

EV'RYBODY LOVES SATURDAY NIGHT

Sierra Leone Round

Ev - 'ry - bod - y   loves   Sat - ur - day   night.
Mo - fe   mo - ni   s'mo   ho____ gbe - ke.

Ev - 'ry - bod - y,   ev - 'ry - bod - y,   ev - 'ry - bod - y,   ev - 'ry - bod - y,
Mo - fe   mo - ni,   mo - fe   mo - ni,   mo - fe   mo - ni,   mo - fe   mo - ni,

Ev - 'ry - bod - y   loves   Sat - ur - day   night.
Mo - fe   mo - ni   s'mo   ho____ gbe - ke.

Other borrowed patterns are encountered occasionally in the repertoire of elementary school music classes. Two notes may occur where three are expected, or five may replace four; any alteration is possible. A borrowed figure may consume more than one beat or less than one. But always there should be a notice of the change, in the form of a number appearing above or below the group of notes. Furthermore, the borrowed figure should not distort the steadiness of the beat when it is performed.

SYNCOPATION

Syncopation occurs in many of the songs sung in elementary school. Essentially, *syncopation* is the removal of an accent where it is expected, or the addition of one where it is not expected.

   In "The Riddle Song," the normal expectation is that the fourth
beat of measures 1, 3, 5, and 7 will have a note that starts at the beginning of the beat, not someplace within the beat. Instead, the last syllable of "cherry," "chicken," and similarly placed words is held over so
that no new syllable occurs at the start of the last beat, where a new
syllable is expected. This creates syncopation. Children can sense it
easily, especially if they examine the song by clapping a steady beat
and compare it with the unusual accents of the words.

THE RIDDLE SONG

American Folk Song

   "The Riddle Song" contains the most common kind of syncopation—the eighth-quarter-eighth pattern. "Down by the Riverside"
features that same figure and two patterns derived from it. All three
patterns reveal the typical "short l-o-n-g short" rhythm of syncopation.

DOWN BY THE RIVERSIDE

Black Spiritual

Gon - na   lay   down   my   sword and   shield___   (clap

clap), down by the ri - ver - side_ (clap clap), down by the ri - ver - side,_   (clap

clap), down by the ri - ver - side,_ Gon-na lay down my sword and   shield_(clap

clap) down by the ri - ver - side,_ oh down by   the   ri - ver - side.

If the claps are omitted and replaced with eighth rests, a typical syncopation device is apparent in the four measures that start with the rest. The clapping actually highlights the syncopation in those measures because it steadies the beat during the unusual rhythm and adds to the spirit of the song.

The third and most recurrent syncopated figure in "Down by the Riverside" is the sixteenth-eighth-sixteenth pattern, which occurs on the words "sword and shield" and "riverside." It is merely a shortened version of the eighth-quarter-eighth pattern—twice as short, in fact, because it consumes only one beat instead of two.

The tie in each of the first six measures is significant in the rendering of syncopation. Theoretically it can be a device for continuing a syncopated figure indefinitely, because it connects into one sound two notes that would otherwise fall into separate, more "normal" groupings. Each series of ties below sounds off-balance because the notes intentionally begin between beats rather than on them.

After the first note above, all sound like quarter notes.

After the first note above, all sound like eighth notes.

Children enjoy the "alive" quality of a spirited syncopated song, and usually have little trouble duplicating the intricacies of its rhythm.

MIXED AND IRREGULAR METERS

By the end of their elementary school experience, children should be aware of the fact that not all music conforms to a few rhythmic patterns and meters. Much of the music familiar to them is regular in its rhythm, but some interesting types of music are not.

One piece in *mixed meter* is "Sim Sala Bim," a Danish folk song that changes meter to accommodate the pattern of the text. Aside from the changes of meter, the song is quite conventional. A teacher might introduce mixed meter this way:

SIM SALA BIM

4. Then came a pretty maiden a- . . . long.

5. She took that poor old crow-ow-ow . . . home.

6. Now comes the happy ending: . . . soup!

"Beverly, which beat in a measure is usually the strongest?"

"The first?" Beverly wonders.

"Okay. Now Beverly, if we change the meter at every measure, will the strong beats fall regularly, like once for every two or three beats?"

"Well, no."

"Why not?"

"'Cause the first beat will land at different places, so you'll have different spacings between all the first beats."

"That's true. So in 'Sim Sala Bim,' some strong beats will occur closer together than others. Let's read the words of the first verse in rhythm, and give a little emphasis to the first beat of each measure."

Children can generally perform mixed meter songs with ease, and recognizing them in notation is no problem because the extra meter signatures are evident after only a brief scan of the music. Reading music in mixed meters is relatively easy if the beat note remains the same; reading is more difficult if the note value of the beat changes often.

Irregular meters, such as those with five or seven beats in a measure, are unusual in traditional American music. "Friend, Since You Want to Take a Wife" is a Greek folk song. Its meter is asymmetrical, and can perhaps best be felt as having three quarter note beats per measure, with an extra eighth note inserted after the first beat. The pattern is not hard to perform after the children get the feel for it. Here is how the meter might be presented.

FRIEND, SINCE YOU WANT TO TAKE A WIFE

M. L. H.   Greek Folk Song

1. Friend, since you want to take a wife, Think how this step will
2. Don't choose a girl with lots of wealth, Rich liv - ing's sure to
3. Don't choose one who is old or young, Too qui - et or too

change your life. I'll ad - vise you, I will tell you
break your health. And of course don't try to take a
quick of tongue. Do not choose a wo - man who is

what to do. Take your time, lis - ten well and think it through.
bride who's poor, or the wolf will be stay- ing at your door.
short or tall. May - be you should not take a wife at all!

"Today we're going to try a song with an unusual meter. I'm writing across the chalkboard the numbers '1' to '7' equally distant from each other. Now say the numbers *evenly,* over and over, rather fast—at this tempo: 1 2 3 4 5 6 7, here-we-go." [The class says the numbers together several times.]

"Fine. This time we'll emphasize certain numbers. I'll circle 1, 4, and 6. Say the numbers again at the same speed as before, only this time 'lean' a bit on 1, 4, and 6. Rea-dy, go." [The class says the numbers again, emphasizing 1, 4, and 6.]

"Now you're getting it! Let's emphasize 1, 4, and 6 even more by clapping on 1, 4, and 6 as we say all the numbers. Don't rush, and keep the numbers coming evenly. Rea-dy, go." [The class says the numbers and stresses the beats by clapping on 1, 4, and 6.]

"Can you just *think* the numbers, but still clap on 1, 4, and 6? Those are the beats in this music. Try it." [The class claps on the beat while thinking the numbers.]

"See how you can 'ride' along with the pattern? I know the three beats aren't equal, but who wants every song to be alike? This time I'll play you a recording of a song called "Friend, Since You Want to Take a Wife." As you listen, softly tap just the beats as you think of the seven numbers."

For a similar drill on another occasion, the class can divide so that some of the children tap or count out the seven background notes while others clap or tap the beats. When the class sings the Greek folk song in its complete form, one or two students can continue to sound the seven background counts on an instrument. As soon as the children are comfortable with the rhythm and text, they can learn the melody in the usual manner.

Actually, students are more likely to encounter mixed meters in the music they hear than in the songs they sing. Many works written in the twentieth century feature mixed meters. One of these is Aaron Copland's *El Salón México*, which is a musical impression of a dance hall in Mexico City. In addition to several Mexican folk tunes and much syncopation, the music contains mixed meters alternating between $\frac{6}{8}$, $\frac{3}{4}$, and $\frac{4}{4}$. It begins with this theme, in which the beats have been marked with lines.

The fourth theme is an alternation between $\frac{6}{8}$ and $\frac{3}{4}$ meter.

El Salón México is a type of music that captures the imagination of ten- and eleven-year-olds.

POLYRHYTHMS

Polyrhythm exists when two or more rhythm patterns occur at the same time. *Polymeter* is similar; it is the presence of two or more metrical patterns at the same time. These aspects of rhythm are seldom encountered in the song literature of elementary school classes, but they are found occasionally in twentieth century art music and in some types of folk music that the children are likely to hear, especially African music.

Presumably the children have had some experience in maintaining a rhythm pattern when others in the class are performing a different pattern. The idea of hearing varied lengths of notes at the same time, therefore, is not entirely new. What happens in most polyrhythmic music is that the patterns are significantly different from one another, and they are likely to be more complex than any the class has previously performed.

The learning of polyrhythmic music can be a creative activity for the class. One way to introduce polyrhythms is to write several rows of numbers, say from 1 to 12, on the chalkboard. Each number represents an eighth note. The children decide the pattern they want for each line by circling the appropriate number. Here is how the chart might look:

1. ①　2　③　4　⑤　6　⑦　8　⑨　10　⑪　12

2. ①　2　3　④　5　6　⑦　8　9　⑩　11　12

3. ①　2　③　4　5　⑥　7　8　⑨　10　⑪　12

4. ①　2　③　④　⑤　6　⑦　⑧　⑨　10　⑪　⑫

When the notes have been circled, the class should set them into notation:

The students then decide which instrument they want for each rhythmic pattern. For example, line 1 might be played on a drum, line 2 on a triangle, line 3 on sticks, and line 4 clapped. Because of the intricacy of the rhythms, it is best in this activity to avoid instruments that are imprecise in their attack and release of sound. Instruments lacking sufficient clarity for this project include chimes and gong, which resonate too long to allow immediate repeating of a note; sand blocks, on which fast notes converge into a continuous brushing sound; and maracas and shakers, which rattle during handling.

When the instruments have been selected, each child needs to practice individually before parts are combined, because it is easy for children to be distracted by another line. Probably only two parts should be combined at first, then a third line and finally a fourth can be added. It may be wise to start with the most difficult part, to give that player more practice and to ensure that the part will remain accurate as other lines are added. Introducing parts one at a time is appropriate not only for practice purposes, but also as a performance technique. Although this polyrhythmic activity will probably never be performed for an audience, the children are experiencing a valid musical procedure by allowing each part to receive attention before it is incorporated into an intricate musical structure.

When children have had experience in performing polyrhythmic music, they usually listen to it more carefully and appreciate it more fully.

READING RHYTHM IN NOTATION

Most of the discussion of rhythm has involved developing an association between what the children hear in the rhythm pattern and what they see in notation. Additional efforts may be necessary to clarify this association.

A visual technique unrelated to the viewing of notation may help children understand the proportionate nature of the note durations that are basic to our rhythmic system. The project is an adaptation of the Cuisenaire rods described in Chapter 6 for the early grades, but developed here in a more sophisticated form. The teacher can follow this procedure:

1. Cut 2″ strips of heavy cardboard into sixteen 16″ lengths.
2. Set two of the strips aside and cut the remaining 14 strips into lengths as specified on this chart; two will be dotted half notes, two will be half notes, and so on:

○	Whole note	16 inches
♩·	Dotted half note	12 inches
♩	Half note	8 inches
♩·	Dotted quarter note	6 inches
♩	Quarter note	4 inches
♪·	Dotted eighth note	3 inches
♪	Eighth note	2 inches
♪	Sixteenth note	1 inch

3. Save the discarded ends of the strips to convert into a reserve supply of smaller note values.

4. Arrange all strips into two identical piles—one set for note values and one set for rests.

5. Make each strip a different color but maintain the same color for the notes and rests that are of equal value.

6. Draw the particular note or rest on each strip, to reinforce what the class is learning.

7. Attach loops of masking tape along the back of each strip, for mounting horizontally onto a chalkboard or large piece of blank cardboard.

The rhythm strips can be used in several ways. Patterns can be displayed for the children to clap or tap at sight, perhaps before attempting to sing them in a song. The advance preparation improves the accuracy with which children sing the song and gives them practice in reading notation in a simplified setting.

Another technique is to display a few measures of rhythmic patterns that include an occasional error for the class to find and identify. A variation of this procedure is to present measures that are not complete, then ask individuals to add the one note or rest that will properly complete the measure.

Finally, the rhythm strips are helpful in illustrating the need for rhythmic accuracy. In the following example, the class has just sung "Clear the Tracks" (p. 199).

> "That first rhythmic figure of a dotted eighth note and a sixteenth needs to be snappier; it sounds too lazy. We'd better find out how to fix it.
>
> "First of all, the pattern lasts for exactly one beat. What note lasts for one beat in this piece, Justin?" [Justin says it's a quarter note.] "Okay, you put up the rhythm strip for a quarter note, please.
>
> "Ted, would you put up right under it the rhythm strips for the dotted eighth note and the sixteenth note?" [The class observes that the two lines are identical in length.]

"Now, class, if you think sixteenth notes in your head, how many of them should go by before you let go of this dotted eighth note?"

[No answers are forthcoming, so the teacher asks Laura to put four sixteenth-note strips directly under the two lines already posted, and to compare the durations of the three lines.]

"Laura says they're all the same length. Is she right, class?" [They agree that she is right.] "Okay, now count the four sixteenths rather fast, like this: *1* 2 3 4 *1* 2 3 4 *1* 2 3 4. Rea-dy, count." [The class counts out the four numbers several times. The process is repeated, each time at a faster speed, until a beat is reached that approximates the tempo of the song "Clear the Tracks."]

"Fine. This time leave out the counts 2 and 3 so that you say only 1 . . 4 1 . . 4 1, and so on. Rea-dy, count." [The class counts, leaving out 2 and 3.]

"Now hold the '1' through the rests; don't make a break before '4.'" [The class says the pattern, holding "1" for three-fourths of a beat.] "Good! That's all there is to it. You're getting the dotted eighth and sixteenth pattern exactly right. Just keep that same accuracy for the first two notes of 'Clear the Tracks.' Sing the whole song now, and pay special attention to the rhythm at the beginning."

There is little consensus among teachers regarding the role of rhythm syllables in the upper grades. If the children learned them in the primary grades and still find them helpful, they can be continued. For most older students, however, they become less useful. In fact, complicated patterns are learned more easily without rhythm syllables.

Some teachers insist that their students learn to count out rhythms by assigning the proper beat number and particular syllables to every pattern. Others believe that counting systems are not as important as many other aspects of music instruction in elementary school. If the children respond to rhythm energetically, produce it accurately, and create it with enjoyment, they are learning this basic element of music.

REVIEW QUESTIONS

1. What are the similarities and differences between rhythm instruction in the primary grades and in the upper grades?

2. What underlying idea should the students understand about the relationship of sixteenth notes to other note values?

3. What are some procedures for guiding students in their understanding of dotted notes?

4. What is the fundamental difference between compound meters and simple meters? What are some methods for making the children more aware of this difference?

5. Sometimes $\frac{6}{8}$ meter is performed with two beats per measure, and sometimes it is performed with six beats per measure. What determines the number of beats that should be felt when performing in $\frac{6}{8}$ meter?

6. How can a performer recognize a borrowed pattern in the notation of a song?

7. In addition to a verbal definition of syncopation, what teaching procedures might help children to become more aware of syncopation in music they hear or perform?

8. How can a teacher help a class to improve in its performance of an irregular, asymmetrical beat pattern in a song?

9. What procedures are appropriate for teaching the class about polyrhythms?

10. What visual material can aid children in their understanding of note and rest values?

11. To what extent are rhythm syllables useful in reading rhythms in the upper grades?

ACTIVITIES

1. Find a song that contains one or more sixteenth note patterns. Teach yourself to sing or play the song. Then decide how you would teach children in the upper grades to sing the patterns correctly. Write down the procedures you would follow.

2. Examine a music series book and find at least five songs that contain syncopation. Select one, and decide how you would teach the syncopated rhythms to upper grade children. Write a brief outline of your plans.

3. Create a short polyrhythmic pattern similar to the one that appears on page 212. After circling the numbers, write the pattern in conventional notation, then decide what instruments might play it. Try to find some people who will form a "combo" to perform your creation.

4. Prepare a set of rhythm strips with lengths varied in proportion to the note and rest values each represents. Arrange them in various combinations to create two measures in $\frac{4}{4}$ meter, two measures in $\frac{6}{8}$ meter, and two measures in $\frac{5}{4}$ meter.

Teaching Timbre
in the Upper Grades

The process of encouraging children to notice differences in tone quality continues beyond the primary grades. The concept of timbre and its role in music is enlarged and refined as the students progress through the upper grades.

VOCAL TIMBRES

Opportunities for examining timbres are evident when the class decides on the type of singing tone that best reflects the mood of a song. For example, should the singers try to achieve a mellow, warm sound? Should they try to sound angry or joyous? How does a singer change the timbre of his or her voice to achieve a desired effect? When the students listen to a recording of a song or choral work, they should notice the vocal timbres that result when the voice is varied for dramatic effect.

In the primary grades, the teacher encourages the children to notice if the music is sung by a male or female. They should expand their powers of observation in the upper grades by learning to recognize the differences in timbre among the four basic divisions of adult voices. From highest to lowest pitch range, they are the soprano and alto (female) and the tenor and bass (male) voices.

The ability to distinguish among voice types must usually be learned by listening to recordings, because trained adult singers are seldom available to perform in elementary schools. It is especially helpful if the class can compare recordings of the same piece sung by different types of voices. Here is how such an example might be introduced:

"The other day we listened to a recording of two songs that were sung by men who sing in different ranges of the male voice. The lower voice, I hope you remember, is called the 'bass' and the higher voice for the male singer is called the—what?" [Several class members volunteer that it is the tenor voice.] "Yes, the 'tenor.' There's a similar division in women's voices. Remember, the voices are women's voices, *not* girls'. Girls at your age have very similar singing voices, and none of you girls has an alto voice. Only a few of you eventually will, and not until about the time you finish high school.

"To let you hear the two types of women's voices, I'll play a song in which both the *alto*—the lower of women's voices—and the *soprano*—the higher of women's voices—sing the same melody. As you might guess, they sing it at different levels of pitch. Barry, which woman's voice will sing the lower version of the melody—the alto or the soprano?"

"You said the alto," Barry recalls.

"Right. The song is from the musical work *Messiah,* by George Frideric Handel. This particular song is called 'He Shall Feed His Flock.' It conveys the feeling of trust in a leader who will take care of his people as a shepherd takes care of his sheep. There's nothing flashy about the music; it just moves at a relaxed pace, sounding comfortable and confident."

The recordings that are provided with the music series books contain songs sung by men, women, and children with unchanged voices. By comparing the voices of adult sopranos and children, the students can learn to distinguish between the timbres of these two types of voices, even though they sing in the same general pitch range. Besides examples of solo singing, the students should hear choral groups such as boy choirs, women's and men's glee clubs, and mixed choruses, so that they can compare the tone qualities in these vocal ensembles.

A more subtle aspect of vocal timbre is the way in which slight changes suggest a different style of singing. As the children learn about other cultures in their social studies classes, they should hear examples of singing from those geographical areas. They will begin to discover the vast differences among singing styles in the myriad cultures of the world. Music series books for the upper grades usually include units on African, Arabian, Oriental, Indian, and American Indian music, to name a few. The children should learn to recognize at least the general characteristics of a culture's vocal music so that, for example, they can identify African singing style and timbre when they hear it. Not only are there differences among cultures and ethnic groups; there are variables within them. The children can appreciate this diversity when they realize how many timbres are employed in singing the various types of music heard in present-day America from country-western music to opera.

Although words are inadequate to describe differences in tone quality, the students should try to find meaningful descriptions for the timbres they hear. For example, they may decide that one timbre is "thin and pinched" and that another is "warm and easy." Their need to find the right word helps them to focus their attention on timbre, which is often a neglected aspect of music as far as the listener is concerned. It is revealing for the class to realize that their descriptions of timbre at a particular passage can almost double for descriptions of the mood at that moment, demonstrating again that there is an affinity between timbre and mood.

INSTRUMENTAL TIMBRES

A good opportunity to promote awareness of timbre occurs when the children add an instrumental accompaniment to a song. Whether they reproduce an instrumental part recommended in the music book or create one of their own, they should consider the characteristics of instrumental sounds and the appropriateness of those sounds for a particular song.

Most music series books contain one or more units on orchestral instruments. These units include photographs and brief descriptions, along with recordings of musical works that feature particular instruments. Older children should become increasingly adept at recognizing instruments by sight and sound.

One work stands out for its musical quality and for the clarity with which it presents orchestral instruments. It is *The Young Person's Guide to the Orchestra* by the twentieth-century English composer Benjamin Britten. Not only does it feature each instrument and each section of the orchestra; it does so by means of finely crafted music that is interesting to every kind of listener—adult or child, musician or nonmusician. In many performances, narration is incorporated into the music, and written commentary is provided with almost all of the several available recordings of the work. Here is how a teacher might introduce it to the class.

"Here's a piece of music for orchestra that's written to show you how the various instruments sound. You won't have any trouble know-

ing which instrument or section is playing, because the narrator on the
recording tells you just before you hear the instrument. Listen for the
theme-and-variation form. You'll hear a solid-sounding main melody,
then many variations on it.

"The music was composed by a man named Benjamin Britten,
who lived in England in this century. For the theme he took the melody of a famous English composer named Henry Purcell, who lived 250
years earlier. I'll play the first half minute of it for you so that you can
get the theme in your mind." [The teacher plays the first 30 seconds
of *The Young Person's Guide to the Orchestra*.]

"That's the theme. This time I'll go back to the beginning and
we'll listen for about 12 or 13 minutes, so that you can hear each instrument play its solo variation. We can hear the rest of the music on
another day."

The last three minutes of *The Young Person's Guide to the Orchestra* is a fugue, which is a type of music in which the main melody
is presented by one part after another in follow-the-leader fashion.
It is a rather distinct section, so for study purposes, either the theme
and variations or the fugue may be heard alone without seeming to
be incomplete.

In addition to music created for an entire orchestra, the class
should hear music featuring particular sections of the orchestra. There
are many fine works for string orchestra, for woodwind quintet, and for
brass ensembles. Even the percussion section has been treated as an independent performing medium. Then there is the wind band, which has
immediate appeal, especially when introduced through one of John
Philip Sousa's famous marches. There are also several recordings of
more sophisticated music for wind band, such as Symphony No. 4
by Alan Hovhaness.

As fine as recorded performances are, they are not as effective
with children as live performances and personal demonstrations of
instruments. In larger communities the local orchestra often provides
children's concerts. If well managed, these programs are a valuable addition to the children's musical and cultural education. Also of value,
again if well planned, are programs presented in the elementary schools
by secondary school music groups. The students in these organizations
benefit from performing before an audience, and the listeners benefit
if the program includes music of quality and is not intended simply
to entertain.

An effective way to teach about instruments is to plan classroom
appearances by the children who play instruments. Such appearances
create much interest in the class because they feature the children's
peers, and they give the performer considerable status. The music performed need not be complicated or polished, but it should be played
competently. Instrumentalists who study privately outside of school

will probably have a few solos ready to play at any given time. Children are usually impressed just to hear a friend play on an instrument a song that they have been singing in class. The player can play the melody or learn the simple descants and accompaniments that most series books provide for student instrumentalists. An instrumental music teacher may be able to help the student prepare the music, but if that is not possible, an elementary school music specialist can do so.

Inexperienced instrumentalists may not realize that their pitches can differ from those printed for the singers. Violin and flute pitches will double the singers' notes exactly, but trumpet and clarinet players will need to raise all their notes one step higher than notated if they are to match the vocal line exactly. That is because these are transposing instruments, and the note that is heard is not the one that is seen on the page. Music for viola, cello, and trombone—plus a few instruments that elementary children seldom play—is written in clefs different from the treble clef that prevails in children's songs. The teacher, therefore, should remind young players to consider the factors of transposition and clef differences as they prepare their parts. This will prevent the dissonance caused by unanticipated pitch discrepancies, and will help to ensure a good experience in front of the class.

Most children are familiar with the timbre of the piano, but few of them are as well acquainted with the sound of the pipe organ or harpsichord. Again the music series books are helpful, with their pictures and their recordings of music played by these instruments. The students should try to hear the differences between a pipe organ and the electronic organ that is sold in music stores and heard in commercial establishments. Although both bear the name "organ," they sound quite different.

Upper grade students should listen analytically to popular instruments such as guitar, electric guitar, and accordion. The differences between the two types of guitars are as great as between the two types of organs. As is true in the case of singing, instruments are played differently depending on the style of music. The clarinet is played with one timbre in a symphony orchestra and with another tone quality in a jazz band. The students can compare the two styles of clarinet playing by listening to the opening portion of Gershwin's *Rhapsody in Blue* and the third movement of Rachmaninoff's Symphony No. 2.

CREATING MUSIC WITH A TAPE RECORDER

The composing of short "sound pieces"—music created out of different timbres and arranged into patterns—was suggested for children in the primary grades. The basic idea is a good one, although the approach to such compositions needs to be somewhat different in the upper grades. Students in fifth and sixth grade do not want to do something in the same way they did when they were first- and second-graders. The change of emphasis can involve either a tape recorder or an electronic synthesizer. These instruments add a new dimension to the creation of "sound pieces." Because few elementary schools can afford synthesizers, and because special knowledge is required to teach music with the instrument, the synthesizer will not be presented in this book.

Working with a tape recorder is attractive to some students. In fact, it often seems to appeal most to those who are not interested in singing. For purposes of creating musical compositions with tape, a reel-to-reel tape recorder is required. A cassette recorder is adequate to record the sounds, but they must be transferred to a reel if anything is to be done with them.

To create music with a tape recorder, the students must learn a few techniques for manipulating tape. One of these is the ability to edit and splice tape. The procedure requires a sharp razor blade or knife and splicing tape. A splicing bar helps, but it is not required.

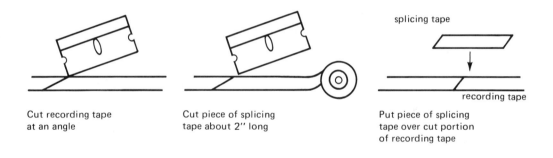

Cut recording tape at an angle

Cut piece of splicing tape about 2" long

Put piece of splicing tape over cut portion of recording tape

The students also need to know how to cover one of the recording heads with masking tape. The steps are as follows: cover one head with tape and record the tape on one track. Then wind the tape back to the beginning. Uncover the first head and cover the other. Record the tape again with different sounds. Rewind the tape to the beginning, and then play the tape with both heads uncovered. This will produce a counterpoint of two simultaneous lines of sound.

Sounds can be altered by changing the speed of the tape and recording the new sounds on a second tape recorder. Most reel-to-reel tape recorders allow for more than one speed. If no change is possible on a particular recorder, a hand held lightly on the feeding reel will slow down the speed and create a new effect.

Tape recorder music does not involve conventional music notation. A composer may assign symbols to certain aspects of an electronic piece, but these symbols are not music notation in the sense that some-one could re-create the music by reading the symbols. Instead, they are like road maps or plans for the composition. Actually, notation is un-necessary in this medium. Because the final tape is the completed work, the music is performed merely by playing the tape. There is no per-former serving as intermediary between the composer's intentions and the listener's perception of the piece.

Creating music by tape recorder is both very easy and very dif-ficult. It is easy to record and "mess around" with a series of sounds. It is difficult, however, to construct a meaningful musical composition, whether with tape or through conventional media. Creating music with a tape recorder requires skill and judgment. In order for a tape com-position to be meaningful, the sounds must have some logic and form. This is achieved, like the orderliness in all music, by conceiving patterns for the phrases and larger sections of the music, or by following the structure suggested by a "program" or story. The tendency of most young composers is to pour too many sounds and ideas into a short composition. Most students will be more successful in creating a work on tape if they are limited to only a few types of sounds for any one composition.

Preparing tape recorder music is best done by individuals or very small groups, not by the entire class working en masse. The process consists of three phases: (1) collecting the sounds on tape; (2) listening to the taped sounds and labeling them; and (3) organizing the sounds to create a composition. Here is how the process might be started:

> "Do any of you have tape recorders at home, either cassette or reel-to-reel? . . . A few of you. Good. I'll tell you people how to prepare tapes at home, but the rest of you need to listen because you'll do the same thing next Tuesday in class.
>
> "Here's the first step in making your own taped composition. Re-cord some sounds on a reel or cassette that you can bring to school. Pick any five sounds that you think would be interesting in a composi-tion. You can record your dog barking, a car starting, someone walking across a kitchen floor in hard-soled shoes, a water faucet running—any-thing you want. You can have the sound source very close to the micro-phone or moderately far away. Record each sound for three or four seconds.
>
> "When you've collected five sounds, write down on a piece of paper what they are. Then listen to your sounds on playback and write on the same paper the words that you think describe each one. You can use words like 'rough,' 'choppy,' 'delicate,' or anything else that means something to you.
>
> "Bring your tape to class on Tuesday. We'll have machines here, so you don't need to bring any from home. We'll record your sounds

onto a reel-to-reel recorder through a patch cord. If you don't have a
recorder at home, don't worry. You can use one of the school's recorders during class next Tuesday. Sorry, but we can't let anyone take
the school machines home."

The procedure just described has the virtue of involving each child in
the first two of the three phases: collecting sounds, and listening to and
labeling them.

When tapes are prepared during the music period, it will save time
if a few groups of two or three students can go with tape recorders into
other areas of the building, or even outdoors, to collect sounds. As in a
scavenger hunt, there should be a time limit on the length of their
search. Allowing them to record outside the classroom will reduce the
number of distractions, both for themselves and for those who are
working on other projects in the room.

The third phase of the composing process is more challenging because it involves more equipment and long-range planning. Here is how
the organizing of the sounds might be undertaken:

"Well, now, we've transferred all of your sounds onto these two
reels of tape. Before we break up into teams, let's do a little bit of
thinking and organizing together, so that you can see how it goes. You
certainly don't *have* to do it this way, of course, but it's a good way to
get started.

"First, look over the master sheet of paper that lists the source of
each sound, describes it, tells which reel it's on, and tells where it is:
the three-digit numbers indicate inches from the beginning of the tape.

"Then make a plan in your mind or on paper about how you'll
put the sounds together. For instance, if you want a rondo, your main
theme might be sound no. 2, which is listed as a 'wild wobble,' and
sound no. 4, which is described as 'steady and dull.' I'll show you later
how to make two sounds occur at the same time. Then find another
sound to contrast with the main theme, say sound no. 7, which is a
'tapping effect.'"

[The teacher proceeds to describe a five-section rondo that probably would last about 20 seconds. Since there is time and the class is
attentive, the teacher demonstrates on two machines how the final tape
or "composition" is developed.]

"That gives you an idea how the process works. Any questions
about the machinery itself?"

"What if somebody presses the wrong button and erases everything?" Blair asks worriedly.

"Yeah," interrupts Theresa, "And what if the tape starts going
real fast and comes off the round thing?"

[The teacher quiets their misgivings in a direct and brief manner.]

"Now we'll form teams of two people. You can work on the equipment whenever the two of you have time, like when you've finished your other assignments, or before or after school. If you compose during class time, you'll need to listen on the earphones so that you don't disturb others. And be sure not to shout when you wear the earphones! For some reason, people talk more loudly when they have earphones on. Now let's decide who'll be partners."

At some point, the teacher must show the class how to splice tape and how to create two sounds simultaneously by covering one head on the recorder. Also, a sufficient number of days must be allowed so that the teams have enough time with the equipment to create the piece they want. A week is often needed for this.

When the students have completed their sound compositions and have shared them with the class, they will benefit from listening to examples of electronic music, to see how recognized composers handle nonconventional sounds. A short section of a work by Subotnik, Luening, or Babbitt should be played enough times so that the class can recognize what the composer is doing. The class members may wish to compare the composer's sound composition with the ones they themselves have created.

REVIEW QUESTIONS

1. How can students be guided in learning to recognize the various types of singing voices and styles?

2. Although no words can adequately describe a timbre, why is it educationally worthwhile to encourage children to attempt to describe timbres?

3. What is one benefit of teaching children about tone quality through performances in class rather than through recorded music?

4. What are some ways in which live performances can be provided for elementary school children?

5. How can children be helped to realize that most instruments use different timbres when playing different types of music?

6. What is the procedure for tape recording two different sounds so that they will be heard simultaneously?

7. How can different timbres and tonal effects be collected and formed into a composition on a tape recorder?

8. Why is music notation unnecessary for music created on the tape recorder?

9. What is one way in which students can learn to create short compositions using the tape recorder?

ACTIVITIES

1. Locate two or three recordings of songs that feature different types of voices. Briefly outline how you would present the recordings to a fifth-grade class.

2. Develop a short unit on teaching the instruments of *one* section of the orchestra to an upper-grade class. Mention specific pictures, recordings, and live demonstrations that are included.

3. In a music series book for the upper grades, find two songs for which the textbook authors have written simple descants or accompanying parts for instruments.

4. Prepare a short composition with tape recorder. Record five sounds from around the classroom. Re-record one sound at a different speed. Combine two sounds on different tracks so that they sound at the same time. Then create a short composition using the original and altered sounds.

Teaching Melody
in the Upper Grades

The process of making children more knowledgeable about melody should start in the primary grades. Through their singing of songs at that level they experience the concept of melody, learn the difference between steps and leaps, and begin to notice phrases. In the upper grades they examine more aspects of melody, learn how melodies function in different pieces of music, and continue to improve in their ability to sing and listen.

WHOLE AND HALF STEPS

In the primary grades the children are introduced to the idea that every note in a melody is either a step or a leap from its neighbor (if it is not simply repeated). This concept of interval is further developed in the upper grades as the students learn to distinguish between whole and half steps. A *half step* is the smallest pitch distance possible on a keyboard instrument, and a *whole step* is a pitch interval equaling two half steps. Most people can easily hear the difference between whole and half steps. The two sizes of steps are apparent on a keyboard because half steps are adjacent white and black keys; where there is no black key, as between B-C and E-F, that distance is also a half step. Adjacent lines and spaces in the staff do not indicate whether the distance is a half or whole step, however. It takes a little figuring to determine whether notes on adjacent lines and spaces are whole or half steps.

A piano or xylophone-like instrument is useful in interval practice not only because it presents consecutive pitches visually, but also because the students' playing of intervals provides physical reinforcement of the distances they see and hear.

The teacher can ask a child to play two pitches either a half step or a whole step apart so that the class can determine, from listening, which was played. To engage an additional student in the interval identification activity, the teacher may display a representation of a keyboard and invite a child to point out the half and whole steps as they are played by a classmate. The teacher can say "Start on G," the instrumentalist plays that note plus one other, and the "pointing" person must decide whether the sound went up or down, and how far it went from the initial G. For variety, the process can be reversed so that the pointer indicates a note on the simulated keyboard and directs the player to "go up a whole step" or "go down a half step"; the class decides whether the directive was carried out properly. The first note need not be named in this procedure, because everyone, including the player, can identify it visually according to its placement on the posted keyboard. When *sounds* are to be identified, however, and either placed into notation or pointed out on a displayed keyboard, the listeners must be told the letter name of at least the first sound. A few persons can name any random pitch they hear, without reference to other information, but this ability is rare even among the adult population and should not be expected of elementary school children.

SCALES AND KEY

Scales and the concept of key, or tonality, are discussed together here, because the two aspects of music are interrelated. A *scale* is an index of the tones occurring in a piece of music, or, more properly, "a series of pitches ascending and descending in a prescribed pattern of intervals." A *keynote* or *tonal center* is "the pitch on which a scale is built and toward which the music tends to gravitate." But these definitions have little meaning unless they relate to actual experiences with music. Of the two concepts, scales are generally easier for children to comprehend, because a lineup of notes is more concrete than the concept of key, which is an "impression" or "effect" created when notes are interrelated. It is discussed in Chapter 15 as an aspect of harmony.

Some songs are especially suitable for conveying the idea of scales. "The Singing School" round is unusual in the fact that it features both a complete ascending and a complete descending scale. Here is how a teacher might present "The Singing School" to introduce the concept of scales.

THE SINGING SCHOOL

Traditional Round

From *101 Rounds for Singing,* published by World Around Songs, Burnsville, North Carolina, 1965.

"Now that we've sung this song, did you hear anything different about the pitches? If you don't remember from the sound, look over the music carefully to see what's different about it. The rhythms are easy, but what about the order of the notes? I'll give you a minute to study the notation by yourselves. .... All right, who's found something unusual in this song? Ron?"

"Well, in the fifth line the notes don't jump around very much. They just go straight up for a while."

"That's right! It's a scale beginning on C. Sing the notes with me, class, with their letter names: C D E F G A B C." [The class sings the scale.] "Does a scale appear anywhere else in the song?"

After a pause, Linda volunteers, "Yeah, in the first line. The notes go down, but a couple of them stop and repeat along the way."

"Good, Linda. Why don't you and Ron go to the bells and play the scales you discovered. Ron, play yours first. Class, sing the letter names along with him." [The scale is sung by the class.] "Linda, you don't need to repeat notes at those two places in your scale. Just play them once in order; class, sing." [The scale is sung in descending order.]

"Now let's do the song again. Notice how the notes all seem to be related to the sound of the scales."

MAJOR AND MINOR SCALES

The arrangement of half and whole steps between the notes in a scale determines the type of scale. In music of the Western world, most scales proceed through seven different notes to the sound that has the same letter name and occurs an octave above or below the starting pitch. The pattern that is called *major* has these distances between its pitches as the notes ascend: whole step, whole step, half step, whole step, whole step, whole step, and half step. The fact that its intervals are not equal is evident in a "stairstep" drawing of the major scale pattern.

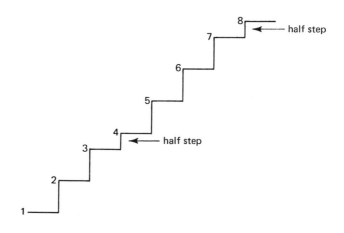

The other type of scale commonly found in the music of Western culture is called *minor*. It occurs in three slightly different forms, but elementary school students do not need to distinguish among them. They should certainly recognize the basic sound of minor, however. In its natural form, the pattern is this:

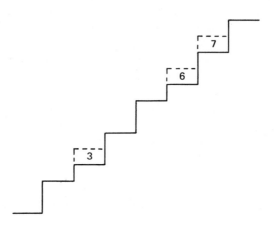

The dotted lines in the drawing show at what pitch steps 3, 6, and 7 would be heard if the scale were major. The main difference between major and minor scales occurs at the third step, which is one half step lower in minor. (Notes near the upper end of a minor scale are sometimes altered, but the lowered third step is the consistent feature by which minor keys can be recognized aurally and visually.) The difference between major and minor scale passages can be heard with a little practice, and students should learn to distinguish by ear between major and minor scales and chords.

An easy first step in learning to compare the difference in sound between major and minor keys is to sing "Go Tell Aunt Rhody" in both tonalities. The conventional version, which is in major, is shown on page 233.

The teacher can write the music on the board (and the words, if they are unfamiliar to the class) and proceed as follows:

> "Here's a song in a major key. It looks like simple stuff, but don't worry—I'll take care of that. Sing it through with me." [The class sings all verses.]

> "That's the way! You either have good memories from singing this song in the primary grades, or you're turning into good sight-singers. Now that you've performed this piece in its traditional major setting, you're ready to transpose the music into the corresponding minor key.

GO TELL AUNT RHODY

Pennsylvania Dutch Song

Go   tell Aunt Rho - dy,   go   tell Aunt Rho - dy,

go   tell Aunt Rho - dy, the   old gray goose is   dead.

2. The goslings are crying . . .

3. The gander is weeping . . .

"You do this simply by lowering the *third step* of the scale from E to E♭ whenever you come to it in the song. Seth, would you come to the board and write downward-pointing arrows over every E as a reminder to the class. The arrow will mean two things: 'This is the note!' and 'Sing it lower!'"

[Seth finds every E, with some coaching from the class, and draws an arrow over each one. As he works, the teacher explains further to the class.]

"E is what step number in this key?" [A few people recall that it is step 3.] "If E is step 3, what note is step 1, where we would start the scale for this song?"

[The class is silent, so the teacher offers help.] "From E, which is step 3, count downward '3 2 1.' Or go backward in the alphabet E D C. C is the keynote."

"Seth has our music ready now. Sing the song in minor this time. Here's your E-flat starting note." [The class sings all verses in minor.]

"Do you notice a difference in sound between this minor version and the original major version? We'll do it again, just for fun. But first, Jim, would you come up and put a flat sign in front of every E? That's how the note E♭ should really look."

[Jim hesitates to leave his seat, but a friend traces a flat in the air, and Jim draws that symbol satisfactorily.]

"Thanks, Jim. This time, class, notice the words and make the music sad! Make me cry with your singing!" [The class laughs and sings the song.]

The students' feeling for key, whether major or minor, should be reinforced frequently. They should be able to sing a scale, recognize aurally and visually whether a phrase stops on the keynote or not, and sing the nearest keynote from any scale step in a song.

CONTOUR

Students in the upper grades should become increasingly aware of the shape or *contour* of melodies. This aspect of music considers the pitches of a melody not as they relate to a key center, but as they relate to one another in the flow of melody. Contour is determined by two factors: direction (does the pitch move up or down or stay the same?) and interval (does the pitch move by step or by leap?) When students notice the contour of a melody, they are scanning a line of music in a way that will help in reading music and in analyzing form.

The Russian folk song "Minka" has a rather even contour with many repeated notes, except for two measures. Here is how a teacher might lead a class to notice the melodic features of "Minka."

MINKA

English words by W. S. Haynie   Russian Folk Song

From E. Boardman et al., *Exploring Music,* Book 6. Words copyright © 1975 by Holt, Rinehart & Winston, Publishers.

"I'm drawing eight blank measures on the board; here are the bar lines. I'm going to make a dot for every pitch in 'Minka,' then one of you can come up and 'connect the dots' to show us the shape or contour of the melody. Sing 'Minka' with me now, on 'la.'"

[The class sings as the teacher draws a dot for every note, in time with the music. By the end of the song, the board reveals this pattern of dots:]

"Who wants to come up now and connect the dots so we can check the contour of the song? Okay, Sheila." [Sheila draws the lines.] "That's good. Thanks.

"Ellen, how would you describe the contour for the first eight measures of 'Minka'? Is it rather even? Jagged?"

"Well, it doesn't move a whole lot. I'd say it's pretty even," Ellen decides.

"Okay, Ellen. Now Clifford, why do you suppose measure 7 has a different contour from the other seven measures?"

Clifford shrugs and speculates, "Maybe if people aren't paying attention, they'll all of a sudden notice what's going on when the music gets to that place."

"Could be," the teacher agrees. "If the music didn't move around, the song probably wouldn't be as interesting. To test your theory, Clifford, we'll all sing the first eight measures, but this time in measure 7 we'll repeat the first note four times while singing 'Min-ka, Min-ka.'"

The class can compare the contours of various songs. "Minka" and "Tum-Balalaika" present two very different contours. When the children have learned the latter song, the teacher can solicit their ideas as to how its melodic contour compares with that of "Minka," and what features in the music might account for the difference.

"Then the consensus of the class is that 'Minka' has a smoother contour and generally smaller intervals than 'Tum-Balalaika.' You say the melody's easier in 'Minka.' Is there any reason for this, do you think? Tyler?"

"Uh, well . . . Maybe this guy's serenading to Minka on a guitar and he doesn't know how to play very well, so he has to make up an easy song." [The class considers this a likely reason and regards Tyler approvingly.]

Francesca ventures, "Maybe the reason 'Tum-Balalaika' has so much variety in the contour is to remind us that there's so much variety in the world, with stones and fire and love and everything."

SEQUENCE

"Tum-Balalaika" features several phrases in which a pattern of pitches is repeated immediately at a different pitch level. This technique is called *sequence*. It is especially clear in the first two lines of the song, when the four measures begin first on A, and then on G. With help, the students should be able to discover other examples of sequence in this and other songs.

TUM-BALALAIKA

Jewish Folk Song
Arranged by Mary Val Marsh

Boys: Maid - en, maid - en, can you ex - plain, What can
Girls: Fool - ish boy, I can___ ex - plain, A stone can

grow with - out an - y rain? What___ can burn for
grow with - out an - y - rain. True love can burn for

man - y a year? What___ can cry, and shed not a tear?
man - y a year. A sad heart can cry, and shed not a tear.

Refrain

Tum - ba - la, Tum - ba - la, Tum - ba - la - lai - ka, Tum - ba - la,

Tum - ba - la, Tum - ba - la, Tum - ba - la - lai - ka, Tum - ba - la,

Tum - ba - la, Tum - ba - la - lai - ka, Tum - ba - la - lai - ka,

Tum - ba - la, Tum - ba - la - lai - ka, Tum - ba - la,

Tum - ba - la - lai - ka, Tum - ba - la - lai - ka, Tum - ba - la, tum!

tum, Tum - ba - la, tum, Tum - ba - la, Tum - ba - la, tum!

From Mary Val Marsh et al., *The Spectrum of Music* 1975, Macmillan Publishing Co., Inc. Used by permission.

ALTERATIONS AND DECORATIONS

A composer or performer can change a melody simply by adding ornamental or decorative notes. If the ornamentation is the idea of the composer, the added notes are written into the notation. Sometimes, however, the singer or instrumental soloist adds them extemporaneously. This is done particularly by singers in the folk and popular idiom.

"I'm on My Way" is one of the few songs in the music series books that contains *grace notes*. In appearance, a grace note is about half the size of a regular note, and it has a slash running diagonally through the stem and flag. Theoretically, a grace note has no rhythmic value, although in fact it must consume a small amount of time. To sing a grace note, the performer must "flick off" the note quickly, so that it sounds like a catch in the voice.

I'M ON MY WAY

Words Adapted by Venoris Cates   Afro-American Spiritual

3. I asked my brother to come with me.
   I asked my brother to come with me.
   I asked my brother to come with me.
   I asked my brother, My Lord, to come with me.

From Mary Val Marsh et al., *The Spectrum of Music* 1975, Macmillan Publishing Co., Inc. Words used by permission of Venoris M. Cates.

Decorative notes are more common in instrumental than in vocal music. Phrases that are conceived instrumentally are usually hard to sing, but the class should hear and study at least a few examples of instrumental music to observe how melodies are enhanced through ornamentation. Here is how a teacher might introduce Chopin's *Fantasie-Impromptu*, Op. 66:

> "As we sing 'I'm on My Way' again, notice those two short, quick notes that are called 'grace notes.'" [The class sings the song.] "The same kind of ornamentation also occurs in instrumental music. Here's a work for piano by a composer named Chopin. His name is spelled this way." [The teacher writes the name on the board.] "But it's pronounced 'Show-pan.'
>
> "This piano piece is in three rather long sections. There are a lot of fast notes in the first section. The music is supposed to sound made up. In fact, the title of this piece is 'Fantasie-Impromptu,' which means 'imagined and made up on the spot.'
>
> "The second section is more singable, and that's the melody to which Chopin adds a lot of decorative notes. The third section returns to the same music that occurred in the first section. Listen carefully to this music now, especially to the decorative notes that Chopin adds to the middle section."

CHROMATIC NOTES

Chromatic notes are those altered by placing to the left of the note head a flat (♭), sharp (♯), or natural (♮) sign to indicate a departure from the prevailing key signature. The signs themselves are called *accidentals* when they are applied for this purpose. Although children in elementary school do not have the time to delve into the harmonic implications of chromaticism, they should be aware of this half-step pitch change and its effect on the melody.

"I'm on My Way" contains two chromatic notes. For example, in measure 7 the sharp sign turns the third note into G♯, which is not a scale tone in the key of F major. Within a span of two notes, the sharp is canceled by the natural sign so that the note once again conforms to the key signature. In measure 11, the natural turns the third note into B♮, a sound that is one half step higher than the B♭ indicated by the key signature. The flat in the next measure serves merely as a reminder that the prevailing key signature is in effect again. If the students sing those passages slowly, it will be easier for them to notice the half step difference in pitch between the G♯ and G♮, and between the B♮ and B♭.

A chromatic note can signify a change of key, or it can serve merely as a passing decoration. If the chromatic note is sustained, if it appears on a strong beat or at a phrase ending, or if it occurs several times in succession, the alteration may signal a *modulation*, which is a change of key that occurs while the music is in progress. Modulation is rare in the short songs that typify classroom repertoire. But if it occurs and the students notice the shift of key center, they should be directed to notice also the eventual return of the music to the original key. Whether the chromatic note turns out to be a long-term modulation or short-term ornamentation, the class should learn to sense its presence and appreciate the variety that it injects into the music.

STYLE OF PERFORMANCE

Sometimes a melody, by its very nature, seems to call for a certain style of performance, regardless of the words set to it. "Greensleeves" is such a melody. It glides along in a smooth and graceful way, partly because of its compound meter, perhaps, and partly because of its tempo. Whatever the reason for the listener's expectation, a choppy, forceful style for this melody would seem to destroy its graceful quality, no matter what the words might be. Actually, other words have been set to this melody, one of the most familiar texts being "What Child Is This?" That text also contributes to the gentle feeling of the melody.

Students can learn more about performance style, or *interpretation*, if the teacher provides opportunities for them to experiment with different types of melodies.

"You're singing 'Greensleeves' very well, with a smooth, graceful quality. You've done one interpretation; now do a different one. How do you think 'Greensleeves' will sound if you sing it loudly, in a choppy style?" [Larry emits an unsolicited "Yecch."] "Larry has let us know his feelings, but keep an open mind, Larry.

GREENSLEEVES

For autoharp, transpose to D minor

Old English Folk Song

"Let's run a comparison in which we sing two songs in the opposite style from the way in which we first sang them. First we'll sing 'Greensleeves' forcefully, with separation between the notes, then we'll do 'Minka' in a smooth and gentle style."

[The teacher sets a brisk tempo for a strongly accented rendition of "Greensleeves," and slows the customary tempo of "Minka" to allow for an expressive legato quality.]

It may not be easy for the class to sing in an inappropriate style; it requires concentration, especially if one interpretation of the song has become habitual for the singers. Occasional altering of the style, as a classroom exercise, can be beneficial to the students, however. It causes them to think about interpretation, and it helps them to be more

flexible in their singing. After each classroom experiment in interpretation, the students should be encouraged to share their impressions of
the musical effect. The following exchange of ideas might occur following the singing of "Greensleeves" and "Minka" described earlier.

> "There now, you've sung the two songs with opposite interpreta-
> tions. What are your impressions?" [A few class members convey their
> reactions by facial expressions of distaste.]
>
> "Joni, you don't seem too thrilled with the results. Why?"
>
> "I don't know. The 'Greensleeves' sounded like someone ahead of
> me, jogging, and I kept wanting them to slow down and get serious
> about the song. I felt like they were running faster than I wanted to
> go," Joni adds uncertainly.
>
> "I know the feeling, Joni. Any other comments about the style?
> Richard?"
>
> "The 'Minka' sort of dragged along and sounded real dull. I like
> it better fast."
>
> "I do too, Richard. Class, both Joni and Richard have made a
> good point about interpretation. Did the rest of you notice that we
> changed several aspects of these songs as we tried to create a different
> style? Joni and Richard mentioned that we changed the tempo, and
> that made a difference. What else?"
>
> [With urging, the class remembers the changes they made in the
> level of loudness. The teacher points out that the accents fall into this
> category, because an accent is a moment of sudden loudness.]
>
> "So you see, class, a lot of factors go into your interpretation of
> a song. Your job as a performer is to notice all you can about the style
> of a song, and then sing or play it in a way that you think will best con-
> vey its meaning to the listener."

In all discussions of style, the teacher must be careful not to say
that certain interpretations are "right" or "wrong," "correct" or "incorrect." It is better to convey to students the importance of keeping
an open mind, especially in matters as subjective as musical expression.
A particular interpretation can be evaluated with words like "appropriate" or "inappropriate," and even "I like it that way" or "I don't
like it that way." But categorical statements as to rightness are hard to
substantiate, even when they are backed by tradition and the consensus of knowledgeable musicians.

"Greensleeves" is an excellent song for familiarizing the class with
chromatic notes and minor keys, especially since the two features are
related in this song. The key is E minor, and the accidentals occur
only on steps 6 and 7 to produce C♯ and D♯, and yet the sharp is not
applied to C and D consistently throughout the song. This may partly
account for the haunting quality of the melody.

RANGE AND REGISTER

The *range* of a melody is determined by simply scanning the melody and noting its highest and lowest pitches. The class can compare a song with a wide range, such as "The Star-Spangled Banner" or "Tum-Balalaika," with a rather narrow-range song like "Minka," to discover whether the range of a song has an effect on the musical results.

The term *register* refers to the general pitch area of a song in terms of the type of voice singing it. For example, a song might be in a low register for a soprano, or in a high register for a tenor voice. Most of the songs in elementary school music books are similar in register, simply because the limitations of children's voices require a register that is not only accessible but comfortable. *Tessitura* is the pitch range within which most notes of a particular melody occur.

All three factors have a bearing on the ease with which most of the children will be able to sing a song. On occasion, the teacher may need to transpose a song into another key to accommodate the pitch limitations of children's untrained voices.

LISTENING TO MELODIES

To many children, "melody" is synonymous with "song." Older students should begin to understand, however, that a melody can be more than a singable tune. When a melody is conceived as the basis for a long work of music, it is called a *theme.* In instrumental music, the theme need not be songlike; in fact, it may be quite unsingable. It can be remembered by the mind, but if it is intended for instruments, it may be too complex or too angular in contour to be sung.

The second movement of a symphony or concerto usually features melodic writing, and such music, if not too long or complicated, is attractive to children who are learning to listen to melodies in instrumental music. Here is how a teacher might present the second movement of Mendelssohn's Symphony No. 4 ("Italian") to help students learn about melody in symphonic music.

> "Here's a portion of a symphony by a man named Felix Mendelssohn, who lived in Germany about 150 years ago. The music has a songlike melody, and to help you remember it, I'll play the first 45 seconds of the music for you twice. Notice that the melody doesn't start right away; there's a short introduction of about 10 seconds. Okay, here we go. Listen carefully and try to remember what you're hearing."

To appreciate Mendelssohn's later treatment of the melody, the listener must be able to remember its original sound, so committing the theme to memory is important. The teacher can aid that process by asking the students to participate in a limited way.

"I'm going to play those first 45 seconds once more. This time, hum along softly with the orchestra as it plays the melody. That will help you remember it."

The class needs to realize that symphonic music generally involves a broad time span. This means that the listener must notice not just the melody itself, but also the thematic changes and transitional material that may occur between appearances of the melody. The teacher might continue:

"The first melody in this music by Mendelssohn is basically a song consisting of four two-measure phrases. You've already hummed it, and it's starting to sound familiar to you. This time I'll let the recording play longer. See if you can keep track of the four phrases as the song is repeated three more times. The first two phrases get changed quite a bit, but you'll recognize the end of each appearance of the song because the notes move evenly downward by step." [The teacher plays about the first two minutes of the movement.]

When students work on an activity that requires intensive concentration, as careful listening does, the teacher should limit the amount of time devoted to that activity in a single sitting. On another day the teacher may want to continue working with the second movement of Mendelssohn's Symphony No. 4.

"I hope you remember the melody that Mendelssohn composed for the second movement of his 'Italian' Symphony, because we're going to study it some more today.

"You'll hear the melody four times. Next, the music takes on what I'll describe as a 'Halloween' feeling, because the instruments sort of quietly sneak around. Then you'll hear something different. At that point, raise your hands. I'll pick up the tone arm and ask you what's different about the music." [The contrasting section is in major and has a rich full sound.]

Following the same basic procedure, the teacher can help the class notice other melodic features of this movement. Perhaps most obvious to inexperienced listeners is the fact that the main theme is accompanied by continuous "walking" notes in the low strings each time it occurs. A somewhat harder assignment is for the class to notice that the two-note figure near the end—the one that serves to unify the movement—is derived from the theme. Still more challenging is to compare relatively long passages that are widely separated, as when two later reappearances of the main theme are found to be shorter and less complete than the first appearance.

Skillful manipulation of themes and melodic ideas is prevalent in most of the music heard in concert halls. In fact, it is the basis for *sonata form*, which has long been a favored organizing technique in movements of symphonies, concertos, and chamber works. Sonata form consists of three large segments, the middle one of which is called the *development* section. That section is expressly devised for thematic development, which refers to the manipulation of melodic ideas. Many other types of concert music also feature an imaginative treatment of themes. A melody can be structurally important and can be recast in different contexts by a skillful composer.

REVIEW QUESTIONS

1. Suppose that a class does not understand the difference between a half step and a whole step. In addition to providing a verbal explanation, what can a teacher do to help the class understand the difference?

2. (True or false?) Complete ascending or descending scales occur fairly frequently in songs.

3. What is the main difference between the pattern of whole and half steps in major scales and the pattern in minor scales?

4. a. The word that refers to the shape or outline of a melody is (scale, tonality, contour, pitch, content).
   b. What are some ways to help a class notice the shape of a melody?

5. a. Repeating a pattern of pitches immediately at a different pitch level is called (contour, repetition, sonata form, sequence, range).
   b. What are some ways to teach a class about this aspect of music?

6. Look at the song "Greensleeves" on page 241. How many different scale steps have been altered chromatically?

7. a. Which song has a wider range, "I'm on My Way" (p. 238) or "Greensleeves" (p. 241)?
   b. Are they in the same register?

8. What is the difference between a theme and a melody?

ACTIVITIES

1. Select a song from one of the music books designed for the upper elementary grades. Then do the following:
   a. Determine what notes appear at least once.
   b. Put the notes into ascending or descending order.
   c. Determine which is the keynote.
   d. Write down the pattern of whole and half steps of the scale.
   e. Decide if the scale is major or minor.
   f. Identify any chromatic notes.
   g. Determine the range of the melody.
   h. Draw on a blank piece of paper the contour of each line of the song.
   i. Indicate any places in the song where there is sequence.
   j. Decide if the melody itself (*not* the words) seems to require a certain style of performance.

2. Referring to the song selected for activity 1, choose two aspects of its melody that you might teach to a class of fifth- or sixth-grade students. Write a plan or strategy for teaching those two aspects.

3. Select a second—or "slow"—movement of a symphony, concerto, string quartet, or piano sonata. (The music series books discuss a few such works.) Listen to the movement enough times to feel familiar with it. After you have in mind how the composer has treated the melody, decide how you might teach this aspect of the music to a class of upper elementary school students.

Pitches Sounded Together: Harmony and Counterpoint

Although primary grade children experience the simultaneous sounding of pitches in the music they hear and in their singing of rounds, they are generally unaware of its significance. In the upper grades, however, they can begin to study harmony as a basic aspect of music.

The purpose of this chapter is to suggest ways in which to teach the students specifically about harmony. The recommendations go beyond the discussion of part singing in Chapter 10, which concentrated on making music. After all, it is one thing to sing in thirds with a melody or to push the buttons on an autoharp; it is something else to understand the organization of the simultaneous sounds that are being produced.

TEXTURE

In music, *texture* is the context in which simultaneous sounds occur. There are two basic textures. One is *harmony*, which is the effect created when the combined pitches form a distinct entity, or chord, at any given moment. In music notation such sounds are aligned *vertically* on the page. The other texture is *counterpoint*, which is a combining of two or more melodies at the same time. Because melodies move from left to right in music notation, this texture is sometimes described as being *linear* or *horizontal*. The sounds, of course, are neither vertical nor horizontal, because music is a temporal, not a spatial art. The directional terms are derived solely from the appearance of music notation. The visual association is helpful, however, as a reminder of the way in which each texture directs the listener's attention.

Each texture contains elements of the other. Harmony is essentially chordal, but it does progress from one moment to the next, so it has a horizontal aspect. Lines of counterpoint do create simultaneous sounds, so they suggest a vertical element. The two basic textures are not absolute, therefore, but are like poles of a continuum. And most pieces of music reveal a combination of textures. Describing the texture of a work is largely a matter of determining which aspect is predominant.

COUNTERPOINT

Elementary school children are experiencing counterpoint whenever they sing a round. Rounds are a logical introduction to such music because the same melody is sung by everyone, but at different times, of course. Furthermore, a round clearly illustrates a characteristic feature of counterpoint, or *contrapuntal* music: the melodic lines should be perceived as being equally important. When the lines are identical, as in a round, they should receive equal attention.

The next step beyond rounds in terms of complexity is music in which two different melodies occur at the same time. It requires a little more ability to conceptualize two different lines of music performed together than it does to think of the same melody being performed a few beats later. A good way to present the varying lines of counterpoint is to let the class sing *partner songs*, which are two different songs that can be sung at the same time. Here is how partner songs might be introduced:

"Let's check out your singing of a couple of songs that you've known for years. First, 'Three Blind Mice.' Here's the starting note. Rea-dy, sing." [The class sings through the song, beginning on E.]

"Fine. Now another old favorite. Here's the starting pitch for 'Are You Sleeping?' Rea-dy, sing." [The class sings through "Are You Sleeping?" beginning on C.]

"Okay. But I need to check out one more thing. Can you keep each song going if only half the class is singing it with you? We'll see. You people from here to the door sing 'Are You Sleeping?' Rea-dy, go." [Half the class sings the song.] "The rest of you sing 'Three Blind Mice.' Rea-dy, go. [The other half sings "Three Blind Mice."]

"All right, here comes the payoff: Sing the two songs together. Remember, no rushing, and no trying to drown out the other song. 'Mice' people, here's your pitch. . . . and 'sleeping' people, here's your pitch. . . . Rea-dy, sing." [The class sings the two songs at the same time.]

"See, it worked! Want to trade sides—or songs, I mean? This time, sing your new song on 'la' instead of with the regular words, so that you can give your attention to the way the tunes combine. Here are your notes. . . . Rea-dy, 'la.'" [The class sings the songs together again.]

"The tunes sound pretty good together, don't they? When you have two melodies or lines of music being sounded at the same time, you have *counterpoint*."

Partner songs are more likely to be successful when the class knows both songs well and the teacher gives clear directions as to tempo and starting pitches. A cue sheet is a helpful aid to the teacher:

Key   **Starting note**

F ⎰ All Night, All Day _____ low C half note ⎰ in $\frac{4}{4}$ meter
  ⎱ Swing Low, Sweet Chariot _____ high A quarter note ⎱

C ⎛ Santa Lucia _____ G quarter note ⎞
  ⎜ ("Now 'neath the silver moon" . . .)   ⎟ in $\frac{3}{4}$ meter
  ⎜ Juanita _____ G half note ⎟
  ⎝ ("Soft o'er the fountain" . . .)⎠

Counterpoint is not always so obvious as in the combining of two known songs. In elementary music series books, counterpoint is usually produced by adding a descant—a musical device that was described in

Chapter 10. The words of a descant are usually similar to those of the melody, but the descant is not just a "shadow" of the melody, even though it is the less familiar of the two parts. A good descant possesses a melodic character of its own. It provides counterpoint because it is an independent line that is attractive in itself.

The following arrangement of "Joy to the World" is interesting for several reasons. First, the composer of the melody is generally believed to be George Frideric Handel, the same man who composed *Messiah*. The descant is by Lowell Mason, who is credited with first instituting music in the public schools of the United States. The music has some unusual features, too. The melody contains one of the rare appearances of a complete scale within a song. It also displays a sequential pattern in measures 12-15.

JOY TO THE WORLD

Words by Isaac Watts (from Psalm 98)   Music Arranged from
George F. Handel by Lowell Mason

The teacher may want the class to notice some of the places where the descant differs from the melody.

"All right; you've spotted several phrases in which the descant goes off differently from the melody. Now here's a harder question. What do you notice about the two lines when each one has the words 'And heaven and nature sing'?" [Silence.]

"Then figure it out with me, class. When the melody is singing 'And heaven and nature sing,' what's the descant doing? Marilyn?"

"Nothing; they have a rest," reports Marilyn.

"Okay. What's the melody doing in the next measure when the descant sings some words? Carla?"

"The melody's holding on the word 'sing' through most of the measure," Carla says.

"Right. Now one more bit of research. Steve, what happens in the next measure when the melody has words and notes? What's the descant doing?"

"Where? . . . Oh, yeah. The descant has just the word 'sing' and then a rest," Steve decides.

"Good. So here's that question again. What can you figure out about the melody and the descant? Rebecca."

"Well, it seems like when the melody has activity, the descant holds more still, and when the descant moves, the melody holds still. The parts sort of trade off in how they move around," Rebecca concludes.

"That's it, Rebecca. It's a basic idea that happens often in counterpoint. If both parts are active all the time, the listeners have a hard time telling which part is which, and they lose interest. But if their attention is directed to one part and then another, the lines of melody stand out better and the piece is more appealing."

INTERVALS

An *interval* is the pitch difference between two notes. (The term when applied to music does *not* refer to a span of time.) Students in the upper grades will find that the basic intervals are easy to compute.

Two facts need to be kept in mind, whether the computation is aural or visual. First, the numerical name of any interval *includes the top and bottom notes*, as well as the intervening pitches that are not heard. To calculate the numerical distance between two notes, apply a "1" to either note and count by step to the other, including it in the tally. If only one note is given, plus an interval number, call the given note "1" and count to whatever note fulfills the numerical distance. For example, the interval from A down to F is a third, because if A is "1," a descending count puts F on "3."

The second fact to remember when identifying intervals is that each number represents a letter of the alphabet, not just a half-step spacing. For example, the interval of G up to B is a third, counted G A B; it is not a fifth, as one might assume from counting each intervening half step—G G♯ A A♯ B. Another computation system, similar to counting by letters, is counting by adjacent lines and spaces on the staff. For example, the note a third above a given line note would be located by counting upward "line space line." A sixth below a given space note would be counted downward "space line space line space line."

The students can take a "sample" of the notes in a two-part song such as "Joy to the World" and from that sample draw an important generalization about music. In the following situation, the teacher has taught the class how to find basic intervals.

"The other day you learned how to tell if an interval is a second, third, fourth, and so on. Today you'll use that knowledge to discover something important about music. We're going to run a survey of every other measure in 'Joy to the World' and find out what intervals occur most often between the melody and the descant. George, would you please keep score of the various intervals as they're mentioned by people in the class.

"Casey, what's the first interval in the first measure?"

"Uh . . . both parts have the same note . . . but I don't know if there's a name for that," Casey hesitates. [The teacher informs the class that such an interval is called a *unison.*]

"What's the first interval in the third measure?" asks the teacher, quickly taking the class through the initial intervals of the odd-numbered measures.

"Now we'll ask George, our record-keeper, to tell us the results for the first notes of the ten measures we looked at."

"There were five unisons, one third, three sixths, and one eighth," George reports. [The teacher reminds him that the name for "eighth" is "octave."]

"Remember, class, that an octave and a unison are practically the same thing, because if you move one note of either interval into a different octave range, you produce the other interval. Thirds and sixths are also the reverse or inversion of each other, so in a sense they're a single interval too. See how much you discovered from your survey?"

[George proposes that the class should now survey the even-numbered measures—a project for which he volunteers to serve again as reporter.]

"Thanks for the suggestion, George. We'd better pass the job around to different people, though, so no one gets lazy. We'll look at other songs later, to see if they have similar amounts of unison/octave and third/sixth combinations."

The following arrangement of "When the Saints Go Marching In" is appropriate as the next step in contrapuntal complexity, because the two lines are dissimilar. An interesting feature of this arrangement is the fact that the melody is slowed to half its original speed when it appears a second time. This is achieved by making the note values for the melody twice as long as they were the first time. The slower notes give the additional line of counterpoint a chance to be more active, a principle that the students discovered when they sang the Mason arrangement of "Joy to the World."

WHEN THE SAINTS GO MARCHING IN

Spiritual
Arranged by Mary Val Marsh

Again, the class can examine the intervals that occur between the two parts of "When the Saints Go Marching In." The tabulation may involve each measure of the two-part segment, or just a sample of those measures. It should be explained to the class that the interval of a tenth is merely an octave plus a third, so the sound is basically a third. The students' attention should also be directed to the temporary nature of the interval of a second that occurs when the melody (lower line) is at the word "number." Careful listening will lead the class to conclude that the E♭, not the F, is the more important note in that measure.

Attention to intervals focuses on the vertical dimension of counterpoint. The horizontal or linear dimension is considered when the melodies are examined as consecutive pitches. It is a simple matter to ask the class to notice similarities and differences between the two lines of "When the Saints Go Marching In."

"Can you find a series of notes in the unison section that comes back in a similar pattern in the descant? Here's a hint: It's a series of five notes, and both patterns have the same rhythm." [Silence.]

"Here's another hint, then." [The teacher whistles or sings on a neutral syllable so that the class will have to locate the spot by following the music rather than by word reading. The passage consists of the five notes in measures 6, 7, and 8 of the unison section. The class is attentive, but no one ventures to describe where the comparable passage appears in the descant.]

"All right, you people; here's your absolutely final hint. Turn
those notes upside down by reversing the direction in which they move.
If a note jumps upward to the next sound, imagine it jumping downward instead." [Further silence.]

"I found it!" Jessica calls out suddenly. "The upper line has that
in measures . . . uh . . . 8 and 9 of the two-part stuff."

[The teacher praises Jessica and points out the similarity of the
inverted pattern by drawing the reverse contours of the two patterns on
the board and having the children sing each of them.]

Students in the upper elementary grades should have a chance to
listen to contrapuntal music. Sometimes this music is like a round—the
theme is heard alone, then other parts enter one after another with that
same theme. In other contrapuntal music, two or more melodic lines
are present throughout the work. For children in elementary school, it
is good to begin with pieces that are relatively short and that contain a
familiar melody. The following contrapuntal works are appropriate for
early listening experiences.

J. S. Bach:	Chorale Prelude on "In Dulci Jubilo"
	Fugue in G Minor ("The Little")
	"Gigue" Fugue
	"Trumpet" Fugue
Handel:	"For Unto Us a Child Is Born" from *Messiah*
McBride:	"Pumpkin Eater's Little Fugue"
D. Scarlatti:	"Cat's" Fugue
Thomson:	Fugue and Chorale on "Yankee Doodle"

HARMONY

Harmony is the simultaneous sounding of pitches, and its primary
function is to provide accompaniment, or background, for a melody.
Most accompanying pitches take the form of *chords;* that is, three or
more different pitches are sounded at the same time. To establish the
concept of chords as accompaniment to a melody, the class can sing a
familiar tune while the teacher devises a strictly chordal accompaniment on an instrument such as the autoharp. Because the autoharp offers an automatic way to play chords easily, the students themselves
can play the simpler accompaniments with minimal teacher direction.
The players can concentrate on the chords as units of sound, and they
are freed from worrying about which notes go into every chord. The

procedures for teaching harmony should enable the class to understand that the notes in the melody determine what chords are played and when they are played. The chord symbols appearing in the notation of a song are someone's decision as to the chords implied by that particular melody.

Harmonizing with a simple and familiar song like "Go Tell Aunt Rhody" (p. 233) is a good way to make the students sensitive to the places where chord changes are needed.

"Karl, take the autoharp, please, and strum a C chord on each beat of "Go Tell Aunt Rhody." [Karl strums the chords feebly.] "Louder!" [He strums more forcefully.] "That's the way! Sing softly, class, so that you can hear the chords on the autoharp. Karl, keep playing that C chord until we tell you to stop, even if it sounds wrong to you. Class, when you think the C chord clashes with the melody, raise your hands. Karl will give us a C chord first so that we get the starting pitch. . . . Rea-dy, sing and play."

[Karl strums vehemently while the class sings softly. A few hands go up in the third measure to indicate that the C chord needs to change. Uncertain students raise their hands in measures 4 and 5, in delayed imitation of their classmates.]

"Listen again, so you can hear for sure when the C chord doesn't fit the melody." [The class sings the song again accompanied by the C chord.] "Okay, now we need another chord, the G7 chord. Joanne, you take Karl's place and strum the autoharp; we don't want to wear him out. Strum the G7 chord loudly." [Joanne starts strumming.] "Yes, like that.

"All right, class, sing again and tell me when the G7 doesn't sound right any longer by raising your hands. We'll sing just the last two measures, where it says, 'old gray goose is dead.' Joanne will give us the chord so that we have the right starting pitch. . . . Rea-dy, sing." [The class sings, and on the last measure hands are again raised to indicate that a change of chord is needed.]

"Trina, what chord do you think we might try on the last measure where a change is needed?"

Trina shrugs. "The C chord is the only other one we've talked about so far," she guesses.

[The teacher asks Joanne to try the C chord, and the class decides that it makes a good ending.]

By introducing the G7 so that it is played experimentally in the last measure, rather than earlier in the song, the class is more likely to hear the dissonance of that chord with the final sustained note of the piece. Judgments about harmony are easier to make when there is time to consider the chord, and no chord follows to distract the young listeners' attention. When the class has determined the chord order that sounds best with this melody, students can take turns accompanying the singing.

An attentive student may ask why some chords have "seven" in their names. That number simply means that one note in the chord is an interval of a seventh above the *root*, the note for which the chord is named. A G7 chord consists of an ordinary G chord plus an F, which is a seventh above G; a C7 chord consists of an ordinary C chord plus a B♭, which is a seventh above C; and so on. In simple songs, seventh chords are almost always confined to *dominant* harmony—that is, to the chord built on step 5 of that particular key. A C7 sounds strange in C major, where C is step 1, but it sounds fine in F major, where C is step 5. If a student's harmonizing efforts sound peculiar, the problem may be that seventh chords are being substituted inappropriately for *triads* (chords of three tones) on the same root.

Harmony can be implied by vocal as well as instrumental accompaniments. After a little experience, students enjoy harmonizing simply by singing chord roots while others sing the melody. For "Go Tell Aunt Rhody," the class might first sing the chord roots with letter names, one note per measure, as follows: "C C G C, C C G C." The pattern can move from C to the G above or below it; there is no difference harmonically. In fact, the class should try the part both ways. When the singers feel secure with the chord roots, they can divide into two sections, one singing the melody and the other the root pattern. They should trade parts frequently, of course.

Learning to hear needed chord changes is a slow process for some students. It takes repeated practice over a number of months for them to learn to fit chords with a melody.

Chord construction

Although students in the upper grades of elementary school do not need to delve deeply into the subject of harmony, they should have a basic knowledge of chord construction so that they can find satisfaction in the harmonizing efforts of themselves and others.

Here is how a teacher might help the class discover the note pattern that is basic in chord construction.

"On the chalkboard I've written the letter names for every note in the F major scale: F, G, A, and so on. The letters are spread way out, and the note lineup extends for two octaves. You see three scales just alike.

"I'm going to tell you the notes that go into three chords. For each chord someone will come up to the board, mark the chord notes, and connect them together with a bracket. The first chord is built on F, and it has the notes F A C. Natalie, would you circle and connect those letters? Mark them from left to right, like the order in which I named them." [Natalie correctly circles the letters and draws the bracket.]

"Fine, Natalie. Gina, on the next line show us the B♭ chord. It's B♭ D F." [Gina draws the three circles and brackets the B♭ chord.] "B♭ D F. That's the way.

"Now, the last chord has one more note than the F or B♭ chords. It's the C7 chord, and its notes are C E G B♭. Jared, would you circle each of those letters on the board?" [Jared, working cautiously and in need of reminders, finally marks the four letters of the C7 chord and places a bracket above them. The scales look like this.]

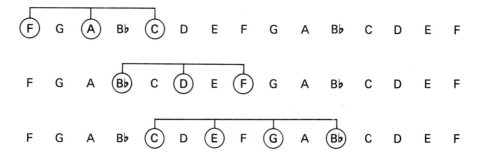

"Thanks, Jared. You see, class, why there's a two-octave scale on the board? Jared's chord won't fit into a one-octave scale unless we scramble the notes, and we don't want to mix them up yet. Sing the chords with me as I point to each note. Here's the pitch for F. . . . Letter names, rea-dy sing." [The class sings the pitches in the chords.]

"Now then. You're about to discover an underlying 'secret' of chords. Who sees or hears a pattern in each of these chords? Hal?"

"They all use every other letter; they have a note and then they skip a note," Hal observes.

"Yeah," Trent interrupts. "The notes go jump, jump, jump, like in checkers."

The teacher confirms their conclusion. "That's the secret combination, all right. That every-other-note arrangement is the basic pattern for almost all the chords you'll ever hear in music. What's the interval between those chord tones, class? . . . Sure, it's a third. Our system of harmony is built on thirds. Chords are built on what interval pattern? Everybody say it! *thirds!*"

Learning about chords should be tied in as much as possible with actual music. Almost any song can serve as the context in which chord construction is examined and harmonization is experienced. "Down in the Valley" is especially suitable because it involves only two chords and moves at a slow tempo.

DOWN IN THE VALLEY

Fitting chords to melodies

When the students can hear the implied changes of harmony in a melody, and when they have some understanding of chord construction, they can begin to consider why certain chords fit a melody and others do not. The clue to good chord selection usually can be found within the melody itself.

As the students learn to recognize thirds harmonically, in chord construction, they become more sensitive to that pattern when they see it in a melody. For example, the first five notes of "Down in the Valley" are C F G A F, and four of those five notes are in the F chord, so that is the logical choice. (The G in that measure is merely a passing tone between F and A.) The first seven notes of "The Star-Spangled Banner" form an unusually extended chord outline. Chord selection is expedited in such a situation because the melody allows so few options.

In the following activity, it is assumed that chord symbols are not printed in the students' version of the song.

> "Jonathan, from looking at the music for 'Down in the Valley,' can you tell which chord is probably going to fit with the melody in the first full measure?"
>
> "Oh boy . . . uh . . . maybe F?"
>
> "Good, Jonathan. Why did you choose the F chord?"
>
> "Well, the notes are A, F, and C, and that's the same as F A C, which is a chord you were talking about."
>
> "Right. See how easy it is, class? Diane, what chord might work in the second measure?"
>
> "Well, there's a G and . . . a C . . . and . . . E . . . ," says Diane in a labored fashion.
>
> "You're right, Diane. What chord do those notes belong to? . . . Okay, Heather."
>
> "A C chord," Heather replies, "because the melody there has a C, E, and G, and they're in a C chord."

Students can check out their suggestions by playing their chords on the autoharp while the class sings the song. The suitability of their chord selections should be judged by how the music sounds.

By working with a round like "Dona Nobis Pacem," students can gain further insight into why certain chords do or do not fit well with a given fragment of the melody.

When the simultaneously sounding measures are aligned vertically, as in the version on page 262, it is relatively easy for the class to see how harmony is achieved in a round. In the first measure, for example, the longest note values in each part form an F A C chord. Experienced students can go on to determine, with minimal help from the teacher, that the basic harmonic progression for this round consists of one chord per measure, as follows: F C7 F C Bb F C7 F.

"Dona Nobis Pacem" is longer and more complex than most rounds that children sing in elementary school. Short rounds like "Are You Sleeping?" and "Three Blind Mice" can be harmonized with a single chord, because when the phrases are short and entrances of the

DONA NOBIS PACEM

tune occur closely after one another, there is not enough time to accommodate different chords. The longer the phrases, the more harmonic variety is possible. Most songs cannot be sung as rounds because the harmony changes at a different spot in each phrase. To be successful, a round must have phrases that are equal in length, identical in harmonic background, and melodically different so that no two phrases will produce an extended unison passage when they are performed simultaneously.

A chord is not required on every note of a melody; only those notes that are longer or more important are harmonized. The meter of the song is also a factor in chord selection, because chord changes are more likely to occur on the strong first beat of a measure than on a weaker beat. A harmonic change occurring partway through a beat is rare.

Chord function and key

When chords are indicated in the music, but not written out in notation, the identification usually consists of simply naming the root, adding any qualifying terms ("dim.," "min.," "7," and so on), and placing this symbol over the staff at the spot where the chord should first be sounded. This type of designation is useful for telling what notes should be played, but it says nothing about the *function* of that chord within the key. Function is the musical effect of a chord in a particular setting or key, and it is indicated by a Roman numeral.

The students can rather easily figure out what chord will serve as I in a key, because it is the chord built on the first step of the scale. Similarly, the IV chord is built on step 4 and the V chord on step 5 of the scale. The letter name of a chord indicates the actual sound to be produced, but the Roman numeral tells what the function or impression of that chord will be. For example, a C chord sounds stable and final when it appears as the I or "home" chord in C major, but the same chord sounds restless and active when it appears as V in F major, or as IV in G major. The musical context, or *key*, determines the function of a given chord.

Almost all of the songs that children sing are based on a certain expectation or syntax of tonal movement within a key. This expectation forms the framework within which chord function operates. The tonic chord and keynote have a kind of "magnetic pull" that makes other notes tend to lead to them. A piece of music that does not end on the tonic chord sounds incomplete, as if it wants to continue toward the point of finality that is provided by the tonic. This point can easily be demonstrated to the students.

> [The class has just sung the song "Down in the Valley."] "Sandra, go to the piano, please, and find the notes B♭, D, and F. After you find them, figure out how you'll place your fingers to play those notes together as a chord. You can use both hands if you want to." [Sandra takes a moment to locate the B♭ major chord and to arrange her fingers on the three notes.]
>
> "Now play the chord for us, just to be sure you have it." [Sandra sounds the chord correctly.] "Good. Now, the rest of us will sing the last line of 'Down in the Valley,' beginning with 'Hang your head.' On the last word, which is 'blow,' Sandra will play the B♭-D-F chord. It has an F in it, like the last note of the melody, so we won't have a clash of sounds and it won't sound like a big mistake. But listen and decide if that chord sounds as if we're 'back home,'—back to the key center." [The teacher hums the starting note, C, and the class sings the last line of the song. Sandra sounds the B♭ major chord in place of the usual final F chord.]

"How many of you thought we were 'back home'? Raise your hands if you think the chord gave a feeling that the song had ended." [Only one or two hands go up.] "How many thought the chord did *not* give a feeling of ending the song?" [Many children raise their hands, including a few who appear to be imitating the responses of their friends.]

"To check your answer, let's sing the last line of 'Down in the Valley' once more, but this time, Sandra, play a chord with the notes F-A-C. Listen, class, to the effect of ending on the 'home' or I chord." [The class sings the last line again.]

"The music sounded finished that time, didn't it? That's the influence of *key* in music."

Closest to the tonic chord in the order of "magnetic pull" is the V or V^7 chord, and the IV chord is less drawn to the tonic. There are other chords in tonal music, of course. In fact, a chord can be built on each of the seven steps of the scale. But manipulating all of the available chords satisfactorily requires a good ear and specialized instruction. Fortunately, the majority of songs sung in elementary school can be harmonized with the three basic chords of I, IV, and V.

Students in the upper elementary grades should become familiar with the two words that describe the relative degree of tension or restlessness in simultaneous sounds: *consonant* and *dissonant*. Most of the songs found in elementary music books contain few passages of extended dissonance in the voice parts. An occasional momentary dissonance adds zest to the music, and the singers can be encouraged to notice the way in which the dissonance resolves to a more consonant sound. They are much more likely to hear dissonance in instrumental music, especially in works composed in the twentieth century. Further development of this concept is usually not undertaken in elementary school.

REVIEW QUESTIONS

1. What is the basic difference between harmony and counterpoint?

2. Why are partner songs especially suitable for teaching the concept of counterpoint?

3. a. What basic intervals occur most frequently between two lines of "Joy to the World" on page 250?
   b. How can a teacher help elementary school students learn to recognize the more frequently encountered intervals?

4. What is the relationship between a melody and its chords?

5. How can children learn to recognize when a change of chord is implied in a melody?

6. How can a teacher help a class to discover the pattern of notes found in almost all chords?

7. What is the main benefit of studying a round with its notation set in "layers," one part above another?

8. What are the three basic chords with which most elementary school songs can be accompanied?

9. What is the difference between the words "consonance" and "dissonance"?

ACTIVITIES

1. From a music series book, select five songs in which a chord is clearly outlined in the melody.

2. Select a short, simple song that has no chord symbols appearing in the music.
   a. With an autoharp at hand, figure out an accompaniment for the song.
   b. Write the text of the first verse on a piece of paper. Then add the names of the chords you selected and the Roman numeral for the function of each chord.
   c. Develop a brief plan for helping children devise their own accompaniments to the song.

3. Select a song with a descant or with two concurrent melodies.
   a. Sample the intervals between the two parts by identifying the interval on the first beat of every other measure. Write a one-sentence summary of your findings.
   b. Compare the amount of "activity" in each line, noticing whether the melodic motion generally alternates between the parts or occurs in each line simultaneously.

Music Has Design: Form

Almost every piece of music has a design or plan, which is referred to as its *form*. Children in the primary grades are beginning to notice form when they discern that some phrases of a song are the same and others are different. A more specific study of form is often successful in the upper grades because the older students' ability to conceptualize helps them to remember and anticipate important structural features in the music they hear. The music itself is usually longer and more complex, and therefore presents more interesting formal patterns.

The understanding of form is predicated on an awareness of phrases, and this awareness should start to develop in the primary grades, as described in Chapter 8. Unless the children can sense and identify the smaller units of a song, they will feel bewildered by the more advanced aspects of form. Because phrases are important to structure as well as to interpretation, children should examine them frequently, at every grade level, and learn to view them in the larger context of the entire piece.

SHORT FORMAL PATTERNS

"Sourwood Mountain" is a good song for introducing older students to formal analysis. If the class in previous years identified phrases through the use of symbols like boxes, triangles, and circles, or through colors, the familiar system can be reviewed. If not, such symbolization can be taught in the upper grades. The form for "Sourwood Mountain" might resemble □ □ ○ ○, or "green-green-red-red," to indicate that the first two lines are the same, as are the third and fourth line.

SOURWOOD MOUNTAIN

Appalachian Folk Song

1. Chick-en crow-in' on Sour-wood Moun-tain, } Hey de-ing dang did-dle al-ly day.
2. My true love's a blue-eyed dai-sy,

So man-y pret-ty girls I can't count them. } Hey de-ing dang did-dle al-ly day.
If I don't get her I'll go cra-zy.

My true love she lives in Letch-er, } Hey de-ing dang did-dle al-ly day.
My true love lives in the hol-low,

She won't come and I won't fetch her. } Hey de-ing dang did-dle al-ly day.
She won't come and I won't fol-low.

In the conventional identification system, phrases or short lines of music are labeled with lower-case letters and long sections are represented by capital letters. To introduce this system, the teacher may proceed as follows.

"This time as you sing 'Sourwood Mountain,' notice which lines of music are the same and which are different. That will help you find the form of the song. Listen for the music, remember, not the words."
[The class sings one verse of "Sourwood Mountain."]
"Sam, are the first two lines of music the same?"
"Let me see . . . yeah, they are," Sam responds.

"Right. We'll label the first two lines with the letter *a*. Is the third line the same as the second, Sharon?"

"No. . . . But it's like the fourth line," Sharon answers quickly, anticipating the next question.

"Anyone disagree with Sharon?" [Silence.] "You're right, Sharon, the last two lines are the same, but they're different from the first two. Debbie, how should we label the third and fourth lines?"

"With a '3' and '4'?" guesses Debbie, taken by surprise during a moment of inattention.

"We're working with letters, Debbie, not numbers. Arthur, what letter comes after *a*?"

"It's a *b*," says Arthur.

"Sure. The first segment is always some kind of *A:* little *a* for a short phrase, capital *A* for a longer section. When you see or hear new material, call it *B*. Still more new material is *C,* and so on. 'Sourwood Mountain' divides nicely into four short sections, so the pattern will have four letters in it. Tell me the form, class, so I can write it on the board. All together, now: *a a b b.*"

As the students become accustomed to finding the design of a song, they can also learn a few terms for particular forms. The *a a b b* form in "Sourwood Mountain" reduces further to *AB*, a form called *binary* because it implies two segments.

Although lines and sections of music determine the form of a song, the class should continue to notice other elements that provide similarity or difference within the song. These features may not affect the form, but they help to give the song unity. In "Sourwood Mountain," for example, the fourth measures of each line are identical in words and music; the rhythm is the same in the third measures of each line; the rhythm in the first two measures of each line is similar, with only the sixteenth note added in the first two lines; the melodic contour of the second through fourth notes in each of the second measures is similar; and the melody ascends on the second beat of each third measure.

Probably the most common structure for songs is *ternary* or *ABA* form, also called *song form*. (The term "song form" applies to instrumental as well as vocal music.) This is a balanced structure that achieves unity by ending on the same material with which it began. The logic of the pattern may explain why the form has been used so widely and has endured for so long. "Go Tell It on the Mountain" is one example of this form. The *A* segment goes through "born" in the third line, the *B* section goes from "When" to the end of the last line, and the final *A* section is a repeat of the first *A* section. Before singing the song, the class may need to be reminded about the D.C. or *da capo* mark at the end of the *B* section, which indicates a return to the beginning.

GO TELL IT ON THE MOUNTAIN

day; I asked the Lord to help me, and He showed me the way.
wall; And if   I   am a Chris - tian, I   am   the least of   all.

As in "Sourwood Mountain," there are several elements that give
a sense of unity to "Go Tell It on the Mountain." Measures 5 and 6 are
almost exactly the same as measures 1 and 2, measures 9 and 10 are
identical to measures 13 and 14, and so on. Incidentally, the song includes a second part that generally parallels the melodic line at the interval of a third or sixth. Syncopation is evident in measures 3, 4, and 7.

When the students listen to instrumental music, they do not often
have access to the notation, so they must rely on their listening skills
to decide whether lines are the same or different. Instrumental works
are usually much longer than songs. For example, here is the theme
from the fourth movement of the Clarinet Quintet by Mozart. (A *movement* is a sizable, self-contained section of a long musical work.) The
theme is a modified binary form, because the final line of the *B* section
(the fourth line) is the same as the final line of the *A* section (the
second line).

TYPES OF FORMS

The theme from the Clarinet Quintet is only one among hundreds of examples of the fact that composers do not follow forms exactly. And there is no rule that says they should. They are free to use a form if they wish, and to adapt it in order to create the musical results they want. The form of a work is extracted by analysis after the composer has written the music; it is not binding on the composer during the creative process. For this reason, there are almost no "perfect" or "textbook" examples of the various musical forms. For study purposes, however, these forms can be grouped into five broad categories or approaches that composers seem to favor when they organize their ideas into a musical work. The five types of organization may be designated as sectional form, variation form, development, imitation, and free form.

Sectional forms

The first of these categories combines sections of music into a form. A three-part sectional form, for example, most often consists of one section of music followed by a contrasting section, which is followed by a return to the music of the first section. The result is *ABA* or song form, which was mentioned earlier.

There may be any number of sections, presented in any order. A sectional form that is encountered in the last movement of many works by Mozart, Haydn, and Beethoven is the *rondo*. The word "rondo" comes from a similar French word referring to "coming around again" in a dance. In a rondo, the main theme returns at least twice after its initial appearance. A typical pattern for a rondo is *ABACABA*, which is actually a balanced form, as is evident when the sections are viewed as *ABA—C—ABA*. Other arrangements of rondo sections, such as *ABACADA*, are possible.

In the following situation, the teacher is adapting ideas from the Orff-*Schulwerk* method of improvisation. Members of the class have devised several melodies of four measures in length.

"Rachel, since you've worked out a melody on the bells, you can play the main theme—the *A* section. Beth, your melody can be the contrasting or *B* theme. Would you play it on the piano, please, so the tone will contrast with Rachel's bells. Eddie, what would you like to hear following Beth's melody in the composition?"

"Rachel can play her melody again," Eddie decides.

"All right. J.T., do you want the piece to end there, or would you like to add something more?"

"Well, Claire had a rhythm on the drum. If she wants to, she could play it next," J.T. suggests.

"Good idea. Rachel, you can finish the piece by playing your melody one last time."

Tammy whispers to a neighbor, "Rachel gets to play all the time." The teacher, overhearing, says, "Tammy, you're probably right in thinking that more people should perform in this piece. If you're volunteering to play Rachel's melody, I'm sure she'll let you take the part at least for one section."

Tammy, looking surprised, shakes her head and admits softly, "I don't remember how it goes."

The teacher summarizes the compositional plan: "So there'll be five sections in the composition. Rachel's melody is first, third, and fifth. Beth will play the second section, and Claire will play the fourth section. You three players, come to the front and line up in order, A, B, and C parts. . . . That's right. Now raise your hands in the order you're going to play for section 1 . . . 2 . . . 3 . . . 4 . . . 5 . . . Good.

"By noticing the order of the sections, class, you can tell the form of the piece. Darryl, what are the letters for this form?"

"*ABACA*?" Darryl suggests.

"Right! When the beginning theme appears at least three times, with other material in between, the form is called a *rondo.*"

Variation forms

Another way to organize a musical work is to present the theme several times but vary it with each appearance. The experience is like viewing similar pictures of the same subject, but seeing each one in a different light or from a different angle. Variation technique is applied more often in instrumental than in vocal music.

A good way to introduce children to variation in music is to play for them a set of variations based on a theme they already know. With the theme clearly in mind, they are better able to concentrate on the variations. Charles Ives' *Variations on "America"* is an excellent example in a modern style. Solo piano works that are more conventional-sounding include Beethoven's *Variations on "God Save the King"* (which we know as "America"), and Mozart's *Twelve Variations on "Ah vous dirais-je, Maman"* (which we know as "Twinkle, Twinkle Little Star").

Pieces of music with the word "variations" in the title are not the only compositions that feature variation technique. Some are constructed on bass lines or chord progressions that are repeated over and over, while new melodic material is heard with each appearance of the repeated bass line or progression. One such form is the passacaglia, while others are the chaconne and basso ostinato (literally, "obstinate bass").

Whatever work is selected for the students' listening, they will learn more about the concept of variation if they start with a simple, familiar theme and try to find out what the composer did to vary the music. To see how Mozart varied "Twinkle, Twinkle Little Star," the class can look at four of the variations. The theme is presented in a straightforward manner:

The fifth variation provides a simple change in the rhythm by adding a rest for half of a beat in each measure of each part:

In the eighth variation (see below), the melody includes additional tones, the left-hand part follows the right in imitation, and the music is in a minor key instead of the original major. There is also a series of suspensions in the right-hand part. A *suspension* occurs when a consonant note is held over (in this case, by the ties) into a new chord in which it is a dissonant note, and then it resolves to a consonant note on the next chord change:

The ninth variation maintains the idea of imitation between the parts for the two hands. The music has returned to a major key and the added notes in the melody are no longer present:

The tenth variation contains rapidly moving sixteenth notes, which if sounded at the same time would form chords. A change of harmony can be seen in the chromatic notes of both the left-hand and right-hand parts:

In these four variations Mozart alters the rhythm, embellishes the melody by adding notes to it, sets lines in counterpoint, and changes the harmony. He even combines these techniques in the eighth variation. His procedures indicate only a few of the many ways in which a theme may be varied.

If the students can hear a recording of a work in variation form while at the same time seeing its notation, they will be able to identify the changes more specifically. In the music class described below, the teacher is preparing to play a recording of Mozart's variations and is directing the students' attention to the notated excerpts in their music series books.

"I'll play the eighth variation again as you follow the notation in your books. Keep the theme in mind as you listen. Then decide how this variation differs from the theme. What exactly did Mozart do to vary it? Here's the eighth variation again." [The teacher plays a recording of the eighth variation.]

"Chip, what's different about this variation?"

"Well, it doesn't sound the same," Chip hedges.

"Agreed. But *what* makes it sound different?"

"I don't know exactly. . . . Um . . . It just seems 'darker,'" Chip tries again.

"Okay, but what makes it 'darker'? Is the music lower, slower, in a different key?"

"Yeah, I think it's in a different key," Chip responds quickly, seizing upon the concrete options that the teacher has suggested to him. "It could be in minor," he speculates.

"It could be, and it is. What else is different about the variation?" [The teacher elicits from the class a few further observations about the eighth variation.]

Development

In writing variations, the composer takes a theme and recasts it by altering the harmony, melody, or rhythm. In writing music containing development of themes, however, the composer takes one or two themes and changes them more completely by dividing them into fragments, turning them upside down, putting them into different keys, and in other ways manipulating them. A variation generally accounts for each measure in the original theme, but a development section often extracts melodic fragments from the theme and treats them as new themes in themselves. Variations need not be musically complex, although they can be and sometimes are. Music with theme development tends to be longer and more intricate, because it is a sophisticated technique and a composer needs time in which to develop a theme. Although these comparisons only touch on the differences between development and variation, they do point out the main distinctions between these compositional approaches.

It is difficult in elementary school to delve into music that involves development. Class time is limited, and the children seldom have the musical background for such study. But they can be introduced to the idea that a theme in music exists not only for its melodic quality, but also for what the composer can do with it.

The first movement of Beethoven's Fifth Symphony begins with a short theme that is hardly a prizewinner in terms of melodic beauty:

Yet after almost 200 years, this symphony continues to be one of the best-known and most frequently played works in the orchestral repertoire. Its appeal surely derives from Beethoven's genius in developing that theme. In fact, that four-note motive can be heard in one guise or another hundreds of times throughout the movement.

A teacher might center the students' attention on the idea of development in this manner:

> "I'm going to play for you a part of a famous symphony, the Fifth Symphony by Beethoven. It begins right away with its first theme. A theme, you remember, is an important melody that the composer treats in different ways to make the movement hold together. You need to get the first theme in mind, so here are the opening measures. You can hear the theme easily, because it's only four notes long." [The teacher plays the opening portion of the first movement.]

> "Can anyone sing the four-note theme?" [No one volunteers.] "No? Then I'd better play it for you again. You need to have it so solidly in your head that you can sing it whenever you want to." [The teacher plays the opening portion again, then sings the first eight notes with the class, urging them to render the theme in a dramatic fashion.]

> "That's the way! This time I'll let the music go on for about 45 seconds. When you *cannot* hear the theme any longer, raise your hand." [The teacher plays the recording to the beginning of the second theme. Hands pop up and down sporadically, but with no unanimity.]

> "You don't seem very sure. You know what that means: we'll just have to listen again to see if we can get more agreement. It's better if you don't look around and raise your hand just because you see someone else doing so. Decide for yourself." [The teacher plays the first minute of the movement. Most of the students raise their hands when the second theme begins.]

The first movement of Beethoven's Fifth Symphony is between six and eight minutes long, depending on whether or not the recording repeats the opening portion of the movement. That is quite short for a symphony movement, and its brevity is one feature that makes it a good choice to play for children.

In fact, the entire Fifth Symphony of Beethoven is a work that invites thoughtful examination and repeated hearings. In a way, that fact presents a problem for the teacher, who must decide which features most warrant the attention of the class. In the situation described above, the teacher wants the students to grasp the concept of theme development without waiting for the development section in a *sonata form* movement, with which the idea of development is usually associated. This form contains a section in which themes are presented, a section in which they are developed, and a concluding section in which the theme is restated. As the students examine a work such as the first movement of Beethoven's Fifth Symphony, the teacher can introduce them to the term "development." The word gives them a verbal "handle" to attach to the musical phenomenon they are hearing and experiencing.

The symphonies and concertos of Mozart, Haydn, and Beethoven are good choices for studying development, because these earlier compositions usually are not as long as the works of nineteenth-century composers. Development also figures prominently in movements of chamber music, such as sonatas and string quartets from the Classical period. When deciding on selections for the class to hear, the teacher should of course check the length beforehand. But it is also advisable to notice whether there is an introduction. Particularly in early symphonies, the introduction is likely to move at a slow tempo and to present material unrelated to the theme that will appear after the introduction is completed. The hardest part of the teacher's preparation may be to locate the opening of the development section on the recording when it is played for the class.

Another consideration in the teacher's planning concerns the form of the first movement in many Classical concertos, if one is to be played for the class. The development section may appear to be delayed, because the composer often repeats the opening portion of sonata form, so that the first time the material is played by the orchestra and the second time it features an instrumental soloist with the orchestra accompanying.

Imitation

Many compositions achieve organizational unity by featuring melodic lines that imitate one another, which means that the music contains counterpoint. The *fugue* is the most notable contrapuntal form, but certain other types of music are likely to involve extended imitative passages, as well: the concerto grosso, choruses from oratorios, and motets and madrigals.

Through their singing of rounds, children are already familiar with the idea that lines of music can occur in imitation. The major difference between a round and the forms mentioned in the preceding paragraph is the complexity and length of the music. A round is a short song that maintains strict and continuous imitation, while the larger imitative forms are more complex and flexible, as seen in the fact that they include additional thematic material and occasionally modify the imitation. Here is how a teacher might introduce the fugue:

"You've been singing rounds for years now, so you know that the main idea of a round is that the same melody is sung by different groups starting at different times. The idea of imitation is also the basis for longer and more complicated pieces of music.

"Today we'll hear an imitative piece called a *fugue*. This one is for organ. It was probably written by J. S. Bach, and it's called the 'Fanfare' Fugue. Do you all know what a fanfare is?" [A few students demonstrate by humming into make-believe trumpets, while others offer verbal descriptions: "It's like a parade," and "You do a fanfare when you want to announce something important."]

"Right! You'll see how this piece got its name when you hear the music." [The teacher plays a recording of the "Fanfare" Fugue, which is quite short.]

"April, what instrument, besides organ, would sound good on this fanfare?"

"It sounds like what a trumpet might play," April responds.

"Yes, it does. And several of you demonstrated a few minutes ago that you know what a trumpet's like. But there's more for you to hear in this piece, so I'm going to play the recording for you again. This time, find out how many different lines are in this fugue. The lines of a fugue are called *voices,* even though the music is for instruments, not singers. You can find out the number of voices by listening at the beginning to the appearances of the theme." [The teacher plays the *exposition,* which is the term for the opening section of a fugue.]

"How many of you think this fugue has one voice? Raise your hands if you do." [No hands go up.] "How many of you think there are two voices?" [One hand goes up.] "Three?" [The teacher goes on to ask about four and five voices.] "Well, as most of you showed by raising your hands, this fugue happens to have three voices. Just to prove that fact to yourselves, listen to the beginning again, and this time raise a finger each time a voice enters." [The teacher plays the exposition of the "Fanfare" Fugue again as the class members raise their fingers with each appearance of the theme.]

Exposition of "FANFARE" FUGUE

"You're doing a good job of listening, class. The theme of a fugue is called the *subject*. So at the beginning of this fugue you heard the subject enter how many times?"

Depending on the time available and the ability of the students, the class can also listen for the change of key as each voice enters in the exposition, and for the type of music that occurs when the subject is absent later in the fugue. The teacher or a student can draw the pattern of the exposition on the chalkboard or a large sheet of paper. To prepare the chart, the class needs to identify the place in the rhythm when each voice enters. Professional musicians count long periods of rest by substituting the number of the measure for every first beat, so they count silently to themselves in this manner: "*1 2 3 4, 2 2 3 4, 3 2 3 4,*" and so on. A class using this procedure can determine, through careful listening, that the "Fanfare" Fugue presents the voice entrances at these exact moments in the exposition:

measure | 1 | | | | 5 | | | | 9 | | | |

Voice I starts here

Voice II starts here

Voice III starts here

The students should realize that a fugue is not the only form that is based on imitation. They need to notice imitative passages in other works as well.

Free form

Many pieces exhibit no standard form such as rondo or sonata form. This does not mean that they are disorganized, but simply that they do not follow one of the recognized formal schemes. Most of these works are short and have a variety of titles such as "fantasy," "impromptu," "prelude," "nocturne," and so on. Many of them are for solo piano, and as their names imply, they are intended to create a particular mood and to sound improvised.

Free form is also evident in *program music*. In this type of piece, the composer associates the music with a nonmusical idea or story, which is its "program." As was mentioned in Chapter 9, musical sounds cannot in and of themselves tell a story; only words can do that. And yet program music is almost always instrumental, with no narration or song text to provide concrete meaning for the listener. The literal telling of a story, therefore, is not the purpose of program music. Its purpose is the same as that of most art music: to provide an interesting and satisfying listening experience through the skillful crafting of musical sounds. The program serves merely as a springboard for the composer's thoughts and as an extremely general idea to which the listeners may refer as they contemplate the music.

Danse Macabre by Saint-Saëns is one of the many program works that are interesting to children. It is a short imaginative piece with definite Halloween overtones. The title and 12 lines of poetry are the only nonmusical associations offered by Saint-Saëns, but the listener can easily imagine the dead rising from their graves and dancing wildly until the rooster's crow announces morning. There is even the tolling of the hour and the clanking of skeletons in a xylophone solo.

"Imagine that you're composers. You've been assigned to write a piece of music based on this poem. I'll read it for you, and as I read, think of what *musical* ideas it stirs up in your mind. You don't need to come up with a complete melody. Just share your ideas for sound effects, maybe, or special rhythms."

Zig, zig, zig, Death in cadence,
Striking with his heel a tomb,
Death at midnight plays a dance-tune,
Zig, zig, zig, on his violin.
The winter wind blows and the night is dark;
Moans are heard in the linden-trees.
Through the gloom, white skeletons pass,
Running and leaping in their shrouds.
Zig, zig, zig, each one is frisking,
The bones of the dancers are heard to crack—
But hist! of a sudden they quit the round,
They push forward, they fly; the cock has crowed.
                                        —Henri Cazalis, 1874

"Patrick, what musical ideas did you come up with?"

"I remember something in the poem about a violin playing a tune, and the story is about spooks and skeletons dancing, so maybe someone could play a scary tune on the violin," Patrick suggests.

"Good idea, Patrick. Who else can think of some special effects?"

Other recommendations follow quickly: "There's a line about bones cracking and skeletons jumping around, so I'd have some clanking and clinking sounds." "At the end the rooster crows, so someone should make that kind of sound."

[On hearing the last suggestion, a few of the more extroverted class members begin, without invitation, to audition for the crowing role. The teacher brings the brainstorming to a close.]

"You all have good ideas. As you may have guessed, I read these lines because a composer named Saint-Saëns has already written an orchestra piece that's associated with them. When you listen to it, you don't need to worry at what point in the music this or that happens in relation to the poem. Instead, notice how Saint-Saëns shapes the music into a good composition. As you listen, try to remember one or two things Saint-Saëns does, and we can talk about them after the piece is finished." [The teacher plays through *Danse Macabre* without stopping.]

LARGE MUSICAL FORMS

The word "form" has several applications in music. So far in this chapter, the term has referred to the overall pattern or design of a musical work. But the word "form" also denotes a type of music such as symphony, concerto, suite, and string quartet. When used in that broader sense, the term suggests both the particular performance medium and the longer nature of the work, which usually consists of several movements.

Time in elementary school music classes is too brief to permit detailed study of these forms, but children should be introduced to them and should know in general what they are. Students who attend children's concerts in the community are likely to hear a movement from a concerto or suite or other large form. It helps their understanding if they know ahead of time that a concerto features contrast between an instrumental soloist and the orchestra, that a concerto grosso contrasts a small group with a large group, and that a symphony is an orchestral work that has several movements (usually four). Above all, the children need to learn how to listen with concentration and open-mindedness, whether the music is a short song or a long symphony.

Planning the lesson

In teaching children to listen more effectively, the teacher should keep in mind the points presented in Chapter 9 concerning repeated hearings and listening for specific points. Those suggestions apply to upper grade students as much as they do to younger children. The greater length and complexity of forms such as the concerto and suite require special planning. The teacher should select compositions or movements that are not too long. Fortunately, there is much music from which to choose, so it is rather easy to find an attractive piece of appropriate length for inexperienced listeners. Often a teacher decides to play only a portion of a work in a single class, as did the teacher in the excerpt involving Beethoven's Symphony No. 5.

Whatever the listening selection, the teacher should give the class something specific for which to listen. That is what the teacher is doing in the following illustration. The listening selection is Haydn's Concerto in E Flat for Trumpet and Orchestra.

"Today we're going to listen to some music by Haydn. It's part of a concerto for trumpet and orchestra. Who remembers the main idea of a concerto? Paula?"

"I think it's the contrast between small and large, like in a trumpet concerto between the trumpet and the orchestra," Paula explains.

"Right. Now, as you listen, decide if the theme comes back or not, or if it ever goes away." [The teacher plays the opening 45 seconds of the third movement of Haydn's Trumpet Concerto. The theme does return, played by the trumpet, after a short section containing contrasting material.]

"Sue, did the theme go away, and if it did, did it come back?"

"I couldn't hear it for a while, so it must've gone away. But then the trumpet played the melody again, so it came back," Sue concludes.

"That's right. Was the second appearance of the main theme exactly like the first appearance? I know that the trumpet played it the second time, but was the theme itself changed, Mike?"

"Yeah, I think the trumpet changed the theme," Mike answers.

"What do you think, Wendell? Was the theme the same or different when the trumpet played it?"

"It sounded the same to me," Wendell shrugs.

"There seems to be some disagreement here. We'd better listen to the music again, class, and see what actually happens to the theme." [The teacher plays the opening 45 seconds again.]

"What about the second appearance of the theme, Mike?"

"Well, it doesn't exactly change," Mike concedes, "but the trumpet makes the music sound different."

The class might go on to discover, through careful listening, that the movement is in rondo form. They might even notice that later appearances of the *A* theme are shorter, while the contrasting sections become longer.

In addition to orchestral forms such as symphonies, suites, and concertos, the students should hear examples of large works written for single instruments, and a representative sampling of chamber music. Young listeners are more likely to appreciate the qualities of chamber music when they understand that it is intended for performance in a room or "chamber" by a small group of musicians with only one person on each part. The more frequently heard combinations are the string quartet and the sonata. The latter form consists of piano and one other instrument, not in roles of soloist and accompanist, but as equal partners. The listeners should look for the clarity and interweaving of parts when they hear chamber music. They will be disappointed if they expect to hear the sweeping dimensions of a large group performance or the loudness of electronically amplified ensembles in the popular idiom.

Opera

Listening efforts in the elementary school should not be devoted exclusively to instrumental music, of course. Although school children in America sing for several years before they become involved in curricular instrumental music programs, most fifth and sixth graders know virtually nothing about art songs, oratorios, and operas. In fact, many children entertain 'a vague idea that they are not supposed to like such music, on the assumption that it is not intended to be understood or enjoyed by the average person. For this reason, teaching children to listen to vocal music presents an extra challenge. And in view of many children's attitudes, such teaching may be particularly important and necessary.

A teacher can facilitate the students' acceptance of opera and other types of vocal art music by carefully choosing the works for study. Even though they may be good music, many vocal works are of little interest to children. The vocal music that appeals to them has something about it to which they can relate. Gian-Carlo Menotti's *Amahl and the Night Visitors* is an opera that fits this criterion very well. The two leads are a mother and her crippled son, Amahl, who is about twelve years old. He has several characteristics of a twelve-year-old, including enthusiasm, curiosity, a tendency to disregard what his mother says, and a flair for exaggerating the truth. Two other features make this work an attractive choice for young people: the opera is in English and is only about 50 minutes long. It was originally composed for television, and it has been restaged regularly.

The music series books contain abbreviated versions of musicals, operettas (which have spoken lines in addition to singing), and operas, including *Amahl and the Night Visitors*. These resources can help a teacher to identify the types of vocal music that are most appealing to young listeners.

Not only the choice of materials but the manner of presentation makes a difference in the students' acceptance of new forms. They should understand, first of all, that an opera is a drama set to music. They will grasp this point more clearly if they read the text as a play, with members of the class taking various roles. If they "walk through" the actions in a scene, the sequence of events will seem more concrete and vivid.

The students also need to realize that the music in operas and art songs is usually created to enhance the text, rather than to stand alone as a dynamic melody in itself. Here is how a teacher might demonstrate this concept to a class.

"We've been listening to *Amahl and the Night Visitors* and study-ing about it for a couple of class periods now. Look in your books at the music the three kings sing as they come nearer to the home of Amahl and his mother. They sing the same melody three times, and each time they sing it louder than before, to give the impression of an approaching sound.

From far a-way we come_ and far-ther we_must go._

How far, how far, my crys-tal star?____

"How Far?" From Gian-Carlo Menotti, *Amahl and the Night Visitors*. Published by G. Schirmer, Inc., 1951, 1952. Used by permission.

"You heard the music when we went through the opera the first time, but let's sing it over again now so that you can learn it a bit bet-ter. Here's the starting note. . . . Rea-dy, sing." [The class sings through the eight-measure excerpt.]

"Arnold, would you say that's a good melody, one that we might sing for a concert or for the PTA?"

"It doesn't seem real good, but then it doesn't seem real bad either," answers Arnold discreetly.

"Robin, what do you think? Is it a good melody?"

"I sort of agree with Arnold," says Robin. "It's okay, but I don't think we'd sing it at a concert." Earl concurs by injecting the opinion that the song is "kinda boring."

"You may be right, Earl. What is it about the melody that makes it seem boring?"

"Well, in the first line the notes wander around so much that you can't tell where they're going to settle down. The second line doesn't do much except go back and forth between two notes," Earl declares.

"Is there any reason for the melody to sound like that? I'll give you a hint: Where does it happen in the opera? Yes, Andrea?"

"The kings are wandering through the desert. They're probably lost, so the music should sound lost, too. Then on the second line, the rocking effect is maybe supposed to sound like walking along slowly for mile after mile," Andrea concludes.

Behind her, Dirk comments, "They weren't walking; they were riding on camels."

Andrea turns around to face Dirk and says, "Camels walk too, y'know." She turns to the front again while the teacher comments, "I like the walking idea. And how about the question in the second line? Class, what's the inflection in your voice when you ask someone a question? Does your voice go up or down?" [Several class members volunteer that the voice rises.] "Sure, it goes up at the end, just like the direction of the notes on the words 'How far?'

"And notice that the note values are longer in the second line, maybe to show that the kings are getting tired. By the end of the line, even the pitch doesn't move; it just stays the same.

"This song may not have a great melody, but it's just right for what the composer, Menotti, wants it to do; it helps set the mood of the situation. All through the opera, the music contributes to the sense of drama and enriches the meaning of the words and stage actions."

One stumbling block to full acceptance of opera in the mind of many people is the fact that the pacing of the stage action seems unrealistic. Students in the upper grades are usually sophisticated enough to understand the reasons for this. Occurrences that would happen quickly in real life are often prolonged in opera so that the characters have enough time to articulate their feelings through music. Conversely, slow-moving events tend to be compressed in opera so that the action will move forward. This flexible attitude toward the time line of the story is of course characteristic of all theater, with or without music.

The impression of unreality in opera is heightened by its most basic and obvious feature—the fact that everything is sung, even the most mundane comments of the characters on stage. To an inexperienced listener the effect seems contrived, at best. So it is especially important for students to understand that opera is not trying to duplicate the realism of everyday life. Its purpose, instead, is to express emotions in a musical and dramatic setting.

Opera, with its blend of acting, scenery, singing, and orchestral accompaniment, represents the combination of several arts. Because the visual element is so important in opera, students are much more likely to understand the form and enjoy it if they can see a live performance. If that is not feasible, performances on film or television are available. Filmstrips with music and narration have been designed for use in the elementary schools, and the companies that offer such filmstrips are listed in Appendix B.

Students in the upper grades of elementary school do not need to know the details of particular musical forms. But when they hear the underlying organization of lines and sections of musical works, they are becoming better educated in music.

REVIEW QUESTIONS

1. In what two ways is the word "form" used in music?

2. Why is the perception of musical phrases a prerequisite to understanding formal patterns in music?

3. What is the basic pattern for binary form? For ternary form?

4. How can a teacher reinforce the students' understanding of rondo form?

5. When a teacher is preparing to present the concept of variation, what is the advantage of selecting a work with a theme that is familiar to the students?

6. a. What are some ways in which a melody can be varied?
   b. How can a teacher help a class to notice more fully how a composer has varied a theme?

7. What is one teaching procedure for helping students to gain a concept of development in music?

8. How might a teacher go about presenting a fugue for the class to hear?

9. Which is a more important focus of attention for a class listening to program music: to hear when events in the story are being represented, or to notice how the music is organized?

10. How might students be made aware of the fact that opera interprets events expressively rather than literally?

11. Suppose that no live performance of opera is available for the class to see. What can a teacher do to provide at least some of the visual element of opera?

ACTIVITIES

1. Locate three songs in a music series book.
   a. Determine the form of each song.
   b. Study the songs for elements that give them unity.

2. Select an instrumental work, perhaps one mentioned in a music series book.
   a. Determine whether the form is basically sectional, developmental, imitative, variation, or free form.
   b. Develop a plan for teaching students about the form of the work.

3. Examine several of the music series books written for the upper elementary grades, and compare their presentations of art songs, oratorios, or operas. Select one unit or example and analyze it according to:
   a. the main points the children are to learn
   b. the method of getting the points across to the students
   c. the appropriateness of the material in terms of difficulty for the age and musical background of the class

Teaching About Music and Culture

Chapters 12-16 discussed the teaching of various elements of music such as melody, harmony, and form in the upper grades. This chapter concentrates on teaching music in its cultural context. Music does not develop in a vacuum unrelated to the people who create it. It reflects the larger culture and its customs and accomplishments. The relationship of a work of music to its culture can be viewed from two perspectives: time and place. Like other expressions of culture, music changes from one historical epoch to another, and reflects the attitudes and practices of a particular time. It also differs from one area of the world to another, and may even differ significantly within a rather small geographical area.

Students in the upper elementary grades learn in social studies about the life and customs of America and other parts of the world. This gives them a certain amount of geographical and historical background for instruction dealing with music in a particular culture.

The cultural significance of musical works is a vast and complex topic. But if "a journey of a thousand miles begins with a single step," the first steps toward understanding are appropriately taken in the upper elementary grades, even though those steps may be small and few in number.

Because culture involves not only the arts but also social studies and history, a classroom teacher is as well equipped as a music specialist to teach this area of study. The classroom teacher knows the students' background in social studies, teaches the subject, and has expertise in that area. Such a person is in a good position to integrate social studies and music. The music specialist, of course, has the advantage of much more training in music, and is likely to approach the subject from a perspective that is slightly different but equally valid.

OPENNESS TO OTHER CULTURES

To appreciate more fully the significance of music in different cultures, both within the United States and around the world, students need to become receptive to unfamiliar sounds and customs. An attitude of openness and curiosity is more likely to be engendered if the teacher helps the class understand the following points.

1. Music is not a cultural manifestation that is limited in time, like the custom of writing with a quill pen, or in location, like the traditional Japanese tea ceremony. Instead, music is a part of every culture throughout the world, and has been throughout the history of the human race. As was pointed out at the beginning of Chapter 1, this fact is an important reason for including music in the school curriculum.

2. Music differs from one culture to another. Just as the people in various parts of the world have different languages, styles of dress, types of housing, religious beliefs, and culinary preferences, they also have different kinds of music.

3. No culture or its music is superior to another. The languages of other countries are as useful and valid for those countries' citizens as the English language is for Americans. The music and dance of other cultures are as interesting and beautiful to those peoples as the art forms of Western civilization are to Americans. It is true that there are methods for assessing in a general way the amount of sophistication in a musical work of a given style, but greater sophistication does not always mean greater cultural value.

Because no culture is better than another, the class should be encouraged to develop an attitude of respect for the music of other cultures. Sometimes people unconsciously adopt the view that in effect says, "If it's different from what I know, something must be wrong with it." Instead, the attitude should be, "If it's different, I want to find out more about it." Although the students should acquire information about the different kinds of music around the world, their attitudes toward unfamiliar types of music may, in the end, be more important than information.

Attitude and knowledge, however, are related. People tend to like what they know, and to be skeptical about what is unfamiliar. They are uncomfortable in situations in which their lack of information makes them feel inadequate, so they tend to develop attitudes of prejudice and dislike toward the unfamiliar area. Increased knowledge, on the other hand, contributes to an attitude of increased respect and curiosity, which in turn encourages a person to want to know more. It is important not only to know that there are many different types of music but also to know what makes the types of music different. Students in the upper elementary grades are advanced enough to learn, for example, that the music of India is improvised, is based on a melodic "formula" called a *raga* and a nonmetrical rhythmic pattern called a *tala*, has no accompanying chords, and is played on instruments such as the sitar and tambura.

RESOURCES FOR TEACHING ABOUT CULTURE AND MUSIC

Although the music series books differ in the depth and method of presenting information about music of other cultures, these books are helpful to the students in learning about the different types of music around the world. Most of the books contain song material and pictures, and there are recorded examples in the supplementary record albums.

Some music series books present material in units, while other books take a one-song-at-a-time approach. Generally, more lasting and effective learning occurs when the material is presented as a unit. The teacher will probably cover fewer types of music, but the presentation is usually more thorough and therefore more likely to be remembered.

A recording can present all the subtle inflections and nuances of pitch, rhythm, and timbre that are important in a particular style of music. Most of these nuances cannot be rendered in music notation. Even in the case of an American folk song, it is important to listen to a version performed in an authentic style. For example, a song from the Appalachian mountains is best performed by a folk singer from that area. The recordings available for use with the music series books contain a number of authentic versions of the music—both Western and non-Western—presented in the textbook. As a further aid to teachers, packages of supplementary material can be purchased from the sources listed in Appendix B.

Teaching the music of different cultures lends itself well to making exhibits. An attractive bulletin board about the life and music of a particular culture or country draws attention to the topic and helps the students learn. Some of the commercially prepared study units have pictures that can be posted, and more general pictures are available from travel services and other sources.

A few residents of the community may be persons from another country. They can talk to a class about their native land, and in some cases even perform some of its music. If such persons are available, they should by all means be invited to share their culture with the class.

One's teaching colleagues can also be approached for ideas and materials. The natural alliance between music and social studies facilitates a pooling of assets among the teachers involved. When a class is studying about Africa in social studies, that is a logical time for the music teacher to introduce African music and for the classroom teacher to emphasize its cultural implications. Communication and cooperation between music specialist and classroom teacher are needed to bring about the most effective learning in both music and social studies.

The total content of the music instruction should not be determined by what is covered in social studies, however. While some integration of the two subjects is desirable, many aspects of music are quite unrelated to other curricular areas. The subject of music needs to be taught systematically, and that is not possible when the music curriculum is organized according to the teaching plan for another subject area.

TEACHING THE MUSIC OF A PARTICULAR CULTURE

Students do not gain much when a teacher simply says, "This song is from France" and points to France on a map. They need to investigate what makes the song French. Is there a characteristic rhythmic pattern, melodic style, instrument, or text?

Singing a song from another culture makes a greater impact on the students than just listening to a recording of it. The amount of satisfaction that they derive from their involvement will depend partly on the syntax of the new sounds. American young people can easily learn to perform music from western Europe and Latin America in a rather authentic style, because it is not too different from the music they already know. But in the case of oriental, Indian, Arabian, and African music, it is unlikely that the singing by Americans is very close to the way the music should actually sound. When the style of music is so unfamiliar, the amount of listening to recordings should be increased and the amount of performance reduced.

The students can still benefit from attempting to sing in the new idiom, but they should understand that the effort is being undertaken for their own experience, rather than as a rehearsal for eventual public performance. They need to realize that the nuances and inflections which they are *not* duplicating may be a more distinctive characteristic of the style than the obvious notes and rhythms they are trying to imitate. The authors observed an example of this at an international conference where a choral group from another country attempted to sing a black American spiritual using black English dialect. The effect was unsettling because basic subtleties of interpretation were missing. Students need to learn that part of their respect for another culture is to recognize the unique qualities of its musical expression.

Although African music is presented in this example, the same basic approach of exploring distinctive characteristics is possible for music of any culture.

"Here's a recording of a piece of African music. Listen and see what you think makes it sound African. It's dance music from the Shona tribe in Zimbabwe."

[The teacher plays *Kalanga Dance,** which features drums and rattles.]

"Bruce, what do you think gives that music an African sound?"

"I guess the drums are different. At least they don't sound like the drums we hear in America. . . . And the rhythms are different, too," Bruce responds.

"That's right. We've talked about the importance of drumming in African culture. What was one of its purposes?"

"Oh, I know!" Several hands go up, and Barbara explains, "The people communicated to places far away through drum language, like a code."

"And was this kind of speech pretty easy, Carol, or was it complicated?"

"It was complicated. At least I'd never be able to understand it," Carol says, to which Phil declares, "Sure you would, if you lived there."

Carol pauses, then agrees, "Yeah, I guess I would."

"Good point, Phil," the teacher says. "We get so used to our own culture that it's hard to imagine ourselves in some other time and place. But let's try, right now, to get an idea how an African drummer might feel when playing complex rhythms.

"You're going to play a measure of music over and over, with *nine* different rhythmic patterns sounding at the same time! I've put nine different instruments on the table. They're not authentic African instruments, but they'll do. To let more of you participate, we'll assign pairs of students to each instrument. One plays and the other person helps the player to keep from getting lost. And yes, we'll trade off."

[The teacher asks the class members to volunteer by twos and take one of the nine instruments, which are also listed on the large rhythm score that the teacher has displayed prominently.]

*Recording for *Silver Burdett Music,* Book 5 (Morristown, N. J.: Silver Burdett, 1974).

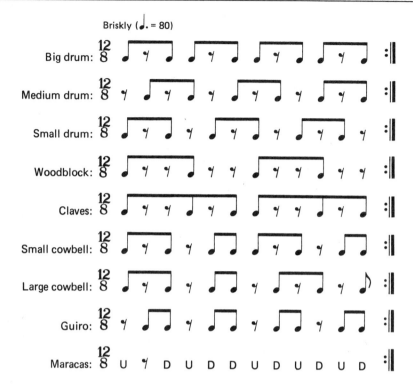

"Notice that you have only eighth notes and eighth rests. There are how many eighths in each measure, class?" [Ben volunteers that there are 12.] "Yes, 12. Count them with me at this tempo: 1 2 3 4 5 6 7 8 9 10 11 12." [The class counts together.] "Good. Are any of the 12 lines the same? No, they aren't. So you people in the teams had better take a minute and look at your parts carefully. Then take another few minutes and practice your part softly by tapping out the notes as you count. All right, practice."

[The teams work quietly together, with occasional giggles and signs of impatience as errors are made. After about two minutes, the teacher hears each line separately, counting aloud for each, in tempo.]

"Now I think you're ready to put the piece together. Above all, keep the rhythm steady."

[The class attempts to reproduce the rhythm in organized fashion, beginning with one line. Other lines are added one at a time. There are several false starts, however, and the class begins to lose its sense of serious effort. The teacher brings the activity to a close and the players return to their seats.]

"If you had been sending a real message, what would it have been?"

> "I don't know," comments Dave, "but if the next room sends us a message back, they're gonna tell us to quit this and get back to something we know how to do."

Experience with a multi-linear drumming pattern is likely to convince even the most casual student that African rhythm is complex, especially when its intricacies are supposed to be shaded with speech-like nuances.

Reproducing the actual speech sounds of songs in another language is difficult. In the following African song there is no English translation, so the African words must be pronounced phonetically. Children can do this after a little practice, and it increases their sense of participating in another culture. The fact that the singers cannot understand the meaning of specific words is a serious flaw, of course. But if the children know the general intent of the text, they can sing with some understanding of the mood of the song.

> "Today we'll try to sing an African song. We'll do our best to sing it right, but remember that we don't know what way *is* right, and an African probably wouldn't like our interpretation at all. We're singing the song so we can find out what goes into African music. A recording of the song will help us decide how it should go.
>
> "The song is from the Bemba tribe in Zambia. Melanie, please point out Zambia to us on the map of Africa." [Melanie looks for the country and soon finds it.] "Right; it's just above Zimbabwe, the home country of the dance music we heard a day or so ago.
>
> "This song from Zambia is accompanied by a dance that's performed only by the women and girls. The dance is difficult, and the song tells how the older sisters need to help the young girls learn the dance. Notice that there are only African words in the music. Why no English translation? Probably because no translation would fit well and contain the same meaning. First let's listen to a recording of 'Bana Cimbusa.'" [The teacher plays the recording.]
>
> "Who noticed something different about this song? Connie?"
>
> "There was a short solo and then the rest of the singers joined in," Connie observes.
>
> "Good, Connie. It was like a statement and answer, wasn't it? That's known as call-and-response technique, and it's common in African music."
>
> [The teacher directs attention the the unusual notation of two consecutive dotted eighth notes, which last as long as three eighths, and can be rewritten as a borrowed pattern:

BANA CIMBUSA

Bemba People, Zambia

Bah - nah see - mboo -sah eh____ Bah - nah see - mboo -sah
Ba - na ci - mbu - sa eh____ Ba - na ci - mbu - sa

moowah-ngah - lah - fooway. Mooway - foo - ndow moowah-nah eh____
mwa - nga - la - fwe. Mwa - fu - ndo mwa - na eh____

Mooway - foo - ndo moowah -nah moowah-moo - shah pah - nshee -lah.
Mwa - fu - ndo mwa - na mwa - mu - sha pa - nshi - la.

Koo - foo-ndow moowah-nah eh____ Koo - foo-ndow mwah - nah
Ku - fu - ndo mwa - na eh____ Ku - fu - ndo mwa - na

koo - kow - sah - poh Seh - nseh - lay - nee eh____
ku - ko - sa - po Se - nse - le - ni eh____

Seh - nseh - lay - nee kah - soo - ba kah - wah.
Se - nse - le - ni ka - su - ba ka - wa.

Refrain

Cha - ndah - ma - sah nsah lah see - lee - kay ngoh -mah,
Cha - nda ma - sa - nsa' la } ci - li - ke ngo - ma,
ah lah }
All a - la }

Ah - lah see - lee - kay ngoh - mah.
A - la ci li - ke ngo - ma.

The teacher points out also that two measures of the refrain present a borrowed triplet figure, which consumes the duration of two "regular" eighth notes.]

"Listen to the song once more. Then we'll say the words with the phonetic pronunciation." [The recording is played again, after which the class recites the words.] "Good. Now that you have the words and melody in your ears, try to sing the song. Here's the starting note. . . . Rea-dy, go." [The class tries to sing "Bana Cimbusa."] "Not bad. So far you've noticed the call-and-response in this song, and the rhythmic patterns that are different from what we're used to. Both these features are typical of African music. What about the amount of repetition in the song, Aaron?"

"Well, patterns in the melody keep coming back . . . and until the last two lines, the solo part stays just about the same. Also, um . . . the response repeats a lot," Aaron concludes.

When presenting music of a different culture, the teacher should convey two points of caution to the class. First, a brief sampling of rhythms and songs can provide only the merest introduction to the many types of music in that culture. Second, the problem of transcribing the pitches and rhythms of African music, for example, into our notation system can be only partly successful. The same problem exists when transcribing the speech sounds of one language into the orthography of another. For this reason, the students should not become preoccupied with the notation of such music. When their attention is directed toward notation, it should be for the purpose of clarifying what they see and hear.

ERAS OF MUSICAL STYLE

History is not usually taught as such in elementary school social studies, although American history receives attention at about the fifth-grade level. For this reason, upper grade students are likely to have had little experience in viewing events from a historical perspective. The music teacher may introduce the usual name for a stylistic period (Renaissance, Baroque, and so on) as the class encounters music of that style, but a detailed survey of music history has little meaning for children whose sense of time span is not well developed and whose experience with different musical styles is still severely limited. With most children it is premature to attempt to convey the sweep of music history.

What may provide them with a better understanding is to relate a style of music and culture to a person. For example, Haydn and Mozart composed during the time of George Washington and the American Revolution, and Johannes Brahms was composing his first works just after the end of the American Civil War and the death of Abraham Lincoln. Associating styles with a few important composers may present a somewhat distorted view of music history, but it helps the children begin to organize their impressions into an orderly time sequence, and it reminds them that history is, after all, a record of human events.

Here is a music class in which the teacher is centering attention on the music and times of Joseph Haydn.

"In your books you'll find some information about Franz Joseph Haydn, and themes from a string quartet that he composed. It's easy to remember the nickname of the quartet: 'The Bird.' Remember: his name is pronounced *High*-din, even though it looks like *Hay*-din. The book points out that Haydn lived about 200 years ago. Who was alive and important in America 200 years ago? Janet?"

"Well, the Revolutionary War was about then, so George Washington and Benjamin Franklin were pretty important," Janet reports.

"That's right. In fact, Washington and Haydn were born in the same year, 1732. Of course, Washington was born in Virginia and Haydn in a country named Austria in the middle of Europe, so they never knew each other.

"The work that we'll hear by Haydn is part of a string quartet. It's played by two violins, a viola, and a cello. The viola, remember, is a little bigger and lower in sound than the violin. Here's the first movement of Haydn's quartet. As you listen, try to think of a word or two that you might use to describe the style of the quartet. Is it 'clear,' 'light,' 'dark,' 'emotional,' or what?" [The teacher plays the first movement of "The Bird" Quartet in C major, Op. 33, No. 3.]

Theme 1

Theme 2

"Patty, what word do you think best describes this music?"

"Chirping," suggests Patty. "You said the name of the quartet is 'The Bird,'" she explains.

"Good thought. Kurt, what word do you think describes the quartet?"

"Clean; everything seemed exactly in place and not cluttered up with a lot of stuff," Kurt decides.

[The teacher elicits other students' ideas about the quartet. Most of the descriptive terms suggest that the music is good-natured and logical.]

"The words you've come up with like 'direct' and 'clean' are good ones for Haydn's music," the teacher summarizes. "In a way, his music is logical like the style of Washington and Jefferson and the other Americans who drew up the Declaration of Independence. For a document that was declaring freedom, it is quite 'cool' and logical. That was the style of art, music, and literature during the classical period. People wanted their art works to be very controlled and unemotional."

On subsequent days the class can discover other features of Haydn's "The Bird" Quartet, including the form and the short, tuneful patterns of the melodies. The class might hear another work by Haydn, perhaps the second movement of his Op. 76, No. 3 ("Emperor") Quartet. That movement is a good choice because it is an example of theme and variations in which the melody is present in all variations. The melody itself is the national anthem for Austria and is sung in churches today under the title "Glorious Things of Thee Are Spoken." Haydn composed 104 symphonies, as well as several concertos, works for small groups of instruments, and oratorios.

POPULAR MUSIC

The students should be encouraged to examine popular music as well as folk and art music. Some music series books for fifth and sixth grade include songs and units on rock and other types of popular music. Whatever type of popular music is studied, the attention should be on learning about music, not on just having fun. The students can engage in that kind of activity on their own outside of school. Both the students and the teacher should approach the music with a "Let's learn about it" attitude.

A good way to encourage the students to think about the musical qualities that make up a type of music is to compare two versions of the same song. The song "Greensleeves" was presented in its original form on page 241 in the discussion of interpretation in singing. The version of "Greensleeves" on pages 300-301 is essentially the same melody but arranged in a rock style. In addition to helping the children sing the song, the teacher can guide them in comparing the rock version with the original.

"We've now sung two versions of 'Greensleeves': the original version from hundreds of years ago and the rock version from our time. How are they different? Emily?"

"The old one is in $\frac{6}{8}$ and the rock one is in $\frac{4}{4}$," observes Emily. "And the rhythm has been changed a lot," Lewis adds.

"You're both right. But what's different about the rhythm in the rock version?"

"It 'swings' and is off the beat," Stephanie volunteers. "I think it has some syncopation." "And the rock version has a second part with sounds on 'bah' instead of words," Nick contributes.

"You're right. But there's another difference that doesn't appear on the pages of the books. Listen as I play the recording of the rock version." [The teacher plays the recording from the album accompanying the series books.]

"Brent, can you name another difference between the old and the rock versions, one that you could hear?"

"They sound different . . . but I don't know why."

"Were there some instruments in the rock version that weren't in the original version from England that we listened to a couple of days ago?"

"Drums?" Brent tentatively suggests.

"And what do the drums and other instruments add to the rock version?"

"Well, they made the rock version seem pretty jumpy. It's like two different songs. I think the old version was nice and smooth and sort of peaceful."

As with many songs, a simple instrumental accompaniment can be added to the rock version of a song like "Greensleeves." There may be students in the class who have studied electric guitar, and they can bring their instruments to school and add much to the accompaniment. They can be asked to create a part for their instrument. Other classroom instruments can also contribute to an accompaniment. For example, the autoharp can play the chords indicated in the music with this pattern:

A drum or tambourine can play:

GREENSLEEVES (ROCK VERSION)

Arranged and Adapted by Buryl Red

Such parts can make the students more aware of the emphasis on the second and fourth beats in rock music.

No type of music should be ignored in school music classes; the only limitation should be the time allotted to any one type. No music, whether art or popular, exists apart from the larger culture. A musically educated person knows about the varied types of music, and has some understanding of where a piece fits, geographically and historically, into the world of music.

REVIEW QUESTIONS

1. What three points should students remember if they are to be receptive to unfamiliar music?

2. How are knowledge and attitude related?

3. Where can a teacher locate materials on music from various countries and cultures around the world?

4. Why will Americans usually sing a German folk song better than they sing a song from Turkey or Indonesia?

5. a. Why is it useful to sing songs when learning about other cultures?
   b. Why is it important to listen to recordings of authentic performances of such music?

6. The integration of music and social studies is desirable up to a point. Why is a combining of the two subjects not recommended for the entire music curriculum?

7. Why is a unit of study recommended instead of a single-song approach when a class is learning about a particular culture?

8. In the music classes involving African music (pages 292-96), how did the teacher help the students learn
   a. the importance of rhythm?
   b. the style of singing?
   c. the call-and-response technique?

9. How can students be helped to gain an initial understanding of historical eras in music?

ACTIVITIES

1. Examine several of the music series books prepared for grades five and six. Find a unit, or combine several pieces of music to form a unit, on any type of non-Western art music. Then develop a plan for teaching the following with your unit:
   a. The features and characteristics of the music
   b. The cultural setting in which the music was created

2. Using the same unit, write a description of how you would incorporate the music into an appropriate social studies unit.

FOUR

OTHER ASPECTS
OF TEACHING MUSIC

The fourth and final section of this book consists of four chapters on topics that are of special interest to teachers involved with music instruction. Unlike the preceding fourteen chapters, these topics do not relate to specific aspects of music. Instead, they discuss the content and methods of music instruction that occur in special situations in the elementary school.

Chapter 18 explores ways to adapt music instruction to the interests and abilities of the individual child by applying the concepts of "open education" and individualized instruction to the area of music.

Chapter 19 deals with the teaching of music as a fine art. Again, the emphasis is on practical application, not on philosophical positions.

The topic of educating children with special learning handicaps has received much attention in recent years, and students from special education classes are increasingly "mainstreamed" with other children. The opportunities and limitations of this practice for music classes are discussed in Chapter 20. Ideas for the music instruction of special education students can also be applied in their own special classrooms or in clinical settings.

Finally, the learning of music should be evaluated, not because children may need to be graded but because the teacher needs to determine what they have learned so that future instruction can be planned more effectively. Evaluation is discussed in Chapter 21.

Individualizing Music Instruction

Music has a long tradition of being performed as a group endeavor. People sing songs together and instrumentalists gather into bands, orchestras, and chamber ensembles. Except for the solo keyboard repertoire and some folk songs, music is almost never performed by one person alone. What place, then, does individual learning have in music instruction in the elementary schools? And if it does have a place, how is individualization accomplished? These questions are best answered by referring to the basic questions presented in Chapter 3 on planning music instruction: What? Why? How? To whom? With what result?

WHAT IS INDIVIDUALIZED LEARNING?

Educators differ in what they mean by the term "individualized learning." Usually it implies that a person is learning a chosen subject in the manner and at the rate he or she wishes. At the very least, it is learning in which not everyone in a class is involved in the same way.

Although the importance of individual differences and learning styles had been discussed for many years prior to the advent of the "open classroom" philosophy, in recent years the concept of individualized learning has become associated with that educational outlook. While individualized instruction is consonant with the tenets of open education, it is certainly not confined to any particular position or program. It does not require a particular scheduling pattern, a special physical set-up, electronic equipment, or extensive resources. The project may be as simple as reading from a book.

Actually, individualized learning is not always one individual working alone; it can involve several children working together as a committee on a project. In short, individualized learning is a flexible and varied concept in which the progress of individual children is emphasized.

WHY INDIVIDUALIZED LEARNING IN MUSIC?

The main reason for individualized learning is the simple fact that each child is different from any other person. Each has individual abilities and interests, and these vary as widely in music as they do in other areas. It follows that if music instruction can build on these individual interests and abilities, it will be more effective.

What about the tradition of group participation in music? Can classroom music instruction be individualized, and if so, should it be? The answer to those questions is a qualified "yes." Some aspects of learning in music can and should be individualized, while other aspects cannot successfully be achieved apart from a group. For example, creating music is almost entirely an individual activity, as has been pointed out earlier in this book. Learning a repertoire of songs, however, is more difficult to accomplish individually, even when the songs are prerecorded and played back for the child to imitate. The stimulation and involvement of a group situation is lacking.

There are several reasons for including individualized learning in the elementary school music program. Studies in educational psychology have demonstrated that children learn better when they take some initiative in the learning activity, a fact that was mentioned in Chapter 3. Individual effort encourages student initiative and involvement, which in turn results in more thorough and effective learning.

Individual learning situations also permit the teacher to assume a different role. The learning situation in most music classes is teacher-dominated, because the nature of group performance requires unity. The performers are not free to decide as individuals what portion of what song they will sing at any given moment, because the resulting sound would be chaotic. So it is necessary for the teacher to render most of the judgments and dispense most of the information. There is nothing inherently wrong with this, but if followed all of the time, it dampens the children's initiative and involvement. They become quite willing to let the teacher do the work, and when they put forth less effort, they do not learn as much. It is good, therefore, if the teacher occasionally assumes the role of guide or helper.

HOW IS INDIVIDUALIZED LEARNING IMPLEMENTED?

The first matter to consider is what the children will learn from the activity. While some incidental learning may happen by chance when they operate completely without direction, school time is too valuable to justify a laissez-faire position. Good teaching requires that the child and teacher have an objective clearly in mind for the individual effort. Whether the expected result is the completion of an assignment made by the teacher or a report in an area of the child's choosing, the objective for the individual activity should be made explicit beforehand.

The way in which the child will pursue the learning task needs to be planned. The method and materials will depend on the nature of the objective. If the child wants to learn about a musical element, a published individualized learning program, such as those available with several of the music series books, is an appropriate tool. If learning to play the recorder, piano, or guitar is desired, prepared materials involving books and cassette tapes are available. Or the child can use other materials not specifically prepared for individual learning projects. Information on many topics can be gathered from the supplementary units available from Bowmar and Keyboard Publications and other sources mentioned in Appendix B. These units often include recordings as well as printed material. If a child is going to create music, then instruments and a tape recorder will be needed. A good record player and an adequate supply of books are helpful, as well as stationery supplies for preparing individualized study units.

Individual study in music is facilitated if soundproof areas are available. The use of earphones makes it possible for many individual music activities to take place in a classroom without disturbing the rest of the children. Sometimes, however, a separate room is required, as when someone is recording sounds on tape.

In many classrooms it is possible to set up a "music center" with materials that the children can use for individual work. The center might include various instruments, tape recorders, record players with earphones, recordings, books, and other printed material. A music center draws attention to the many possibilities for individual music study, and also makes the equipment and materials easily accessible.

Several resources offer suggestions to teachers on how to create units for individual study in music. Devising materials for one's students is a commendable project, but it is not a practical one for most teachers. Classroom teachers are responsible for a wide range of subjects in addition to music, and they may not have a strong music background. Music specialists have excellent training in the subject, but most of them see several hundred children each week. Neither classroom teachers nor music specialists, then, have time to do much writing of individual units, as desirable as that might be. Furthermore, the published materials are likely to be of better quality because of the experience of the authors, the time they spend preparing materials, and the fact that most publishers carefully review and screen their prospective publications. Both classroom teachers and music specialists should first make sure that the materials already in existence are available to their classes. After that is done, the writing of materials may be attempted.

A teacher who is guiding individual learning efforts should be sure that the child has the knowledge and skills required to undertake a particular project and complete it successfully. This safeguard is necessary to prevent disappointment for a child who is attracted to a project that is beyond his or her present capabilities. If a child is going to prepare a tape composition, knowledge of how to operate a tape recorder and splice tape is a prerequisite. In some cases the teacher can give the necessary instruction on the spot, as when a child needs to know simply how to operate a tape recorder. In other cases, individualized study of a particular topic and concomitant skills must be undertaken first. In general, as is pointed out later in this chapter, it is wise to begin with modest achievements and work up to larger projects.

WHEN CAN INDIVIDUALIZED LEARNING TAKE PLACE?

Sometimes an entire class can be assigned to work on individual projects at the same time, but because of limited equipment and materials, that cannot happen very often. Seldom are 25 tape recorders available, for example. Individual learning efforts must usually take place while other activities are going on in the classroom. They are not confined to music class time. Because of the music specialist's commitment to many classes, often involving travel to more than one school daily, the classroom teacher needs to cooperate with the specialist and share the responsibility for conducting individual learning activities in music.

Individualized learning is most successful when the classroom teacher is flexible about the time schedule followed in the classroom and about allowing children to develop special interests. If time is allocated in the daily schedule for individual and small group activities, children can pursue projects in music as well as other areas. For example, while one group is working on a social studies project and another group is doing supplemental reading, a few students can be working at the tape recorders on a music project. In the elementary school it is seldom possible to point to a time slot on a daily class schedule and say, "This is when individual learning in music takes place."

HOW IS INDIVIDUALIZED LEARNING EVALUATED?

As in all learning situations, evaluation of individual projects should be considered in terms of the objectives of the learning activity. The reason for evaluating the outcome is to help the child learn and to improve instruction; it is not primarily to gather data with which to grade the children. Whether they are given grades and how grading is done are matters for each school to decide for all areas of the curriculum, including music.

What distinguishes the final assessment of individualized work is the fact that the individual child is much more involved in deciding what is to be evaluated and how the observations are to be made. Almost by definition, evaluation in individualized learning efforts is not solely a responsibility of the teacher. The teacher may help the child decide whether an objective has been met, but that is quite different from acting as adjudicator.

Quite often the evaluation of individual learning involves the use of "contracts" or "commitment cards," on which the child states the objective of the individual effort. A sample of such a contract appears here.

While such a specific plan may appear to be unnecessary, most students in the upper grades of elementary school react well to its concreteness. They want to know exactly what they are to do, and they like the sense of achievement they feel when a task is completed. When conferring with a student who is preparing such a contract, the teacher should make sure that the student's goal is realistic and the steps to its implementation are explicit. When that is accomplished, evaluation becomes an easy matter, even though there are no references to "quality of work" or "final grade" on the form. This omission is intentional. If the goal and required steps have been conceived as realistic behavioral objectives, their completion will be assurance enough that learning has taken place. The contract's emphasis on self-evaluation, and work completed, is a reminder to the child that the ultimate responsibility for learning depends on his or her individual effort.

The contract forms are useful in other ways. The teacher can gain insight into the children's interests by noting the types of projects they choose to do. In some cases, the teacher may be able to adapt these ideas into group activities that the whole class will enjoy. The forms also help the teacher maintain a record of what a student has done as an individual in music. The record can be helpful to a music specialist too. A specialist who sees a few hundred children each week appreciates any information or experience that helps to distinguish each child as an individual.

Name _____ Date _____

Given _____ _____ , I will do the following:
       (number)   (days, weeks)

_____
(Student's signature)

Steps required:	Self-Evaluation	
	Accomplished	Needs more work
1.		
2.		
3.		
4.		

Contract completed? _____

_____ _____
(Teacher's signature)   (Date)

HOW SHOULD A TEACHER BEGIN INDIVIDUALIZED INSTRUCTION?

As was stated at the beginning of the chapter, the question of individualized instruction is not so much "Should there be some?" as it is "How much individual study should there be, and of what type?" The answers depend on a number of factors.

1. What is the age of the children? Students in the upper grades can usually manage individual learning efforts better than six- or seven-year-olds. Certainly the type of projects available to the children should differ according to their ages.

2. Are the children accustomed to working alone? If they are not, the individual efforts in music will need to be simpler and shorter.

3. What is the classroom teacher's attitude toward individualized instruction? If time for such learning is limited by the way in which the teacher operates the classroom, the amount and complexity of individualized learning in music will have to be reduced.

4. What equipment and materials are available? If there is only one tape recorder in the classroom, the opportunity for tape-recorder compositions will necessarily be restricted.

5. Is an individualized approach the best method for teaching what the children need to learn? Traditional techniques may be more appropriate for conveying certain aspects of music.

If answers to the previous questions indicate that some individualized efforts are desirable, the teacher may begin. Initial plans should be modest in scope, so that mistakes and problems will be minimized. If the children are not accustomed to working independently, more class time will be needed to discuss with them what they will do. Otherwise, the mechanics of individual study can be explained quite briefly.

Initial efforts should be an outgrowth of regular class activity. For example, if the class is studying same-and-different phrases in songs, each child might be asked to examine a song independently and prepare a brief verbal report on its pattern of phrases. The activity requires no special equipment and no analytical procedures other than those that have already been taught in class. All class members will be doing essentially the same thing, so there is no need for many different explanations. The children should begin the practice of completing commitment cards, however.

The next stage of independence in pursuing individual projects is similar in that the class members work toward the same goal, but each decides how to approach the activity. Some children might want to listen to songs to determine same-and-different phrases, while others might choose to look at the notation. Or if a song accompaniment is to be devised by each class member, individual decision-making will be evident in the various choices of instrument.

Some children develop confidence for later individual study by first working with a few friends on a committee project. Four children might work together on an autoharp accompaniment, four on a piano accompaniment, four on a ukulele accompaniment, and so on. Small committees allow the more able children to help the less able ones, and the experience of hearing ideas being proposed, rejected, and adapted is beneficial to children who will soon be making such decisions for themselves.

An idea that seems to work well is to give the children options from which to choose. A list of "Music Lab Ideas" offers several activities for the children to consider. An example is shown here.

MUSIC LAB IDEAS

Projects for learning about Mexican music:

Singing — I will learn one Mexican song, in English or Spanish, either by myself or in a small group. Of course, I will sing it for the class!

Listening — I will listen to two Mexican songs, and be able to describe four things about them that make them sound Mexican. Of course, I will describe these features to the class!

Playing — I will learn the melody of one Mexican song on the bells, piano, or recorder. Or I will learn the accompaniment to one Mexican song on the autoharp or guitar. Of course, I will play the song for the class!

Moving — I will learn the dance pattern for one Mexican song, either by myself or in a small group. Of course, I will perform the dance for the class!

Related arts — I will study and prepare a written report on one type of Mexican art, and I will relate that art form to the music of Mexico. Of course, I will share my report with the class!

Information — I will study and prepare a report on the music of one area of Mexico. Of course, I will tell the class what I learned!

Some children may hesitate to undertake an individual project because of the stipulation that they share their results with the class. The teacher may simply point out that this expectation provides a tangible goal for their work, gives them experience in front of a group, and provides information for the rest of the class.

In the following list of options, the obligation to perform is implicit rather than explicit, and the language is less contractual in tone. Like the preceding compilation of "Music Lab Ideas," the following suggestions enable the children to make individual choices within broad guidelines—this time in the creating of music.

MUSIC LAB IDEAS

Projects for creating music:

1. Compose three variations on this four-measure theme. You may write the variations in notation or play them on an instrument.

2. Compose a short "sound piece" involving four different sounds. Record the sounds and then manipulate them with a reel-to-reel tape recorder to make the final composition.

3. Develop an instrumental accompaniment for any song in the music book. You may use any instrument you wish. Your accompaniment does not need to be written out in notation, but be sure you can play it the same way twice!

4. Compose an eight-measure melody that the class can sing. It should be written in notation so that the class can read it. Words are optional.

5. Compose a rhythmic rondo with five sections (*ABACA*). You may use any instruments you wish, including body sounds. Each section should be at least four measures long.

As the children demonstrate increasing ability to handle independent work, they should be given more freedom in what they study and how they study it.

If introduced and managed carefully, individual learning efforts enhance music education in the elementary school by supplementing the group instruction and providing for richer and more effective learning experiences in music.

REVIEW QUESTIONS

1. What are the characteristics of individualized learning?

2. Why is some individualized learning needed in music instruction in the elementary school?

3. What determines whether a music learning activity can take place on an individualized basis?

4. Why is it important to have the objective for an individual project clearly in mind before starting on the project?

5. What are the benefits of a "music center"?

6. Why is it that few teachers develop units or projects for individualized music study?

7. How can individualized learning activities be worked into the classroom schedule?

8. What is the main purpose of evaluating an individual learning project?

9. What are the reasons for using "contracts" in individualized learning?

10. What are some factors that a teacher should consider before introducing individualized learning in a music class?

11. How can individualized learning be introduced?

ACTIVITIES

1. Examine the *Macmillan Music Center Materials*.
   a. Write a summary of the program's contents.
   b. Briefly describe how the materials might be used in elementary music instruction.

2. Examine several supplementary units available from publishers such as Keyboard Publications, Silver Burdett, Bowmar, Macmillan, and others. (See Appendix B, "Elementary Music Series Books" and "General Enrichment.") Make a list of what you examine, and compile the following information about each unit:
   a. The grade level for which it is most suitable
   b. The nature of the content
   c. Ways in which it could be used for individualized music learning

3. Devise a short music project that a child could undertake successfully. Include the following:
   a. The objective of the unit
   b. The way in which the child will accomplish the objective
   c. The materials and equipment needed
   d. The prerequisite knowledge and skills
   e. The method of evaluation

Teaching Music
and the Fine Arts

A well-balanced education in music requires attention not only to the subtleties of sound but also to the fact that music is only one type of artistic endeavor. Sculpture, painting, dance, drama, poetry, and music are areas of human achievement referred to as the *fine arts*. Although each art exists in its own medium—poetry in words, music in sounds, painting in color and shapes on a two-dimensional surface, and so on—the fine arts fulfill a basic human need. They are valuable not for the practical benefits they offer but for the psychological satisfaction and stimulation they provide. They make life richer and more interesting. They provide human beings with a mode of thinking and a type of experience found nowhere else in life.

The fine arts often reveal the similar viewpoints that have prevailed at various times and places in human history. The blurred outlines in impressionistic paintings result from the same approach to art works that influenced Claude Debussy's impressionistic music. Admittedly, there are differences among the arts because of the techniques that each employs; the painter Monet worked with paint on a flat surface, while Debussy organized sounds to be heard within a span of time. But aside from the obvious differences in the media of expression, the arts at times have shared a similar outlook.

Because the arts are characterized by a common purpose and a shared view of time and place, the study of one art medium can be enriched by an examination of the others. A comparative study of this

317

nature makes the students more sensitive to the expressive properties of sound, color, and form. The fundamental mode of thought needed for understanding the arts is reinforced and enlarged, and the students become more conscious of the qualities that distinguish artistic endeavor from the more functional forms of human activity.

There are two basic approaches for correlating music instruction with the fine arts. One approach is to supplement the music study by alluding to other arts at appropriate places in the music curriculum. The other approach is to combine all the arts, and sometimes the humanities as well, into an integrated program of study. These two approaches merit further explanation and discussion.

ENRICHMENT WITH THE ARTS

At first glance, any distinction between the "enrichment" approach and the integrated study may seem negligible. Their basic premises are different, however. In the enrichment type of teaching, music study is enhanced by including aspects of other arts where appropriate *for music*. Music has first priority, and the other arts are consigned to second place. In the integrated approach, instruction is organized around a unifying factor other than music, and that makes a considerable difference in what is taught.

The main virtue of the enrichment approach is that music is taught systematically and as thoroughly as time permits. This outcome is necessary if music is to be a significant part of the elementary school curriculum.

The negative aspect of an enrichment format is that the other fine arts are not taught in a systematic way. While the music educator may be pleased to have other arts contribute to music instruction, an art teacher or dance instructor may feel, justifiably, that such minimal coverage in his or her area is completely inadequate, especially if it is the only education the children will receive in that area during elementary school. This problem is alleviated if art is taught as a subject in itself, and if physical education experiences stress free movement as well as games and sports.

There are several ways in which music can be enriched by references to the other arts. In the following example, the teacher is referring to architecture to help the children understand the concept of form.

"You've been learning about form in music, and you know how to analyze it by assigning letters to the lines of songs and sections of pieces. Today let's consider form from another point of view, and see

Notre Dame

Seagram Building

what form is like in architecture. On page 32 in your books, look at the picture of the two buildings. One is the Cathedral of Notre Dame in Paris, France, and the other is a modern office building.

"Concentrate first on the Cathedral. Who can point out some-thing about the design or form of it? Josh?"

"It has two towers, one on each side," Josh reports, "so they give the building balance."

"That's right; the Cathedral is evenly balanced. Monica, what do you see in the center of the Cathedral, about halfway up?"

"Well, it looks like a big round window," Monica says.

"Yes; it's called the 'rose window.' What about the doors and doorways, Gavin?"

"The middle door looks like it's a little bigger . . . and the door-ways have lots of decoration around them . . . and they're shaped like an upside-down 'U' with a point at the top," Gavin concludes.

"Okay. Now what about the up-and-down form of Notre Dame? Becky?"

"It has sort of three levels or layers, and then the towers are on top of that," Becky decides.

"Good. You're all very observant, and you've recognized that there's a design to the Cathedral of Notre Dame. Is its form anything like the forms we've learned about in music, Ethan?"

"Some of our music forms have three parts."

The teacher nods. "Which three-part form is like the three sections of Notre Dame, Ethan?"

"I guess the *ABA* form. It's got the tower, a center part, and another tower," says Ethan.

"That's a good comparison. Class, notice that the *ABA* form and the three-section form of Notre Dame are similar, even though the *ABA* form happens in a period of time, and the three-part structure of Notre Dame exists in space. Both show planning, and both have a logical balance of two parts with something different in between. Now, what about the modern building? Does it have form? [The teacher helps the students to contrast its form with that of Notre Dame.]

The music series books offer several examples of enrichment, like the picture of the Balinese musicians and dancer shown here. Typical of the classical dance of Bali, India, and other countries of southeast Asia is the attention given to facial expression and the position of the hands and fingers. Children should learn that there is artistic dance in Bali and that it differs in several ways from ballet in the Western world. They should also observe the instruments that the musicians are playing and try to imagine the timbres that each would produce.

Other musical concepts can be enriched through the use of poetry. In this example the teacher asks the class to read the poem "Everyone Sang" by Siegfried Sassoon.

Everyone suddenly burst out singing;
And I was filled with such delight
As prisoned birds must find in freedom,
Winging wildly across the white
Orchards and dark-green fields; on—on—and out of sight.

Everyone's voice was suddenly lifted;
And beauty came like the setting sun:
My heart was shaken with tears; and horror
Drifted away . . . Oh, but Everyone
Was a bird; and the song was wordless; the singing will never be done.

"Craig, does the poem have a form?"

"Well, it has two stanzas. Is that form?" Craig wonders.

"Could be, but keep looking. What do you notice about the first two lines of each stanza?"

"They're sort of alike. Both lines have the words 'everyone . . . suddenly.' Um . . . and both of the second lines begin with 'and,' so I guess there's a plan," Craig discovers.

"Okay. Now, Claudia, are there any lines where the sounds of the words or first letters of words contribute to the effect of the poem?"

"Ah . . . you have three 'W' words where it says 'winging wildly across the white,'" Claudia says.

"Good for you. Another way to unify a poem is through rhyme. Is there some rhyme in this poem, Dale?"

"Yeah. In the first stanza the last words of a line sometimes rhyme, like 'delight,' 'white,' and 'sight' . . . And the same thing happens in the second stanza" Dale notices.

"So the poet is thinking about the sound of the words as well as their meanings. Is there anything similar about what a poet and a composer do when they work? Penny?"

"Music is sounds, and a poem is partly sounds, so I guess they do some things the same," Penny answers.

"Here's a trickier question. Can people enjoy hearing the sounds of a poem in a foreign language when they can't understand the words? . . . Yes, Molly?"

"Maybe, but it bothers me when I don't understand the words," Molly volunteers.

The teacher nods, "I know what you mean. Poetry communicates on several levels, and one of those has to do with word meanings. But what about this poem? Do you understand completely what it's saying?"

"Well, not completely," Molly admits.

"But you still enjoyed hearing it and reading it aloud, didn't you?"

"Yeah . . . so I guess sounds have something to do with it, even if you can't understand everything the words say," Molly decides.

The teacher could go on to compare other aspects of the poem with music. Just as music demonstrates the power of human imagination, so does the poem "Everyone Sang" in phrases like "And I was filled with such delight/as prisoned birds must find in freedom." Also, as the sounds in music convey a feeling that cannot be adequately expressed in words, the first stanza gives a sense of "winging wildly" that goes beyond the nouns and verbs that make up the lines, and the second stanza with its "beauty came like the setting sun" seems to project a more subdued and sublime mood.

Most of the music series books realize the value of enriching music with poetry, dance, and art. For this reason, it is not difficult to find appropriate materials. A teacher should not overlook other sources, however. Copies of many excellent art works from the National Gallery of Art are available in inexpensive reproductions. In many cities the public libraries loan pictures in much the same way they loan books. In recent years several programs funded from federal and state sources have made dancers, poetry readers, film makers, and other artists available for performances in schools. A live performance by a qualified artist is a stimulating experience for children. The ways of enriching music instruction through the arts are many and varied.

COMBINED ARTS PROGRAMS

As was mentioned earlier in this chapter, a second way to correlate the fine arts in the elementary school is to combine them into a single program. Such an integrated course of study is usually organized around a unifying aspect other than music. One example is an approach called "three arts" or "allied arts," which combines art, music, and dance through the study of common elements such as line, rhythm, form or design, and so on. Some combined programs present the arts from the standpoint of style periods like Baroque, Classical, and Romantic, although this organization is probably too advanced for elementary school children.

A somewhat different type of combined course involves not only the arts but also philosophical concepts such as truth, love, and freedom. This combination is often called a "humanities" program, since it involves more than just the arts. An example of a humanities approach for elementary school children can be found in a series of books titled *Self-Expression and Conduct: The Humanities.** These attractive books are organized around the concepts of truth, beauty, justice, love, and faith, and are studied through art, dance, drama, music, and language. The arts are included whenever they can help develop the humanistic concepts. Shown here is an example from one of the primary-level books in which the children are encouraged to relate sounds from their environment—in this case the weather—into visual images and words, many of which are also used in music.

Weather is full of the nicest sounds.

Please listen.

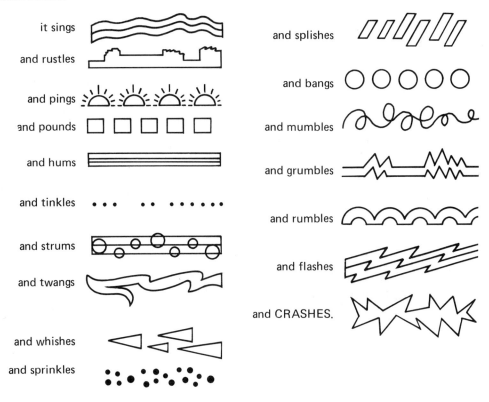

it sings

and rustles

and pings

and pounds

and hums

and tinkles

and strums

and twangs

and whishes

and sprinkles

and splishes

and bangs

and mumbles

and grumbles

and rumbles

and flashes

and CRASHES.

---

*Harcourt Brace Jovanovich, Inc., 1974.

Bringing several areas together in this manner clearly overarches the traditional subject-matter boundaries. It enables children to think about an idea in a way that is seldom possible in the subject-matter classes. Love and truth are topics that transcend arithmetic, spelling, punctuation, and music.

There are limitations to the combined approach, however. When such programs are examined from the perspective of what is learned in music, the results are disappointing. There is little systematic study of the subject, and virtually no development of skills such as playing the recorder or singing. The main problem is lack of time. It is nearly impossible to do justice to five subject-matter areas in a single program of instruction unless one has an hour or more each day to devote to the program. When there is only so much time available, adding more subjects simply means subtracting time from all areas.

There are other problems, too. One concerns the training and interests of the teacher. It is a rare teacher indeed who is competent to teach art, music, dance, drama, and poetry. If a teacher tries to do so, almost always one area receives more attention than the others. It is possible to form a team of teachers for the program, if there are specialists available for the school. But teaching in a team is a bit like teaching by committee. The venture requires much time and patience on everyone's part if it is to be successful. Sometimes team teaching is little more than "turn teaching." Each teacher takes a turn with the class, but there is little integration of the various areas.

Another problem involves the false parallels that are sometimes drawn between one art and another. For example, the fact that the word "line" is found in both music and painting does not indicate that they refer to the same thing. A line or melody in music evolves rather slowly because it is a series of pitches occurring consecutively through a span of time; a line in art is seen within a millisecond. A musical line cannot be represented in physical space, and a visual line cannot be represented in a time span. (It is possible to draw a picture of a clock, but that is not the same as a picture of time. Nor is notation a pictorial representation of music. It is a blueprint for reproducing sound, not a substitute for aural experience.)

Looking for parallels between the temporal and spatial arts only confuses the children. Comparisons should not suggest that a chord in music is like a pillar in a building, or a clarinet tone is like a certain color. Children can see that dance involves both time and space in a continuously evolving motion that casts the dancer as a design-maker within three-dimensional space. And they can see that drama involves literary elements in addition to time and space manipulation. But the distinctive advantages and limitations of each medium should not be compromised in order to make them appear interchangeable. Each art form stands by itself without direct support from any other. In fact, any attempt to establish direct relationships only detracts from each art.

What does all this mean for the teacher who is considering the feasibility of a combined approach? First, because it does not include the teaching of music in much depth or order, the integrated program should not be the only music instruction the children receive. There should be a good program of music study; then, and only then, should a combined course be added to the curriculum.

Second, the teacher will need to devote extra effort to the planning and teaching of an integrated program. Such instruction is not everyday fare in elementary school, so most teachers have had little experience with it. Furthermore, it requires a greater amount of subject-matter preparation. Only a few materials are available, and only one series of books* in the fine arts/humanities area is published for use in elementary school.

Third, the other teachers, administrators, and parents may not have a clear understanding of what the combined instruction is trying to accomplish. There is no problem in explaining the need for instruction in reading or arithmetic, but the advantages of learning music are more difficult to pinpoint, and the benefits of fine arts or humanities programs seem even more obscure. Telling a principal or parent that the instruction "seeks to make the students into better human beings" does little to clarify the goals. This fact does not mean that integrated arts or humanities programs should be avoided. It does indicate that the teacher should develop the course in such a way that it can be explained adequately to everyone.

ENRICHING OTHER SUBJECTS WITH MUSIC

This chapter has discussed bringing other arts into the music instruction to enrich it, and combining the arts into a single program. There is another practice: taking the arts into other areas of the elementary school curriculum. The idea of infusing the rest of the curriculum with the arts has been promoted in recent years by several foundation and governmental grants, one of which was the IMPACT project mentioned on page 10. Although the objectives of some of the projects have been fuzzy and the claims of success exaggerated, the idea has merit if handled carefully. A curriculum infused with the arts is more interesting for the students, which means that more learning is likely.

*Self-Expression and Conduct, op. cit.

Because the infusion process is one of bringing the arts into other areas of the curriculum, the classroom teacher must be the person to do this, and not the music specialist who teaches only one subject and who sees a classroom for only a limited time each week. The specialist can help by offering ideas and materials appropriate to the topics the class is studying. The more the classroom teacher and the music specialist work together, the better will be the educational results.

The enrichment of social studies with music was mentioned in Chapter 17. It is the area in which infusion is most easily accomplished. Other areas can be enriched with the arts, too. The combining of poetry and songs is another logical choice, since almost all songs have texts and many poems have been set to music. If one of the objectives of the reading program is to have children read "with expression and meaning," then a poetry-music study can be valuable.

Even science can be enriched with the arts, if the teacher is alert to the possibilities. In this example, the class has been studying the solar system, and the teacher is building on that study by playing a movement of Gustav Holst's *The Planets*.

"You've learned a lot of scientific things about the planets and the solar system. Now let's switch to a different way of thinking about them. Listen to how the idea of the planets influenced a composer named Holst. He wrote this piece in 1915 and called it *The Planets*. It has seven sections or movements, one for each planet.

"Why seven instead of nine planets? Because he left out Earth, and Pluto wasn't discovered until 15 years after Holst wrote the music.

"Anyway, Holst wasn't interested in telling us how many miles away a planet is, or what kind of atmosphere it has. Instead, he was attracted by the names of the planets, which come from the names of ancient Roman gods. One of the sections of *The Planets* is called 'Mars, the Bringer of War,' and another is called 'Mercury, the Winged Messenger.'' Usually you see pictures of Mercury with wings on his helmet and his feet; he's the character you see in the ads for telegraphing flowers.

"Holst wanted these sections of *The Planets* to give a sense of the Roman gods for whom they were named. See if you can sense the quality of these two movements. I'll play one of them, but I won't tell you which one. Listen carefully, then decide which it is." [The teacher plays the movement titled "Mercury."]

"Duane, which movement was that: Mars or Mercury?"

"The music goes pretty fast, so I think it was Mercury," Duane answers, moving in his seat as if dancing vigorously.

"You're right, it was Mercury. In a day or two we'll hear the Mars movement of *The Planets*."

The teacher may want to introduce some works of art and literature related to the planets. The children can attempt to create musical compositions or draw pictures based on the idea of the planets and their names.

The main reason for infusing the study of planets with music and art is to provide enrichment and variety. Holst's *The Planets* does not try to give factual information about the solar system. Instead, it demonstrates the inventiveness of a human mind that was stimulated by the idea of the planets to create a fascinating musical composition.

The arts have much to offer, both as subjects for specialized study in themselves and as components of other areas of the elementary school curriculum. They stimulate the imagination and make the school day more interesting and richer for the children. Such benefits are reason enough to look for ways to integrate the arts and subject-matter areas in the classroom.

REVIEW QUESTIONS

1. What are two fundamental points that the fine arts have in common?

2. a. What is the basic difference between the "enrichment" approach to including the other arts in music instruction, and the combined or integrated approach?
   b. What are the strengths and weaknesses of each approach?

3. Why is it desirable to enrich music instruction with the other arts in elementary school?

4. What are some sources of pictures and poems with which a teacher can enrich the study of music?

5. What is the difference between a fine arts program and a humanities program?

6. Why is it more demanding on the teacher to instruct in a fine arts or humanities program?

7. a. What are "false parallels" among the arts?
   b. Why should they be avoided in teaching the arts?

8. a. What are some ways of infusing the arts into other curricular areas in the elementary school?
   b. Why is the classroom teacher in a better position than the music specialist to infuse the arts into other areas of the curriculum?

ACTIVITIES

1. Select a music series book and examine it for the amount and type of enrichment it contains from the other arts. Prepare a report on your findings.

2. Develop a plan for a music lesson into which another art can be incorporated.
   a. State the objective of the instruction.
   b. List the materials needed.
   c. Describe the teaching procedure.

3. Examine one book in the elementary humanities series *Self-Expression and Conduct: The Humanities.* Select one concept for careful analysis.
   a. Describe how the concept is introduced and taught.
   b. Determine the proportionate amount of music included in the unit.

4. Select a topic from any area of the elementary school curriculum except the fine arts. Then select two items from music, art, or poetry to infuse into the non-arts learning. Develop a short plan to describe how the material will be integrated.

Music
and Special Learners

Almost all children can learn to enjoy music and to participate in it to some degree. In fact, music can be of particular value to children who are handicapped in their ability to hear, see, think, move, or respond.

Identifying the nature of a child's handicap is sometimes difficult, particularly if there are no obvious manifestations of disability, or if multiple handicaps are present. For this reason, any label for classifying children, even when used accurately, is of limited value to teachers. As Nocera points out: "The medical profession most often labels by etiology, or the cause of the disability. The psychology profession most often labels by the dysfunction itself. Although these terms may be meaningful to *those* professions, they do not provide much insight that will enhance the *educational* management of children. . . ."[1]

Although children do not fit neatly into categories of disability, the teacher may find it helpful to note the seven areas which the U.S. Department of Education recognizes in identifying handicapped children. They are children who are mentally retarded, physically handicapped, visually impaired, hearing impaired, speech impaired, learning disabled, and emotionally disturbed.

MAINSTREAMING

The federal government has mandated a "free appropriate public education" for all handicapped children. Prior to the passage of Public

Law 94-142 in 1975, only about half of the eight million handicapped children in the United States were being given educational opportunities, and about one million had been excluded from school. Now these children are not only involved in a school setting but are being placed in the "least restrictive environment"—that is, with nonhandicapped children of comparable age and ability. This practice is called *mainstreaming*.

The Education of the Handicapped Act requires each public agency to insure that "to the maximum extent appropriate, handicapped children . . . are educated with children who are not handicapped . . ." and that "special classes, separate schooling or other removal of handicapped children from the regular educational environment occurs only when the nature or severity of the handicap is such that education in regular classes with the use of supplementary aids and services cannot be achieved satisfactorily."[2]

The regulations make it clear that when possible, handicapped children are to be educated with nonhandicapped students. For this reason, virtually every classroom includes one or more handicapped learners. The teacher's responsibility to these children is the same as it is for all children: to educate them to the fullest extent of their ability.

If mainstreaming is to be successful, the following conditions should be met:

1. All teachers should have at least minimum competencies in teaching handicapped children.

2. School districts should provide or support in-service activities through which teachers can acquire the needed competencies.

3. Music teachers should be consulted in decisions regarding the placement of handicapped children in music classes. Not every handicapped child can be mainstreamed in all areas.

Recognizing the interests of the non-handicapped children in a mainstreamed situation, the law states that "where a handicapped child is so disruptive in a regular classroom that the education of other students is significantly impaired, the needs of the handicapped child cannot be met in that environment. Therefore, regular placement would not be appropriate for his or her needs."[3]

MUSIC EDUCATION FOR THE HANDICAPPED

The basic goal of music instruction for all children, including those with handicaps, is to educate them to be sensitive to music, knowledgeable about it, and somewhat skilled in its performance. Enjoyment is a legitimate outcome of good music instruction.

With handicapped students, the nonmusical benefits of music, discussed in Chapter 1, assume greater importance. The difference is more a matter of instructional emphasis than course content. Handicapped children learn music in much the same way that nonhandicapped children learn it: they begin with the same fundamental experiences and proceed through the same sequence of learning.

When alterations in the program are needed, they most often involve the *rate of learning* and in some cases the *scope* of what is learned. The handicapped child may take significantly longer to accomplish the same amount as the nonhandicapped child. Nor can every handicapped child succeed at every task. Blind students cannot read printed music, although they can be taught Braille notation. Children who cannot walk will not be able to march with the music, but they can keep time in other ways. Retarded children may never be able to conceptualize some aspects of music, but most are able to participate in music and enjoy the experience.

Although it is not the purpose of this chapter to explore the various categories of disability in depth, suggestions are provided to help the teacher develop the musical abilities of learners with special handicaps.

The mentally retarded

Several terms have been devised to classify varying degrees of mental retardation, but they all refer to below-average intellectual ability. The mentally handicapped children who are mainstreamed into regular classrooms are likely to be only mildly retarded, and they can do many things in music. They learn more slowly and in smaller increments, however, and they require more repetition. Their attention span is short. Because they are less able to generalize, concrete learning experiences are more effective. Their language ability is limited, so work with a book or written notation is not successful in most cases. Despite these limitations, a mentally handicapped child who is mainstreamed into a music class should be placed with students who are close to his or her chronological age. A social problem can be created if the age difference is too great, and the words of songs enjoyed by young children may not be suitable for the older retarded student.

Mentally handicapped children are usually quite receptive to music, and a teacher can enhance their enjoyment by keeping these points in mind when teaching them, whether in a homogeneous class or in a mainstreamed situation:

1. Choose songs that have repetition in words and music, and a text that has concrete imagery and relates to the children's experiences. Include American folk music and selected popular songs for older students, to give them a social bond with their non-handicapped peers.

2. Base the learning on active participation. A song with motions requires the child to attend to the words, and helps the teacher assess the extent of the child's understanding.

3. Keep verbal directions and explanations short and to the point.

4. Change songs and activities frequently, to accommodate short attention spans.

5. Praise each child frequently, by name, for a specific accomplishment, but do not be effusive or dishonest in the commendation.

6. Do not confine instruction to simple tasks that the students can always do; they need to be challenged at times.

Improving self-image through names. Mentally handicapped children need to hear their names often. Severely retarded children who are unable to speak or to maintain interest in activities around them sometimes show momentary alertness when their names are spoken. The teacher may need to speak or sing the name directly in front of the child, and bend down or touch the child lightly to make contact.

Names can be incorporated into music class in several ways. A simple procedure is to substitute a child's name for other words in a song. To the melody for "He's Got the Whole World in His Hands," the class can sing, "He's got Gloria Porter in his hands," or "He's got Joyce and Stewart in his hands." If the class members each want a turn as a subject of the song, the latter version, referring to two children at a time, is a good way to move through the class quickly. In fact, each verse can accommodate several different names, but it is better to limit the number in each verse, and then repeat them. In this way, the children will be more likely to notice when their names occur, and they will derive more pleasure from hearing their names repeated.

Names can also involve a directive for each child. In the song "Michael, Row the Boat Ashore," the class can sing "Gordon plays upon his drum, Hallelujah!", or "Nicole, shake your tambourine, Hallelujah!" Again, a full verse should be devoted to one child so that the slower responses can be accommodated.

The song "Little David, Play on Your Harp" can be similarly altered to allow for specific names and actions. The teacher may want to eliminate the word "little" in the substitute phrases, since it connotes small stature and immaturity. Names can be incorporated into the song "Little David, Play on Your Harp" in several ways, while still retaining the characteristic syncopation of the music: "Here's Howard clapping his hands," or "Christina, smile as you sing," or "Neil Johnson, tap with your foot."

Children who can associate their names with letters will enjoy the song "Initials." Songs of this type should provide an early clue to the children that this is "their" verse, so that they have sufficient time in which to recognize the initial letter and stand. The words should be

INITIALS

M.L.H.   German Folk Song

If your name starts with a(n) "A," you may stand, stand up now.

If your name starts with a(n) "A," stand and take a bow. (Chord for bow.)

adapted, of course, to accommodate the needs of children with limited mobility.

Body awareness. Mentally handicapped children need to have their sense of self enhanced not only by hearing their names frequently but by knowing the names for the parts of their bodies and how they work. The following four songs, and many others, are good ones for increasing the children's awareness of their bodies, and all can be done from a seated position if necessary.

　　1. "If You're Happy and You Know It" (p. 98). Further motions can include "tap your foot, pull your ear, blink your eyes, touch your nose, wave your hand, pat your hair, nod your head, bend your knee, show your teeth, make a fist."
　　2. "Tony Chestnut" (p. 120).
　　3. Mentally handicapped children generally like to sing the song "Head and Shoulders" several times in succession, at increasingly faster tempos, while pointing to the body parts being named.

HEAD AND SHOULDERS

Head   and   shoul - ders,   knees and   toes,   knees and   toes,

Head and shoul-ders, knees and toes, knees and toes,____ Eyes and ears and

mouth_ and_ nose,   Head and shoul-ders, knees and toes, knees and toes.

4. In the song "Johnny Works with One Hammer," the children's names should be substituted for "Johnny" to involve them more completely in the music. The singers should pound with one fist for "one hammer" and with two fists for "two hammers." Unless the children are able to move confidently from a standing position, they should remain seated as they do this song, because the "three hammers" verse requires balancing on one foot and tapping the other, "four hammers" requires jumping (to tap with both feet), and "five hammers" requires jumping plus nodding the head in a way that may cause dizziness if attempted too vigorously.

JOHNNY WORKS WITH ONE HAMMER

American Folk Song

John - ny works with one ham - mer, one ham - mer, one ham - mer.

John - ny works with one ham - mer, Now he works with two.

2. Johnny works with two hammers (etc.) . . . Now he works with three."

3. Johnny works with three hammers (etc.) . . . Now he works with four."

4. Johnny works with four hammers (etc.) . . . Now he works with five."

5. Johnny works with five hammers (etc.) . . . Now he takes a rest."

The physically handicapped

Sometimes called "orthopedically impaired," these children are limited in mobility and may lack control of gross or large muscle movements, which means that they have trouble moving their arms, legs, or entire body. They may lack fine motor skills, which involve the use of small muscles and the manipulation of objects, usually with the hands and fingers.

Physical activity in music may be altered to accommodate orthopedic handicaps, but it should not be eliminated. A child in a wheelchair can participate by moving rhythmically while others march with the music. Musical instruments can be adapted for playing, too, even to the extent of hitting a bell with a beater held between the teeth. In such a case the instrument's height may have to be adjusted, or other arrangements made for the child's comfort. Most physically disabled children who are not in other ways deficient are ingenious in thinking up ways to overcome their disability. With a little help they can do nearly everything that other class members do, but sometimes their participation takes a different form.

There are several ways in which a music teacher can help physically handicapped children to move with music.

1. Encourage the children to develop lateral balance by using both sides of their bodies for foot-tapping, finger-snapping, waving, winking, and so on. Transferring a motion occasionally to the other side of the body is not likely to upset the child's sense of handedness, and it is beneficial because it engages more body parts in the activity and sustains interest during review of the music. The song "Hokey Pokey," with its references to "right" and "left," is a good choice to reinforce the concept of equal body sides.

2. Stress that the children need to stop moving when the music stops. Some handicapped learners seem unable to break the focus of their attention when they are engaged in a repetitive activity. Because an abrupt stop to the music may catch them off balance, prepare a cadence or a slowing of the tempo to alert them to the approaching end. An exception can occur if the class is playing a game of "Statues" in which the children try to hold perfectly still when the music stops abruptly.

3. Do not play elimination games in which children are removed from a music activity one by one on the basis of physical skills.

4. Encourage spatial orientation by helping the children produce sounds through body movement at different levels: a foot tap at floor level, a thigh slap or *patsch* (a German word for which the plural is *patschen*), a clap at waist level, and a finger snap at shoulder level (achieved by slanting the forearms upward so that the hands are above the elbows). Don't worry if some children cannot snap; a hand bounce is a good substitute. Let the children make up rhythmic patterns of these four motions, and apply them as accompaniments to songs.

5. Look for ways in which wheelchair-bound children can participate in every music activity involving movement. Encourage them to think up motions to resemble the class activity. Let responsible students who are more mobile volunteer to help those who are not ambulatory.

6. When handicapped children are to join together in moving about the room, let them rest palms under neighbors' elbows if a substitute for hand-holding is needed. Linking elbows pulls bodies too close together for free movement, and shoulder-holding emphasizes diverse heights.

7. If the class is to proceed in a circle while neighbors touch, remember that it is unnatural to walk sideways. If you direct the children to turn and face in one direction, looking at a neighbor's back, let

them hold onto the waist of the child in front. They should not be expected to have arm contact with the person behind, because that would require their arms to twist and to be pulled back uncomfortably.

8. Call fast steps "jogging" instead of "running." Jogging suggests a more comfortable pace and is a more realistic activity for children whose coordination is impaired. Remember that walking, stepping, marching, or jogging in place is more difficult than normal forward motion. Be sure that the cleared area is large enough to permit physically impaired children to move together freely and safely.

9. To encourage buoyancy in skipping activities, choose music in compound meter—or provide a drum beat—that starts with a pickup:

This suggests a lift, in contrast to a long first note that is too static to help uncertain skippers begin to move. Notice the floor surface and the children's shoes before involving persons in this activity; carpeted floors and crepe-soled shoes make skipping difficult.

10. For square dancing, help the children visualize the format of the dance by delineating a square on the floor with tape. Help them remember their "home" positions by pointing out a stationary object toward which they should face. Choose a dance that does not require frequent changes in activity or direction of movement. The following words, sung to the tune of "Turkey in the Straw," are easy to follow and comprise an effective square dance. Insert slurs as needed to make the italicized syllables occur on the strong beats:

> Now *stand* up tall as you *make* a square,
> And *face* your partner *stand*ing there,
> Then *back* to back in a *do*-si-do,
> Now *swing* your partner, *here* we go!
>
> (Verse 2: Change "partner" to "corner" and repeat action with the
>   other neighbor.)

For children in wheelchairs, sing "hold yourself up tall . . ." and "face your partner beside you there."

The visually handicapped

Students with vision problems are usually able to function well in music classes, probably because their condition has forced them to listen attentively and to remember what they hear. Sight-impaired persons also depend heavily on tactile sensations, as well as on hearing.

Their limitations in music involve reading printed music and other visual materials. Braille, an international system of reading through the fingertips by feeling embossed dots on paper, has a code for music as well as for letters and numbers. Reading Braille music is no easy matter, however, and few children in elementary school have mastered that skill. Even an experienced blind performer who knows the Braille system for music notation must painstakingly figure out the dots in terms of each particular piece, so sightreading at tempo is not possible in the sense that it is with sighted persons.

Another area in which children with sight limitations encounter difficulty is in moving to music. They cannot see how others move, so they cannot imitate movement. They must also contend with the ever-present possibility of physical injury when they move in an unfamiliar situation.

The teacher should keep these points in mind when teaching children with sight impairment:

1. Give concrete directions, such as "Put the drum on the shelf that's waist high about two feet to your right," rather than "Put the drum away."

2. Remember not to rely on instruction by visual means; repeat verbally for sight-impaired children.

3. When possible, use raised-line drawings and other tactile materials. Raised visuals can be made on a Thermoform Brailon Duplicator. Use wide-lined staff paper and large print for the partially sighted.

4. Encourage the children to identify instruments by touch as well as by sound.

5. Label bells and autoharp buttons with tactile symbols or Braille letters. The student can make the letters if the teacher does not know them.

6. Arrange for vision-impaired children to practice parts on an independent basis so that they are prepared ahead of time for the music class.

7. Assign a sighted partner to help a sight-impaired child in activities that involve moving about the room.

8. Develop activities to increase the child's confidence in moving independently.

9. Devise games that require children to find objects by sound only, or to move in unusual ways.

10. Do not let the ears of a visually impaired child be covered.

Visual perception. Some children find it difficult to discern the visual properties of objects, distinguish between a figure and its background, relate symbols to objects, remember visual images, and judge distance. In the above situations, the problem often lies not in a physical disorder of the eye but in faulty perception. Perception is a result of the brain's ability to interpret and evaluate the stimuli that come to it. Flaws in visual perception impede a child's educational progress because so much of what is learned is obtained through the sense of sight.

Music contributes to the development of visual perception by relating sounds to symbols. Initial help is possible through the teacher's use of hand motions that indicate the level of pitch, or through the hand signs associated with the Kodály method. The teacher can present simple patterns of pitch, relate the sounds to hand motions, then translate the hand motions into visual symbols on the chalkboard or on paper to represent pitch patterns.

Children with visual-perception problems should learn to be more sensitive to facial expressions and cues such as body movement and gestures. They can make up games like "Musical Charades," or volunteer to show the class "how this song might make you look," or mirror the motions of a "conductor."

Simple instrumental parts of three or four notes can be made up using colored dots or different shapes to represent different bells. A shape or color can be pasted on the bell, so that a child seeing that symbol in notation knows that it is time to play a particular sound. Even form in music can be graphically represented through the use of colors or other symbols that the children devise. Finally, experience with conventional music reading also aids in the development of visual perception.

The hearing impaired

In clinical diagnosis, "deaf" refers to profound hearing loss, while "hard of hearing" describes less severe impairment. Very few children hear nothing at all. Some are unable to hear pitches in certain ranges, while others cannot hear soft sounds. With the improvement of hearing technology, the trend today is to develop whatever hearing potential the child has, rather than to rely completely on lip-reading or signing. Fewer than 50 percent of speech sounds are visible, so lip-reading is limited in effectiveness, and signing is limited by the small number of persons who can communicate in that way.

A hearing aid amplifies the sound entering the ear, and must be fitted to the individual by a specialist in that work. The teacher needs to know the child's hearing ability with the aid, because it is with the aid that the student will be functioning in class. Although it is a remarkable invention, the hearing aid is limited in terms of the distance at which it can pick up sounds and its fidelity for reproducing timbres. Like listening to music over the telephone, hearing through an aid provides less richness of timbre than normal hearing does. Loud sounds must never be produced directly into a hearing aid, because the device has already been adjusted to provide the best sound level for that child's needs. Further amplification can be a painful experience for an aid-dependent person.

Although most sounds are transmitted to the brain through the ears, vibrations are also felt through other parts of the body, as anyone can report who has stood by a bass drum when it is struck. The tactile sense complements the ear, and it is for this reason that children with hearing problems are encouraged to touch sound sources. Hearing-impaired persons can learn to feel a difference between high and low pitches, and this helps them to sing. Often singing is aided by experience with blowing wind instruments such as kazoos and commercial devices such as Pianicas. Hearing-impaired children have been taught to play conventional wind instruments such as the clarinet and saxophone, on which pitches can be located without careful hearing.

As might be expected, hearing-impaired children exhibit poor speech development as a result of their auditory limitations. Often what they try to say is difficult to understand and lacking in inflection. They require much work on language development, even in music class. The teacher should point out rhymes, explain words, employ chants to develop lively speech that has rhythmic drive, and stress high/low, loud/soft, and fast/slow to encourage inflection. It is likely that some deaf children are not surrounded by language in the home because their families mistakenly think that the spoken word is of no use to the deaf. But they can respond to sound vibrations in parts of the body other than the ear, and the social benefits of being involved in some form of language communication are incalculable.

Many hearing-impaired children are tense and lag in motor development, perhaps as a result of overprotection, lack of socialization skills, or their inability to receive information about the environment that surrounds them outside their immediate field of vision. They need music activities that provide relaxation and self-confidence in both bodily movement and social situations.

The teacher should remember these points when teaching children with hearing problems:

1. Do not startle the children by touching them after approaching from outside their range of vision.

2. Do not speak when turned away from the class, as when writing on the chalkboard.

3. Speak directly to the child, even if it means bending down in the case of small children. They cannot see the facial expression or lips well when looking in an upward angle.

4. Speak clearly, with normal fluency and inflection, but do not talk loudly.

5. Encourage the children to talk, not merely to gesture. Feel free to correct their speech or to admit that you do not understand what they said, but do so in a positive and constructive manner. Cut out catalog pictures of instruments and mount them; then let the children point to the instrument they hear as they attempt to say the word.

6. Use visual as well as verbal symbols to indicate the beginning of a song and similar activities. To teach breath control, ask the children to pretend to blow a feather when they see a flashlight shine, and to stop blowing when the light stops. Or let them respond to a stop-and-go sign previously prepared with appropriately colored paper on opposite sides of a stick.

7. Do not expect a high degree of timbre discrimination.

8. Encourage hearing-impaired children to touch sound sources directly, so that they can feel the vibrations and sense the beat. Obtain a cello, string bass, or large tone bell and let the children encircle their bodies around the instrument as it vibrates. Or play a large cymbal *softly*, with a padded stick, over their heads, to immerse them in sound. Over a period of time, have them gradually move away from the sound source.

9. Do not let the eyes of hearing-impaired children be covered. If it is necessary to hide sound sources for later identification, or game objects for later discovery, do this before class or work outside the children's range of vision, rather than ask them to close their eyes and thereby cut off a valuable link with their environment.

Auditory perception. As has been mentioned before in this book, hearing is not the same as listening. One can hear a sound, but if that sound has no meaning to the hearer, no perception has taken place. Deficiencies in auditory perception include an inability to identify sounds, locate the source of a sound, relate sounds to visual cues, remember what is heard, organize sounds, and pay attention to a particular sound while others are heard at the same time. The last-named disability involves a flaw in figure/ground perception, which causes sounds to assail the brain in a confusing jumble. Children with this perceptual problem need help in learning to discern which sounds are important and which ones should be disregarded.

Because music instruction teaches students to listen more carefully, it contributes significantly to alleviating problems in auditory perception. Basically this is done by helping children to pay attention to the elements of music (pitch, rhythm, timbre, and loudness) that are discussed in Chapters 6-9 and 12-16. Most of the many suggestions presented in those chapters can be applied to the teaching of children with auditory perception problems. Since the rate of learning is slower for some of these children, the suggestions for teaching in the primary grades are especially suitable.

Whatever the class activity, it should call for a response from the perceptually impaired children so that the teacher can note individual progress and ensure that music is not regarded as a passive experience. As the children improve in auditory perception, they will be able to move from playing an instrument, which is relatively easy because of tactile and visual reinforcement, to singing, which involves subtle internal bodily actions and requires a mental impression of each sound before it is produced. Eventually the children should be able to devote complete attention to a music listening experience, sorting out the complexity of sounds with both knowledge and enjoyment.

A teacher can further auditory perception by engaging the children in activities such as the "Stretching Song." The rhyming words are emphasized by being sustained for a longer time in the song. Such combinations as tall/small/ball, wide/hide/side, and high/lie/sky help hearing impaired children to discriminate among words with different initial sounds, and their concreteness helps the children to respond appropriately. The teacher can then assess the children's understanding of the words by observing their actions.

STRETCHING SONG

Words and Music by Eunice Boardman

```
1. I'm  stretch-ing  ver - y    tall,   And  now  I'm  ver - y   small.   Now  tall!
2. My    hands  I  stretch  out  wide,   Be - hind  me  they  will  hide.  Now  wide!
3. My    hands  I  stretch  up   high,   Now  on  the  floor  they  lie.   Now  high!
4. Now   with  my  head   I  shake,  Now  not  a  move  I  make.   Now  shake!
5. Now   all  the  girls  and  boys  Don't  make  a  sin - gle  noise!  Sit  down!
```

```
Now    small!  Now  I'm  a     ti - ny   ball.
Now    hide!   I  put  them  at  my   side.
Now    lie!    Now                           way  up  to  the  sky.
No move  make!  Now  my  whole  bod-y  I  shake.
No     sound!  And  dream  of  man - y   toys.
```

Speech impaired

Communication disorders are evident in poor articulation, stuttering, voice irregularities, unnatural pitch range, and use of faulty word sequence. The fact that music helps overcome stuttering and stammering was mentioned in Chapter 1. Music is helpful in aiding over 92 percent of all such problems—an extremely high success rate.[4] Perhaps it is successful because vocal music treats speech in a way that differs from the students' usual experience with language. In singing, vowels are sustained, and the rhythmic flow of the music encourages fluency of expression. Some songs require the performer to simulate animal noises, whistles, wind, and other nonverbal sounds. Other songs contain echos, which are beneficial in providing phrases to be imitated. All of this attention to mouth-sounds makes children more sensitive to spoken language. Needless to say, all musical experiences related to speech for nonproficient children should be undertaken in a relaxed and nonthreatening atmosphere.

To encourage inflection in speech, the teacher may want to have the class engage in the "talking drum" idea that is found in some African languages. The technique in the classroom is to take simple word phrases and to render them on drums of two different sizes (perhaps on a pair of bongos), or on notes of more specific pitch (probably on two bells forming the interval of a minor third).

Notating the patterns is a helpful aid to visual perception. The written symbols indicate the factors of rhythm (fast/slow) and pitch (high/low). The other aspect of inflection is sound level (loud/soft). The teacher can help the children control this factor by encouraging them to inject accents and nuances of phrasing into the musical fragments.

The learning disabled

This category as defined in the 1977 *Federal Register* includes any "disorder in one or more of the basic psychological processes involved in understanding or in using language, spoken or written, which may manifest itself in an imperfect ability to listen, think, speak, read, write, spell, or to do mathematical calculations."[5] These children are of average or above-average intelligence, although at times they exhibit some of the characteristics of mental retardation. It takes them longer to organize information that comes to them from two or more senses, and they are slower in making judgments, evidently because they are trying to process information that has become distorted before they can sort it out. Some of them have trouble judging distances and direction, so they cannot play catch with a ball. Some cannot use two senses at the same time, so they cannot simultaneously sing and walk. Others have a poor concept of time, so they have little sense of past or future. Still others fail to remember for more than a few seconds.

Children with learning disabilities often have one sense that is stronger than the others, and some are quite talented in music. When possible, the teacher should work with the stronger capability to build the child's confidence, then seek to improve performance in the weaker areas. The child should learn one point thoroughly before attempting another—that is, learn to sing a song well before adding an activity such as clapping. These children do not profit from repetition to the extent that mentally retarded children do, because the same drill may elicit a different response each time.

The teacher should follow these guidelines in teaching learning disabled children:

1. Get the child's attention before trying to communicate.

2. Present only one directive at a time.

3. Limit the number of choices offered to the child.

4. Use visual materials that are uncluttered with distracting images or printing.

5. In action songs, be ready to help the child identify the right and left sides, or recall the sequence of motions, when these patterned responses are required in the music activity.

6. Expect short attention spans, or overattention, as when the child seems unable to break the spell of interest in a prior activity and move on to something new.

7. Do not pressure a learning-disabled child for a response before he or she is ready to respond. If there has been a pattern of responding impulsively, encourage the child to take time to think.

8. Praise the child for specific accomplishments, especially in matters involving attentiveness, sequencing, and problem-solving.

9. Maintain order and consistency in classroom operation.

The emotionally disturbed

This handicap is manifested by an inability to learn that cannot be explained by intellectual, sensory, or health factors. Emotionally disturbed children exhibit inappropriate types of behavior or feelings under normal circumstances, and are unable to work well with others. Their antisocial behavior sometimes resembles autism and takes the form of withdrawing into a shell, but more frequently the behavior is characterized by hyperactivity, clowning, defiance, or aggression. Children who are antisocial generally have a poor opinion of themselves and feel insecure, despite frequent displays of bravado. Their self-control is tenuous, and they appear to have little regard for the future benefits or discomforts that are likely to result from their present actions.

Music instruction can help both withdrawn and aggressive children. Music by its nature is a different "language." Furthermore, music periods are relatively short and are often taught by someone other than the classroom teacher. For these reasons, music instruction frequently suggests a different atmosphere from the classroom setting, which the disturbed child may perceive as frustrating. Music class is not a retreat, however. Except for individual study projects, music instruction also takes place in a social setting. Part-singing, playing instruments, moving to music, and sharing ideas are accomplished in conjunction with other students. The benefits of responsible social interaction are available to a troubled child in music instruction as well as in other areas of the curriculum.

The teacher can reinforce a child's progress toward emotional stability in several ways.

1. Choose songs with texts that contribute to a positive self-image and encourage sensitivity to others. The child may be quite sophisticated intellectually, so choose relevant materials that do not talk down to the student.

2. Plan activities to accommodate a short attention span.

3. Limit the number of choices available to the child. An emotionally disturbed person often feels more secure when simply told what to do, and following directions provides an orderly focus for behavior.

4. Plan carefully for any activities involving movement. An emotionally vulnerable child may feel threatened when surrounded by persons engaged in free movement.

5. Provide orderliness by establishing procedures that are expected when the child passes out and collects materials such as instruments.

6. Recognize that the child will have good days and bad days for no apparent reason. Expect swings of mood but do not cater to them.

7. Enlist the support of the class in bringing pressure to bear on disruptive behavior. Make clear to all the children why a certain action causes a problem: "When you talk out of turn, we can't listen to the other person's ideas."

8. Apply behavior modification techniques, which reinforce desired behavior through a system of rewards.

9. Provide opportunities for independent study, adapting the suggestions offered in Chapter 18 for individualized learning.

10. Find time to help the child on a one-to-one basis, since individual attention is often what is needed and wanted by the child.

The health impaired

A child's educational performance can be adversely affected by chronic health problems. Any condition that limits the strength, vitality, or alertness of a child must be taken into account by the teacher. Music activities should be adapted to meet the special needs of the ill child. In many cases, approaches designed for the handicapped will apply equally well to children who are disabled for health reasons.

To help every child feel relaxed and confident in the learning situation, some teachers teach their classes a "welcome song" which is sung for each new child who enters the group, handicapped or not. It is a valuable social gesture for every incoming child, but especially so for handicapped youngsters, who may feel particularly fearful and insecure as they try to join into a new situation. The song is equally appropriate as a welcome to adults and other persons who visit the room. In conjunction with the "welcome song," a few of the class members should shake hands with the new student or guest. Children like to do this, and they benefit by learning to become more compassionate and caring.

The task of helping handicapped children is demanding and difficult. Even with good support services in terms of counseling and materials, the responsibility falls largely on the teacher, who must be knowledgeable, patient, understanding, and inventive. In the end, the teacher's positive attitude may be the most important factor in a successful learning venture. If the teacher sees handicapped children as a challenge rather than a burden, the music experience can be exciting and productive for both the teacher and the students.

NOTES

1. Sona D. Nocera, *Reaching the Special Learner Through Music* (Morristown, N. J.: Silver Burdett Company, 1979), p. 3.
2. *Federal Register*, Vol. 42, No. 163 (121a.550), August 23, 1977, p. 42497.
3. Analysis of the regulations for Section 504 of the Rehabilitation Act of 1973; cited in *Federal Register*, op. cit.
4. Richard M. Graham, comp., *Music for the Exceptional Child* (Reston, Va.: Music Educators National Conference, 1975), p. 35.
5. *Federal Register*, Vol. 42, No. 163 (121a.5), August 23, 1977, p. 42478.

REVIEW QUESTIONS

1. What is the goal of music instruction for handicapped students?

2. In what ways does music instruction for handicapped students differ from that given nonhandicapped students?

3. Describe three techniques for teaching music to mentally retarded students.

4. Describe three techniques for improving the motor skills of physically handicapped children.

5. What limitations in music do sight-impaired children have, besides being unable to read music?

6. What activities associated with music instruction will help to develop children's visual perception?

7. What are the limitations of a hearing aid in terms of music?

8. Describe three techniques for teaching music to hearing-impaired children.

9. In what way does music help children learn to speak better?

10. Describe three techniques for teaching music to children who are learning disabled.

11. What is the principle of behavior modification techniques?

ACTIVITIES

1. Select any song or other music activity you wish. Then decide how you would teach the material to improve the children's
   a. auditory perception
   b. motor skills

2. Decide whether you wish to concentrate on aiding the children's visual perception, auditory perception, or speech. Then select another song or another music activity to help you toward that goal. Plan a short lesson in which you use the material.

3. Observe a music class with one or more handicapped children in it. Answer the following questions from your observation.
   a. Were the handicapped children easily noticeable?

b. What handicaps were evident?

c. What special procedures did the teacher use to help the handicapped children?

d. Were the handicapped children able to participate successfully in the class?

e. What were the attitudes of the other children toward the handicapped students?

f. What was the teacher's attitude toward the handicapped students?

Evaluation in Music

Evaluation in education has two purposes. One purpose is to assess the results of instruction in terms of what the class as a whole has learned, and the other is to evaluate the progress of individual students in a subject. Both types of evaluation are useful, but the assessement of instruction is a more vital concern for the teacher.

EVALUATING INSTRUCTIONAL PROGRAMS

"What did the children learn in music?" This is an important question, for two reasons. First, a teacher needs to answer it in order to plan for further learning. Without evidence to indicate what the children know and can do, decisions about future instruction are guesswork based on hopes and assumptions.

Second, other people want to know what the students are learning in school, and their concern extends to music. These interested persons include administrators, other teachers, parents, school board members, and taxpayers. Many people, then, have a stake in how the citizens' money and students' time are being spent. A teacher needs to present clear evidence of learning in music when this area is scrutinized by concerned citizens.

Objectives

Evaluation begins with the formulation of clear and specific objectives. A teacher who plans a music lesson without objectives is like a man who walks up to the ticket window at the bus station and asks to buy a ticket. To the clerk's question, "Where do you want to go?" he replies, "I don't know, but I need to get there."

Teachers should know "where they want to go," educationally speaking, and they need to state their objectives specifically. "To understand the form in songs" is certainly a desirable objective, but as a statement of what the children are to accomplish, it is not very good. What does "understand" mean? Assigning formal letters to the phrases of a song? Being able to define the word "form"? Recognizing the names of forms such as "binary" and "ternary"? Some word more specific than "understand" is needed.

If, for example, the objective is actually to assign letters to the phrases of a song, it should be so expressed: "To be able to assign the correct letters to the phrases of a song." Words in addition to "understand" that are usually too general to be useful in a statement of objectives include "know," "discuss," "appreciate," "be familiar with," "learn," and of course "*really* understand."

Observable results

When the teacher has formulated a specific objective, the next step is to find out to what extent the objective has been achieved. The only way to determine this is to observe the children do something that requires application of the learning. It is not enough to ask them, "Do you understand?" or to presume on faith that there will be eventual accomplishment. A teacher looks for something the children can do. Traditionally, a written test has been the vehicle for confirming what they have learned, but there are other ways to do this. The teacher can ask a child to raise a hand when a chord change is heard, or to play the autoharp with chord changes at the right places, or to sing the root of a chord, or to look at a melody and indicate which chords fit.

Conditions

It is not enough to state an objective specifically in terms of what the children will be able to do to show that they have learned. The teacher also needs to spell out the conditions under which they will show their competence. If the objective is "To sing a melody accurately," the teacher should state whether the melody will be sung at sight from reading notation, in imitation of the teacher or a recording, alone or with others, and with or without accompaniment. The conditions make a significant difference in whether or not the children can demonstrate what they have learned.

As Chapter 3 pointed out, if the evaluation is for purposes of assessing instruction, it is not necessary to check all the students in order to determine the general level of understanding. The teaching can question a small sample of the class, and those randomly selected students will give a rather accurate impression of how well the class has learned. Time is saved and student interest maintained in this way. More extensive efforts can be undertaken when needed for individual grading or more formal evaluation.

Criterion level

How good is good enough? There is a fourth component in evaluation, along with the statement of the objectives, the observation of results, and the conditions under which the learning is to be assessed: the passing or criterion level. How many items (or notes, or questions) do the students need to get right in order to demonstrate an acceptable level of performance? The question is not easy to answer. For example, a tennis instructor might set the criterion level at eight out of ten services in the correct court. Fine; but on what basis was the number eight selected? Why not ten out of ten, or possibly nine out of ten? If the students are beginners, why not set the level at five out of ten? Much judgment is involved in setting the passing level, so the process is not as objective as it first appears.

There is another problem with setting the criterion level. If the number of services in the correct court is the only standard for passing the tennis class, the students might just slap the services over the net to make sure they fall in the right place. This practice would meet the criterion, but at the expense of an effective service. To put the matter another way, is the *quantity* of services in the correct place the only criterion, or is there also an element of *quality*? If there is, then the idea of a quantitative measurable standard must be partially abandoned.

Although certain aspects of tennis are hard to evaluate, the game does define excellence quite tangibly in one respect. As in most sports, the action is judged on how many points each side earns. The rules are so definite that no subjective judgment is necessary to determine the outcome. The impartial scoring system declares a winner.

It hardly needs saying that evaluating quality in music performance is a much more subjective undertaking. Different adjudicators look for different things. Even recognized authorities often disagree among themselves in their evaluations of a musical performance. Since it is difficult to devise standards for music performance that are completely objective, the teacher should work toward documenting growth and improvement, and this can be the basis for evaluating music learning in the elementary school. For example, the degree of accurate pitch in the singing of a song in January can be compared with the singing during the previous November.

To test for musical knowledge in the elementary school, a teacher may want to administer a standardized test such as the *Music Achievement Test* by Richard Colwell, which is designed for upper-grade students.[1] Through the use of a recording and an answer sheet, the students are examined on pitch, intervals, major/minor keys, and meter discrimination; auditory-visual discrimination; feeling for tonal center; tonal memory; melody, pitch, and instrument recognition; and identification of style, texture, and chords. The reported reliability of the test is high, and its validity was established in several different ways. Norms are available by which scores can be compared to a national sample of 9,600 students. Another significant published achievement test in music is *Achievements Tests in Music* by William Knuth.[2] It is neither as comprehensive nor as well standardized as the *Music Achievement Test*.

TYPES OF LEARNING

The action or behavior that the teacher observes differs according to the type of learning. The word "learning" involves several areas of human behavior, which can be reduced to the three basic types mentioned in Chapter 3. *Cognitive* learning refers to the retaining of information and related mental processes, *affective* learning refers to the shaping of attitudes and beliefs, and *psychomotor* learning involves the development of physical skills. Since each type of learning requires somewhat different methods of evaluation, they are discussed separately here.

Cognitive learning

The easiest way to assess learning of this type is to ask the children questions, either orally or in writing. The questions may be direct, requiring only a single-word response that is unaffected by opinion:

What is the name of the highest note in this song?

How many eighth notes equal one quarter note?

A self-contained section of a symphony or concerto is called a

_____ .

What is the musical term for soft?

Although these specific questions are perfectly satisfactory, comprehensive questions are also useful in evaluating cognitive learning. Students should be able to organize facts, make comparisons, and solve problems with the information available to them. Here are examples of questions that require comprehensive thinking and higher levels of understanding.

[The opening portion of a theme and variation work is played.] Is this music a theme and variation or a fugue?

[An example of music from the Classical period is played.] Is this music from the time of George Washington or John F. Kennedy?

[A song is presented in notation or performed.] Is this song in a major or minor key?

[A song is presented in notation, with text.] Should this song go rather fast or rather slow?

Affective learning

The affective area presents a challenge to anyone wishing to evaluate that type of learning. When asked if they like a certain song, children can easily guess the answer the teacher wants to hear. If they are in a congenial mood, they will say "yes" even if they don't care for the song. A teacher exclaiming "Boys and girls, wasn't that a nice song?" and the class answering "yes" is not a valid assessment.

To evaluate students' attitudes, the teacher needs to observe behaviors that indicate attitudes and then interpret that information. The teacher informally observes what the children do and say, especially in situations where they do not realize they are being evaluated. For example, does a child ever come up to the teacher and tell about music heard on the radio or at a concert? Do the children respond as positively to music as they do to other subjects? Do they participate in singing? What songs do they ask to sing? Have their choices changed or enlarged? Do they ever mention music when studying other cultures in social studies? When a piece of music is played for them, are they more inclined to listen than they were two months ago? Do they take care of music books and equipment as well as they do other school materials? How often do they make use of a music center in the classroom?

Observations of these and other behaviors tell the teacher whether attitudes toward music are generally becoming more positive. Observations are not foolproof, of course, nor can they be subjected to statistical analysis. But they do provide evidence about attitudes. Researchers have tried to devise projective psychological techniques, but these procedures are rarely practical for the everyday classroom setting. Even after the projective test has been administered, the interpretation of the results is a subjective matter.

Psychomotor learning

Evaluating musical skills in the elementary school is relatively easy, if the teacher intends merely to determine which of the children can sing or play a song and which of them cannot. A teacher who wants an accurate assessment of their progress, however, will need to undertake comparative judgments over a span of time. For example, if singing improvement is the objective, do the children sing a particular song better now than they did two weeks ago? Only a careful analysis of specific points in the song can provide the answer. The children need not know that the teacher is evaluating their singing and noticing certain points in the music.

Suppose that a teacher selects the Swedish round "Come and Sing" for assessing the psychomotor skill of singing. If the song is already in the children's repertoire, they will feel comfortable with it and will probably remember the teacher's previous suggestions for making the music sound good. At any rate, the teacher should choose three or four points for specific attention. These might include the intonation of the octave at the second phrase, or the accuracy of the rest and eighth note in the second measure, or the tone quality on the highest notes in the fourth phrase.

COME AND SING

Words by Sarah Jacobson

Swedish Round

Come now and sing, And let your voi - ces ring.

A song can make your trou - bles light - er,

hap - pi - ness it soon will bring. Come now and sing.

More objectivity is possible when one performance is compared with an earlier performance of the same song. For the purpose of general assessment, however, observing similar points in two different songs provides sufficient information. A person engaged in elaborate research would require a tape recording of each child for careful analysis, but that is not needed in most school situations. The teacher can catch most of what there is to hear without resorting to such rigorous and time-consuming procedures.

Does the assessment of learning skills need to be done individually? Obviously the judgments are more accurate when undertaken on an individual basis, and testing each person alone is necessary if grades are to be given. The disadvantage of individual testing is that it takes a considerable amount of time, and some children do less well in an obvious test situation.

One way to alleviate both problems is to send the children to a room one by one to sing or play into a tape recorder. A student helper operates the machine and announces the name of each person for the recording, and the child being tested performs. The teacher may listen to the tape at leisure, and valuable class time has been saved. Most children are delighted to operate the tape recorder, partly because they like the responsibility and partly because they are curious to hear their classmates perform. Student helpers need careful instruction, however, so that an entire recording session will not have to be repeated because of a "technician's" mistake. A teacher of primary-level children can make a game of the recording procedure by suggesting that the children pretend they are performing on the radio or preparing a record album.

Listening is a skill that requires application of knowledge. It can be assessed by a paper-and-pencil test in conjunction with a recording. In fact, several of the music series books contain such tests, in which these are typical items:

What is the form of this song?

        ABA   _____
        AABB   _____
        AABA   _____

What do you hear along with the melody?

        An accompaniment of chords _____
        Another, different melody _____
        No accompanying part _____

What happens to the level of loudness in this song?

        It stays the same _____
        It starts softly and gets louder _____
        It starts loudly and gets softer _____
        It starts softly, gets louder, and gets softer again _____

You will hear a series of five notes played twice. The second time the series is played, one note will be changed. Count, and decide if the changed note is the first, second, third, fourth, or fifth note in the series.

First _____
Second _____
Third _____
Fourth _____
Fifth _____

Listen to this song and tell what word is sung on the climax or "high point" of the music.

_____

GRADING STUDENTS IN MUSIC

The grading of elementary school children in music and other subjects is a matter of perennial debate, because the issues are complex and the interests of teachers and parents differ. Elementary school teachers tend to think of reporting in terms of a child's progress and potential, while some parents want to know primarily how their child compares with others in the class. The question of whether or not grades motivate students to do better work has never been resolved, probably because grades motivate some students but not others.

Music seems to present more questions about the validity of grades than do most other subjects in the elementary school curriculum. The amount of instructional time for music is significantly less, so the teacher has relatively little contact with the children in a music situation. Furthermore, the objectives of music instruction have not always been articulated clearly enough to provide a basis for evaluation. Regardless of whether grading in music is difficult, it should be undertaken according to the same system that applies to other subjects in the school. Because music is an integral part of the elementary school curriculum, it enjoys both the benefits and obligations of that position. If music teachers ask to be exempt from grading children because music is "special," they are tacitly saying that music is not an equal partner in the educational enterprise. Teachers cannot have it both ways; music cannot be both an established part of the curriculum and a peripheral activity in the school day when it comes to grading.

The main factor to consider in grading a pupil in music is the progress of the individual in terms of his or her potential, especially in the primary grades. The idea of fixed standards for grading in music seems premature for elementary school children.

If individual progress and accomplishment are to be considered, it is a good idea to involve the child in the evaluation process, at least to some extent. In the discussion of individualized study in Chapter 18, there were suggestions for helping children assess for themselves how well they have fulfilled an objective. In fact, prior to evaluation they can propose objectives that they feel they can realistically meet in terms of singing, listening, and information-gathering. Negotiation is even possible in setting up objectives. For example, a student who is weak in singing may offer to do extra work in other aspects of music. Substitutions should generally be discouraged, however, because areas in which a child feels uncertain need more work, not less.

Students can also chart their progress by keeping records of their work. In one music class, the children listed the songs they had learned to sing from memory, even specifying a minimum of two verses before a song could count as being learned. Class members can keep track of the instrumental parts they learn, the compositions they create, and the recordings they hear. The teacher can spot-check their work to make sure that what was claimed was actually completed to a reasonable degree. Student record-keeping is not so important if the music grade is the responsibility of the classroom teacher, but it is a help for the music specialist, who sees several hundred students each week.

If a teacher considers grading in relation to the child's potential, how does the teacher know what that potential is? Sometimes this must be guesswork, especially in the primary grades. To an extent, it is associated with the student's other school work. There is a tendency for children who generally do well in school to do well in music class also. Either the classroom teacher or music specialist should know about children who are studying music privately, and it does not seem unfair to expect greater accomplishment from those who are receiving specialized instruction outside of school.

For students in the upper grades, music aptitude tests can be administered. These tests are by no means infallible, but they are the best means available to gain an estimate of a person's musical potential. The test manuals contain norms that are adjusted for the age level of the students. The first such tests were developed more than 60 years ago, and despite some faults, they have demonstrated remarkable durability and validity over the years. Two such tests are *The Seashore Measures of Musical Talents*[3] and the *Musical Aptitude Profile.*[4] They are easily available. The tests provide information to help the teacher assess a child's potential in music; they do not predict that one child will find music satisfying and another will not.

Ultimately, a child's enjoyment of music depends not only on an innate potential for recognizing aural subtleties, but on successful experiences in listening to music, performing it, and creating it. Music instruction in the elementary school classroom is uniquely able to provide these experiences.

NOTES

1. Richard Colwell, *Music Achievement Test* (Chicago: Follett Educational Corporation, 1968-69).
2. William Knuth, *Achievement Tests in Music*, rev. ed. (Monmouth, Ore.: Creative Research Associates, 1967).
3. Lewis Seashore and Joseph Saitveit, *The Seashore Measures of Musical Talents*, rev. ed. (New York: Psychological Corporation, 1938).
4. Edwin Gordon, *Musical Aptitude Profile* (Boston: Houghton Mifflin, 1965).

REVIEW QUESTIONS

1. Why do teachers need to evaluate the results of their teaching?

2. a. Why must evaluation begin with the formulation of specific objectives?
   b. What words are too general to be of much value in statements of objectives?

3. Why are observable results important in evaluation?

4. Why is it necessary to specify the conditions under which the actions of a student or class will be observed for evaluation purposes?

5. Indicate which type of learning—cognitive, affective, or psychomotor—is evident when a child
   a. Plays an F major chord on the piano
   b. Indicates a liking for band music
   c. Hears the change from minor to major in a piece of music
   d. Names the strings on a violin
   e. Evaluates the quality of a performance of a song
   f. Identifies syncopation in a melody from looking at the music
   g. Asks to sing an Irish folk song
   h. Sings a song in tune

6. Why is it difficult to evaluate students' attitudes?

7. a. What is a criterion level in evaluation?
   b. Why must the criterion level be partly a matter of judgment?

8. Name one standardized test of music achievement designed for use in the elementary school.

9. a. Why does grading seem to be more difficult in music than it is in other subjects?
   b. Why should children be graded in music if they are graded in their other school subjects?

10. In what ways can a child's potential in music be estimated with at least a moderate degree of accuracy?

ACTIVITIES

1. Write an objective for a specific outcome in music that represents
   a. cognitive learning
   b. affective learning
   c. psychomotor learning

2. For each of the three objectives you wrote for the preceding activity, develop the conditions and state what student actions will be observed.

3. Choose a song from any source. Examine the song and identify four places in it that are especially good for evaluating children's singing. Decide what you would evaluate at each of the four places you select.

4. Listen to a sample of items from the *Music Achievement Test*. Decide what each subtest can tell you about the students' achievement in music.

5. Discuss with other members of the class what grade in music should be given to each of these children:

   Wayne, grade 2.   Can't carry a tune; seems to like music but talks a lot in class.

   Felicia, grade 4.   Able student who takes piano lessons; sometimes does well in music, but is not good about paying attention.

   Elizabeth, grade 3. Conscientious and able student; can hardly be heard singing, and never volunteers in class, but appears interested in every music activity.

   Zachary, grade 5.   Poor singer, but brings records to school and likes to make up tape-recorder compositions; seems to enjoy music.

Appendix A
The Notation of Music

RHYTHM

Rhythm: the progression of music in terms of time.

Beat: the recurrent pulse or throb in music; the unit of measurement by which the duration of a musical sound is judged.

Tempo: the rate of speed at which the beats recur.

Meter: the grouping of beats according to the heaviness or lightness of the various beats. Example:

> *Beat* beat *Beat* beat *Beat* beat (suggests a grouping of twos)
> *Beat* beat beat *Beat* beat beat (suggests a grouping of threes)

Measure: the visual representation of meter, in which the notation of each metrical pattern is written between two vertical bar lines.

Note value: the duration of a particular musical sound, figured in relation to the beat.

Whole note	𝅝	usually lasts for 4 beats
Half note	𝅗𝅥	usually lasts for 2 beats
Quarter note	𝅘𝅥	usually lasts for 1 beat
Eighth note	𝅘𝅥𝅮	usually lasts for ½ beat
Sixteenth note	𝅘𝅥𝅯	usually lasts for ¼ beat

The mathematical relationship among these note values is illustrated by the following chart. The arrows here represent the passing of time; they do not appear in actual music.

Consecutive notes may share *flags* for ease in writing and reading. The shared flags, when they appear as connecting horizontal lines, are called *beams*. The stem (straight portion) of a note can point up (𝅘𝅥𝅮) or down (𝅘𝅥𝅮) without changing the note value or pitch.

Rest: silence. For each kind of note there is a rest with the same name and time value.

The whole rest may also indicate an entire measure of rest, regardless of the number of beats in the measure. In such cases it is called a *measure rest*.

Dotted note: a note with a dot on the right, indicating that the sound is lengthened by half of the original note value. The value of the dot depends, therefore, on the value of the note preceding it. Assuming in each case that a quarter note lasts for one beat, the duration of each dotted note is:

$$\text{♩.} = \text{♩} + \text{♪} = 1\frac{1}{2} \text{ beats}$$

$$\text{♩.} = 2 + 1 = 3 \text{ beats}$$

$$\text{♪.} = \text{♪} + \text{♪} = \text{¾ of a beat}$$

$$\text{○.} = 4 + 2 = 6 \text{ beats}$$

Meter signature or **time signature:** the two numbers at the beginning of a piece of music. The top number tells how many beats are in each measure. The bottom number tells what kind of note lasts for one beat. A 4 on the bottom stands for a quarter note, a 2 for a half note, and an 8 for an eighth note. A meter signature is not a fraction; $\frac{3}{4}$ or 3/4 does not mean three-fourths, because it does not represent a portion of anything.

Two abbreviated meter signatures are seen frequently:

C means $\frac{4}{4}$; **¢** means $\frac{2}{2}$ (also called cut time or alla breve)

Meters are of two types: *simple meter* subdivides the beats into twos, and *compound meter* subdivides the beats into threes. A beat having three equal subdivisions must be a dotted note, since undotted notes such as quarter and eighth notes divide into twos. However, there is no system for indicating a dotted beat-note in the bottom number of a

meter signature. So compound meters are indicated by signatures that tell the number of beat *subdivisions* per measure, and the note value of that subdivision:

$$\frac{6}{8} = \frac{6}{\text{♪}} = \begin{array}{l} \text{Number of subdivisions} \\ \text{Note value of each subdivision} \end{array}$$

PITCH

Pitch: the highness or lowness of a musical sound, determined by the number of vibrations per second.

Note: a sign placed on the staff to indicate the pitch and duration of a musical sound.

Staff: the five horizontal lines and four spaces on which notes are written.

Leger lines: short horizontal lines indicating the pitch of notes too high or too low to be placed on the regular staff. Leger lines extend the range beyond the staff.

Clef: a sign placed on the staff to show the exact pitches of the written notes. The two most common clefs are:

Treble clef   Bass clef

The treble and bass clefs indicate definite pitches, all named for letters of the alphabet from A to G. (See below.)

Sharp (♯): a sign placed before a note to raise the pitch one half step.

Flat (♭): a sign placed before a note to lower the pitch one half step.

Natural (♮): a sign placed before a note to indicate that it is neither raised nor lowered. This sign cancels a sharp or flat previously applied to the note.

PITCHES ON THE PIANO KEYBOARD

The black keys of the piano are found in groups of twos and threes. All white keys are identified in relation to these groups of keys. For example, every C on the piano is a white key immediately to the left of a two-black-key group; every F is a white key immediately to the left of a three-black-key group. The white keys are named consecutively from left to right, using the letters A through G:

"Middle C," the note midway between the treble and bass staffs, is also the C nearest the middle of the piano keyboard.

middle C

lower pitches   higher pitches

To find the sharp of any white key on the piano, find the black key touching it on the right. To find the flat of any white key, find the black key touching it on the left. If there is no black key on one side, the nearest white key in that direction is the sharp or flat.

Each black key has two names, such as the key called G sharp (because it is to the right of G) or A flat (because it is to the left of A). See below.

Interval: the difference in pitch between two notes. The name of an interval is determined by the number of letters it includes, counting the lower tone and the higher tone. (See next page.)

Examples:

| fourth | second | fifth | third | octave | prime or unison |

Half step: the smallest interval that can be played on the piano; also called a semitone or a minor second. It is produced by sounding adjacent black and white keys or adjacent white keys that have no black key between them.

Whole step: an interval or two semitones; also called a major second. It is produced by sounding any two keys that are separated by only one other key.

Scale: a series of pitches ascending or descending by a specific pattern of intervals; an "index" of the pitches that occur in a section of music. A scale can be built on any note, which is then called the *keynote* (or *tonal center* or *tonic*). A scale usually consists of eight notes, with the eighth pitch having the same letter name as the first, or keynote. Numbers are often used to indicate the successive steps of the scale, as in this example that has C as the keynote:

Step number: 1 2 3 4 5 6 7 8

When eight-note scales are written, they must utilize each successive line and space —every letter—between the low and high keynote.

Key: the effect created when several tones are related to a common tonal center. If these notes are rearranged to form a scale, the starting note of the scale (step 1) is the name of the key.

Key signature: a group of sharps or flats placed after the clef at the beginning of the staff. Every sharp or flat in the key signature applies to its particular note throughout the composition, unless it is later canceled by a natural (♮). The key signature indicates the keynote or tonal center of the composition. The order in which flats appear in a signature is exactly the reverse of the order of sharps.

Accidental: a sharp (♯), flat (♭), or natural (♮) used within a composition to show a pitch not indicated by the key signature. An accidental remains in effect for one measure; after a bar line it is assumed to be canceled unless it is specifically indicated again in a succeeding measure.

Modulation: changing key within a composition, usually with no break in the music.

Transposition: changing the key of an entire piece, so that it is performed at a higher or lower pitch level than the original.

MAJOR KEYS

Major scale: a scale having the pattern of whole and half steps shown below:

| 1 | | 2 | | 3 | 4 | | 5 | | 6 | | 7 | 8 |

| whole step | whole step | half step | whole step | whole step | whole step | half step |

It can also be visualized as a flight of steps of unequal height—steps 3 and 4 are close together, as are steps 7 and 8.

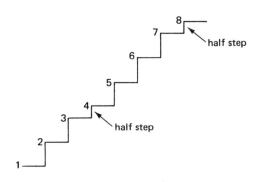

Major key: the effect created when steps 3-4 and 7-8 are a half step apart. Below are the key signatures for all major keys. If the signature is in sharps, the last sharp to the right is always step 7 of the major scale; therefore the eighth step, or keynote, is a half step above this last sharp. If the signature is in flats, the last flat to the right is always step 4 of the major scale. (If there is more than one flat, the keynote has the same name as the next-to-last flat in the signature.) If there are no sharps or flats in the signature and the key is major, the keynote is C.

MINOR KEYS

Minor key: the effect created when the third step above the keynote is lowered. Other notes may be lowered also, but a lowered third step is a consistent feature of music in minor keys. The unaltered pitch relationships in a minor piece produce the sound called "natural minor."

Natural minor: a pattern in which steps 3, 6, and 7 are lowered from their positions in a comparable major key.

In the diagram below, the dotted lines show at what pitch steps 3, 6, and 7 would be heard if the music were major:

Harmonic minor: a pattern in which steps 3 and 6 are lowered as in natural minor, but step 7 is raised so that it is now only a half step away from the keynote. This gives a feeling of "leading into" the keynote, but it creates a larger gap between steps 6 and 7:

Melodic minor: a pattern in which steps 6 and 7 are raised when the notes ascend and lowered when the notes descend (see below). The raising of step 6 eliminates the awkward interval found between steps 6 and 7 in the harmonic minor pattern and is easier to sing or play; it is more "melodious," as reflected in its name. In descending passages, these two notes are lowered to make the music sound more distinctively minor again, as in the natural minor form.

Minor key signatures: The key signature of a minor piece assumes that the notes will conform to the pattern of natural minor, so any deviations from natural minor must be written into the piece as accidentals. Here are the signatures for all minor keys:

A comparison of the foregoing chart with the chart of major key signatures will disclose that *each minor key has three more flats—or three fewer sharps—than the major key built on the same note.* These additional flats (or canceled sharps, as the case may be) indicate the lowered steps 3, 6, and 7 of natural minor. For example,

C major   C minor lowers
                 step 3 from E to E♭
                 step 6 from A to A♭
                 step 7 from B to B♭

E major   E minor lowers
                 step 3 from G♯ to G
                 step 6 from C♯ to C
                 step 7 from D♯ to D

D major   D minor lowers
                 step 3 from F♯ to F
                 step 6 from B to B♭
                 step 7 from C♯ to C

Parallel major and minor keys: a major key and minor key that share the same keynote but require different key signatures. The keys of C major and C minor—and other pairs of keys like those cited immediately above—illustrate parallel keys.

Relative major and minor keys: a major and a minor key that share the same key signature but have a different keynote. The signature charts for major and minor keys illustrate relative keys, because they show that every key signature does double duty: it can represent either a major key or a minor key. The keynote of a minor key is always step 6 of its relative major key. Examples are:

> B-flat major and G minor each have two flats; G is step 6 in the key of B-flat major.

> D major and B minor each have two sharps; B is step 6 in the key of D major.

F major and D minor each have one flat; D is step 6 in the key of F major.

HARMONY

Harmony: the effect created when tones are sounded at the same time.

Chord; a combination of three or more tones sounded simultaneously.

Triad: a chord of three tones, each a third apart.

Root: the note on which a chord is built. In any key,

> The triad built on step 1 is called I or *tonic* triad.
> The triad built on step 4 is called IV or *subdominant* triad.
> The triad built on step 5 is called V or *dominant* triad.

These three chords are basic because they occur so frequently. The roots are scale steps, as in this example in the key of C major:

1   2   3   4   5   6   7   8

Triads can be built on any step of the scale and are named accordingly: II if the root is step 2, and so on. In harmonic analysis, a Roman numeral indicates a triad, and an Arabic numeral indicates only one tone—one particular scale step.

Chord function: the role of a chord in a particular key. In the music example above, the G triad (G B D) functions as V. It suggests restlessness, and the listener wants it to resolve to the home triad of C E G, which is I. But in the key of G major, the same G B D triad has a different function; it is the home triad and gives the listener a feeling of repose and rest. The purpose of Roman numerals is to indicate chord function—to tell how a particular chord works in a particular key.

Seventh chord: a chord of four notes, consisting of a root plus intervals of a third, fifth, and seventh above the root.

The most common seventh chord is the V^7, or dominant seventh chord. The term "seventh" refers to the interval from the root to the top note in the basic chord; it does not mean the seventh step of the scale.

Inverted chord: a chord that does not have its root sounding as the lowest tone. Inversion does not affect the name or function of the chord.

A chord may be sounded in many ways. Some of the basic methods are shown below. (Inverted chords can be included for ease of playing, to reduce the necessity for big jumps from one chord to another.)

Appendix B
Additional Resources

ELEMENTARY SCHOOL
MUSIC SERIES BOOKS

Addison-Wesley Publishing Company, Reading, Massachusetts 01867. *Comprehensive Musicianship through Classroom Music*.

American Book Company, 135 West 50th St., New York 10020. *New Dimensions in Music*.

Holt, Rinehart & Winston, 383 Madison Ave., New York 10017. *The Music Book*.

Macmillan Publishing Co., Inc., 866 Third Ave., New York 10022. *The Spectrum of Music*.

Silver Burdett Company, 250 James St., Morristown, N. J. 07960. *Silver Burdett Music*.

BOOKS ON ASPECTS OF TEACHING
MUSIC IN THE ELEMENTARY SCHOOLS

General

Adler, Marvis S., and Jesse C. McCarroll, *The Elementary Teacher's Music Almanack* (West Nyack, N. Y.: Parker Publishing Company, 1978).

Andress, Barbara, et al., *Music in Early Childhood* (Reston, Va.: Music Educators National Conference, 1973).

Aronoff, Frances W., *Music and Young Children* (New York: Holt, Rinehart & Winston, 1969).

Athey, Margaret, and Gwen Hotchkiss, *A Galaxy of Games for the Music Class* (West Nyack, N. Y.: Parker Publishing Company, 1975).

Baird, JoAnn, *Using Media in the Music Program* (New York: Center for Applied Research in Education, 1975).

Batcheller, John M., *Music in Early Childhood* (New York: Center for Applied Research in Education, 1975).

Bramscher, Cynthia S., *Treasury of Musical Motivators for the Elementary Classroom* (West Nyack, N. Y.: Parker Publishing Company, 1979).

Carabo-Cone, Madeleine, *A Learning Theory and Music Methods for Teachers of Elementary and Pre-School Children: A Sensory-Motor Approach to Music Learning* (New York: MCA Music; or Melville, N. Y.: Belwin-Mills). Four books.

Crews, Katherine, *Music and Perceptual-Motor Development* (New York: Center for Applied Research in Eduation, 1975).

Gingrich, Donald, *Relating the Arts* (New York: Center for Applied Research in Education, 1974).

Graham, Richard M., compiler, *Music for the Exceptional Child* (Reston, Va.: Music Educators National Conference, 1975).

Graham, Richard M., and Alice S. Beer, *Teaching Music to the Exceptional Child* (Englewood Cliffs, N. J.: Prentice-Hall, Inc., 1980).

Hotchkiss, Gwen, and Margaret Athey, *Treasury of Individualized Activities for the Music Class* (West Nyack, N. Y.: Parker Publishing Company, 1977).

Landis, Beth, and Polly Carder, *The Eclectic Curriculum in American Music Education: Contributions of Dalcroze, Kodály, and Orff* (Reston, Va.: Music Educators National Conference, 1972).

Marsh, Mary Val, *Explore and Discover Music* (New York: Macmillan, Company, 1970).

Monsour, Sally, *Music in Open Education* (New York: Center for Applied Research in Education, 1974).

Mulligan, Mary Ann, *Integrating Music with Other Studies* (New York: Center for Applied Research in Education, 1975).

Nash, Grace C., *Creative Approaches to Child Development with Music, Language, and Movement* (Port Washington, N. Y.: Alfred Publishing Company, 1974).

————, *Today with Music* (Port Washington, N. Y.: Alfred Publishing Company, 1973).

Nocera, Sona D., *Reaching the Special Learner Through Music* (Morristown, N. J.: Silver Burdett, 1979)

Nye, Vernice, *Music for Young Children* (Dubuque, Iowa: William C. Brown Company, 1975).

Nye, Vernice T., Robert E. Nye, and H. Virginia Nye, *Toward World Understanding with Song* (Belmont, Calif.: Wadsworth Publishing Company, 1967).

Palmer, Mary, *Sound Exploration and Discovery* (New York: Center for Applied Research in Education, 1974).

Reeder, Barbara, and James A. Standifer, *Source Book of African Materials for Music Educators* (Reston, Va.: Music Educators National Conference, 1972).

Willman, Fred, *Electronic Music for Young People* (New York: Center for Applied Research in Education, 1974).

Zimmerman, Marilyn P., *Music Characteristics of Children* (Reston, Va.: Music Educators National Conference, 1971).

Dalcroze

Driver, Ethel, *A Pathway to Dalcroze Eurhythmics* (New York: Thomas Nelson and Sons, 1963).

Findlay, Elsa, *Rhythm and Movement: Application of Dalcroze Eurhythmics* (Evanston, Ill.: Summy-Birchard, 1971).

Gell, Heather, *Music, Movement and the Young Child* (Sydney, Australia: Australian Publishing Company, 1969).

Kodály

Choksy, Lois, *The Kodály Method: Comprehensive Music Education from Infant to Adult* (Englewood Cliffs, N. J.: Prentice-Hall, 1974).

Daniel, Katinka S., *The Kodály Approach* (Belmont, Calif.: Fearon Publishers, 1973). Three books.

Lewis, Aden, *Listen, Look and Sing* (Morristown, N. J.: Silver Burdett, 1971). Four books.

Richards, Mary Helen, *Threshold to Music* (Belmont, Calif.: Fearon Publishers, 1964). Four books.

Szabo, Helga, *The Kodály Concept of Music Education* (New York: Boosey and Hawkes, 1969).

Szönyi, Erzsébet, *Kodály's Principles in Practice*, trans. John Weissman and Raymond Alston (New York: Boosey and Hawkes, 1974).

Wheeler, Lawrence, and Lois Raebeck, *Orff and Kodály Adapted for the Elementary School* (Dubuque, Iowa: William C. Brown Company, 1972).

Orff

Keetman, Gunild, *Elementaria*, trans. Margaret Murray (Melville, N. Y.: Belwin-Mills, 1974).

Keller, Wilhelm, *Introduction to Music for Children* (Mainz, West Germany: B. Schott's Söhne, 1974). Obtainable from Belwin-Mills, Melville, N. Y.

Nichols, Elizabeth, *Orff Instruments Source Books, I and II* (Morristown, N. J.: Silver Burdett, 1970).

Orff, Carl, and Gunild Keetman, *Music for Children* (Mainz, West Germany: B. Schott's Söhne, 1950). English edition adapted by Margaret Murray; obtainable from Magnamusic-Baton, St. Louis, Mo. Five books.

Wheeler, Lawrence, and Lois Raebeck, *Orff and Kodály Adapted for the Elementary School* (Dubuque, Iowa: William C. Brown Company, 1972).

SOURCES FOR MUSIC TEACHING MATERIALS

Because the producers of materials to be used in teaching music in the elementary schools frequently add and delete items, it is suggested that interested persons contact the company to secure the current catalog.

General Enrichment

Bowmar, 4563 Colorado Blvd., Los Angeles, Calif. 90039. Recording and enrichment units, especially of music of various countries.

Children's Music Center, 5373 West Pico Blvd., Los Angeles, Calif. 90019. Enrichment material on American Indians.

Keyboard Publications, 1346 Chapel St., New Haven, Conn. 06511. Recordings and enrichment units on various types of music; also publishes a magazine for students, *Man and His Music*.

Films and Filmstrips

American Book Company/Keyboard Publications, 7625 Empire Drive, Florence, Ky. 41042.

BFA Educational Media, 2211 Michigan Ave., Santa Monica, Calif. 90404.

Churchill Films, 622 North Robertson Blvd., Los Angeles, Calif. 90069.

Educational Audio Visual, Inc., Pleasantville, N. Y. 10570.

EMC Corporation, 180 East 6th, St. Paul, Minn. 55101.

Film Associates, 11559 Santa Monica Blvd., Los Angeles, Calif. 90025.

Franson Corporation, 225 Park Avenue South, New York, N. Y. 10003.

National Geographic Society, Washington, D. C. 20036.

Prentice-Hall Media, 150 White Plains Road, Tarrytown, N. Y. 10591.

Shetler, Donald J., ed., *Film Guide for Music Educators*, Music Educators National Conference, Reston, Va. 22091.

Society for Visual Education, Inc., 1345 Diversey Parkway, Chicago, Ill. 60614.

Humanities—Fine Arts

Harcourt Brace Jovanovich, 757 Third Ave., New York, N. Y. 10017.

Individualized Learning

Macmillan Publishing Company, Inc., 866 Third Ave., New York, N. Y. 10022.

MuGin Publications, P. O. Box 36528, Los Angeles, Calif. 90036.

Kodály Method

Boosey and Hawkes, Oceanside, N. Y. 11572.

Music Reading

Shawnee Press, Delaware Water Gap, Pa. 18327.

Orff Method

Magnamusic-Baton, Inc., 10370 Page Industrial Blvd., St. Louis, Mo. 63132.

Special Education

Abingdon Press, 201 8th Ave. So., Nashville, Tenn. 37202.

Educational Activities, Inc., Freeport, N. Y. 11520.

Kimbo Educational Records, Box 246, Deal, N. J. 07723.

Magnamusic-Baton, Inc., 10370 Page Industrial Blvd., St. Louis, Mo. 63132.

Myklas Music Press, P. O. Box 929, Boulder, Colo. 80306.

Glossary

(Terms associated with rhythm, pitch, harmony, and notation are defined in Appendix A.)

Accidental: see pp. 239, 362.

Acoustics: the science of sound.

Affective learning: the shaping of attitudes and beliefs as a result of learning.

Art song: a composed song that displays an expressive unity of text and music.

Autoharp: an instrument on which the player sounds a chord by pressing a button and strumming across the strings.

Beat: see pp. 89, 359.

Behavioral objectives: outcomes stated in terms of what the students should be able to do as a result of the instruction.

Bells (Melody Bells, Resonator Bells): a xylophone-type instrument on which the player strikes bars that conform to the pattern of a piano keyboard.

Binary form: a musical structure consisting of two segments—*AB*.

Borrowed patterns: a rhythmic pattern in which the note values represent durations different from those indicated by the prevailing meter, as when three eighth notes are expected.

Canon: a contrapuntal composition in which the imitation between two or more lines of music is not always at the same pitch level; it is usually instrumental.

Chamber music: instrumental music intended for performance in a small room or "chamber," by an ensemble having only one person on each part.

Chant: a repeated phrase spoken rhythmically, with strong accents.

Chord: see pp. 256, 365.

Chord function: see pp. 263, 365.

Chromatic notes: notes altered on the left side by a flat, sharp, or natural sign to indicate a departure from the prevailing key signature.

Clef: see p. 360.

Coda: a concluding section that is not essential to the form of a piece of music.

Cognitive learning: the retaining of factual information and the developing of intellectual understanding.

Compound meter: See pp. 202-05.

Concerto: an extended musical work for an instrumental soloist with orchestral accompaniment.

Concerto grosso: a musical work for a small ensemble of instrumentalists—one on a part—in contrast to the accompaniment provided by a larger instrumental group.

Consonance: the effect of simultaneous sounds that the listener considers agreeable or pleasant.

Contrary motion: melodic lines that move in opposite directions at the same time.

Countermelody: a melodic line designed to occur simultaneously with a given melody and to contrast with it.

Counterpoint (adjective form is **contrapuntal**): the simultaneous sounding of two or more equally important melodies.

Creativity: the ability to think in new and different ways or to see relationships that others do not see in a given situation.

Crescendo: becoming gradually louder.

"Cuckoo" call: the descending interval of a minor third found in many children's songs throughout the world.

Da Capo (abbreviated form is **D.C.**): return to the beginning of the music.

Dalcroze method: techniques devised by the Swiss music educator Emile Jaques-Dalcroze to refine the physical experience of body movement and rhythmic response.

Decrescendo or **diminuendo:** becoming gradually softer.

Descant: a decorative line performed with a more important melody, generally in a higher pitch range than the basic melody and in contrast to it.

Development: manipulation of a musical theme by such techniques as fragmentation, inversion, and other alterations.

Dissonance: the effect of simultaneous sounds that the listener considers discordant.

Distributed effort: learning that is accomplished in numerous short sessions rather than in a few long ones; also called *spaced practice.*

Dominant triad or chord: see pp. 258, 365.

Dotted note: see pp. 201-02, 360.

Echo-clapping or **echo-singing:** performing a musical task by immediately imitating another person's performance of it.

Ensemble: a group of musicians; also the effect of unity achieved when they perform together.

Exposition: the opening section of a fugue.

Fine arts: the body of subjects, including music, painting, sculpture, dance, drama, and poetry, that are pursued not for their functional benefit but for their aesthetic qualities.

Flat: see pp. 239, 361.

Form: the design, plan, or structure of a piece of music; also the type of work as suggested by a particular performance medium (concerto, string quartet, and the like).

Fragmentation: manipulation of a short segment of a melody as a theme in itself.

Free form: a musical structure that does not follow an established pattern.

Frequency (of pitch): the number of vibrations per second that occur when a sounding medium is activated, with a faster frequency producing a higher pitch.

Fugue: a musical form in which the theme or subject is presented by one part after another in imitative style; it may include additional thematic material.

Half step: see pp. 228, 362.

Harmonic minor: see p. 364.

Harmony: the effect created when pitches are sounded simultaneously.

Humanities: the branches of learning, such as fine arts and philosophy, that are regarded as dealing primarily with culture and humankind.

Improvisation: varying a theme while performing spontaneously; music that is performed without first being notated.

Interpretation: the style of musical expressiveness in a performance.

Interval: see pp. 252, 361.

Inversion: turning a melody upside down so that an ascending interval descends, or vice versa; also, rearranging the notes in an interval or chord so that the lowest note is no longer on the bottom.

Inverted chord: see p. 366.

Irregular meter: asymmetrical beat patterns within a measure.

Key: see p. 362.

Key signature: see p. 362.

Keynote: see p. 229.

Kodály-Hungarian Singing School: techniques devised by the Hungarian composer Zoltan Kodály to develop musicianship by emphasizing good vocal tone, freedom of musical expression, and music reading.

Leger lines: see p. 360.

Mainstreaming: placing handicapped learners in a classroom setting with nonhandicapped students.

Major key: see p. 363.

Major key signatures: see p. 363.

Major scale: see pp. 231, 362.

Measure: see p. 359.

Melodic minor: see p. 364.

Melody: a series of consecutive pitches that form a cohesive musical entity.

Meter: see pp. 99, 359.

Meter signature: see p. 360.

Metronome: a mechanical device for producing repetitive taps, the tempo of which can be regulated to mark the beats.

Minor key: see pp. 232, 363.

Minor key signatures: see p. 364.

Mixed meter: several changes of meter within a composition, causing a shifting of stressed beats.

Modulation: changing key as the music progresses, usually without a break; see p. 362.

Motive: a short melodic or rhythmic fragment that is important because of its frequent appearances in a musical work.

Movement: a sizable, self-contained section of a long musical work.

Music: an aural art consisting of organized sound.

Music consultant: a music specialist whose role is not primarily to teach but to provide help for classroom teachers and others who do the actual music teaching in a school district.

Music literature: the body of music that has been created through the ages.

Music reading: the ability to look at music notation and to translate its symbols into sound.

Music specialist: a teacher who holds certification in the subject area of music, and whose function is to teach music to children and help classroom teachers to provide appropriate music experiences.

Music supervisor: an administrator with certification in music, who provides leadership for the music program and serves as a liaison between music teachers and the central administration of the school district.

Music theory: a study of the way in which musical sounds are organized.

Natural: see pp. 239, 361.

Natural minor: see p. 363.

Note: see p. 360.

Note value: see p. 359.

Octave: the pitch distance between a note and the nearest pitch with the same letter name.

Opera: a sung drama involving staging, costumes, acting, and orchestral accompaniment.

Orff-*Schulwerk*: techniques devised by the German composer Carl Orff to develop musicianship by involving the child in movement, speech, rhythm, singing, and playing specially designed instruments in an improvisational manner.

Ostinato: a rhythmic or melodic pattern that is repeated persistently.

Parallel major and minor keys: see p. 365.

Parallel motion: simultaneous melodic lines that move either upward or downward at the same time.

Patsch (plural is **Patschen** in German): a thigh slap.

Pentatonic scale: a five-tone scale in which all intervals consist of a whole step or 1½ steps, like the black keys of the piano.

Phrase: consecutive sounds that belong together as a musical thought, like a phrase in language.

Pickup note: an unstressed note, usually less than one beat in length, that begins a musical phrase.

Pitch: see pp. 117, 360.

Polymeter: several meters occurring simultaneously.

Polyrhythm: several rhythms occurring simultaneously.

Program music: instrumental music associated with nonmusical ideas or a story.

Psychomotor learning: acquiring physical skills that involve the senses and muscles as well as the mind.

Range: the upper and lower pitch limits of a voice, instrument, or piece of music.

Recorder: a wind instrument, generally of wood, on which notes are produced by covering finger holes.

Register: the general pitch area of a song, defined in terms of the voice or instrument performing it.

Relative major and minor keys: see p. 365.

Repertoire: the body of music that has been prepared for performance by an individual or group; also, the body of music that has been created for a particular medium, such as "the piano repertoire."

Rest: see p. 359.

Rhythm: see pp. 88, 359.

Rondo: a piece of music in which one melody returns several times, with other music interspersed between its various appearances.

Root: see pp. 258, 365.

Rote: learning by imitation of another person.

Round: strict imitation occurring between two or more lines of music for the duration of a song; usually vocal.

Rubato: a performer's slight deviation from strict rhythm, for interpretative purposes.

Scale: see pp. 229, 362.

Score: music written down in such a way that the parts for different performers appear vertically above one another.

Sequence: the immediate repetition of a musical phrase at successively higher or lower pitch levels than the original.

Seventh cord: see p. 366.

Sharp: see pp. 239, 361.

Sight reading: the ability to look at music notation and translate its symbols into sound without experimentation or prior study of the music.

Simple meter: see p. 202.

Solfeggio (Italian) or **solfège** (French): a system of syllables for identifying pitches in relation to a key center.

Sonata: a multi-movement work of chamber music performed by one instrument alone, or by piano and one other instrument as equal partners.

Sonata form: a movement of three sections, the second of which is called the "development" section because of its intricate treatment of thematic material.

Staff: see p. 360.

Subdominant triad or chord: see p. 365.

Subject (of a fugue): the theme of a fugue.

Suspension: a dissonant tone that was consonant in the preceding harmony and that eventually resolves downward to become consonant in its present harmony.

Symphony: an extended orchestral work of several movements, usually four.

Syncopation: the removal of an accent or stress where it is expected and/or the addition of one where it is not expected.

Tempo: see pp. 93, 359.

Ternary form: a musical structure consisting of three segments; also called *ABA* or song form.

Tessitura: the pitch range within which most of the notes of a melody occur.

Texture: the context in which simultaneous sounds occur, either as harmony (chords) or as counterpoint (concurrent melodies of equal importance).

Theme: a melody that is structurally important because it is the basis for a long work of music.

Theme and variations: a composition in which a theme is presented in different ways, but with the basic identity of the original version implied in each version.

Tie: a curved line connecting two notes of identical pitch to indicate that they should be combined into one continuous sound.

Time signature: see p. 360.

Tonic triad or chord: see p. 365.

Transfer effect: engaging in an activity that causes behavioral changes in another area.

Transposition: rewriting music (or performing) at a pitch level other than the original; see p. 362.

Triad: see pp. 258, 365.

Upbeat: an unstressed note, usually the last beat of a measure, that begins a musical phrase.

Whole step: see pp. 228, 362.

Index of Songs

Index of Music
Recommended for Listening

Index